# Powerline365

*Choose NOW Ministries
Nicole O'Dell*

© 2015 by Nicole O'Dell
ISBN 978-0-9847816-0-7 (print)

All rights reserved. No part of this publication may be reproduced or transmitted for commercial purposes, except for brief quotations in printed or electronic reviews, without written permission of the publisher. Churches and other noncommercial interests may reproduce portions of this book not to exceed 500 words or five percent of the book without the express written permission of Choose NOW Publishing, provided that the text is not material quoted from another publisher. When reproducing text from this book, include the following credit line: "From Powerline365 published by Choose NOW Publishing. Used by permission."

Printed in the United States of America.

All scripture references contain in-text citations of the version used. Used by permission. All rights reserved worldwide.

Choose NOW Publishing
Paxton, IL
www.choose-now.com

# Acknowledgements

I want to thank all the contributors to Powerline365. Your hard work and contributions have made this a go-to resource for parents of teens. I so appreciate your partnership!

*Cassie Beck*
*Takiela Bynum*
*Valerie Comer*
*Claire Culwell*
*Shannon Deitz*
*Mary DeMuth*
*Dr. Tara Fairfield*
*Wendy Fitzgerald*
*Amber Frank*
*Sara Goff*
*Tricia Goyer*
*Tim Hageland*
*J. Alden Hall*
*Jill Hart*
*Bethany Jett*
*Sherri Wilson Johnson*
*Amy Joob*
*Laura Kurk*
*Wil O'Dell*
*Lyn Parker*
*Cara Putman*
*Jason Lane*
*Debi Lee*
*Dori Powledge Phillips*
*Steve Repak, CFP®*
*Janet Sketchley*
*Laura L. Smith*
*Vicki Tiede*
*Brenda L. Yoder*

Also, to all of the parents who will read this book: Thank you for reaching out for tools to help you with your parent-teen relationships. Your efforts at raising godly teens are what will make a difference in the next generation.

Powerline365

# A Good Work
### Nicole O'Dell

*He who began a good work in [your teenager] will carry it on to completion until the day of Christ Jesus. Phil. 1:6, NIV*

Welcome to Powerline365! It's going to be an amazing year, and I'm so happy you're willing to do the extra work to be an amazing parent.

I began my work with families out of fear for my own. I know, I know, fear is not of the Lord. But you know what? I was terrified my kids would turn out just like me! And I had to do something about that. I felt like all of my kids' choices, mistakes, failures...were my fault as they were surely payback for my own mistakes. I feared those struggles would be a direct reflection on me as a parent. I wanted more for them than what I had claimed for myself. I was terrified that no matter how much I wanted God's best IN them, I wouldn't be able to make it happen FOR them.

I was right.

It wasn't until I realized I was right that I could parent in freedom. God really put me in my place. He spoke to my heart from Philippians 1:6 (above). "Who do you think you are? You didn't start this beautiful work in your kids; I did that when I drew them to their knees as they surrendered to me. You aren't going to bring it to finality; I did that on the cross. You aren't going to complete the work in them in this life; I will do that when they stand with me on That Day."

Friends, what a relief it was to realize it wasn't about me. From that moment, I could just enjoy them and revel in the privilege of parenting those precious souls whom my Savior loves so very much.

As we embark on this year together, can you take refuge in that promise? Read those words from Philippians — speak them aloud until they really sink in— print them out, and paste them around your house if you need regular reminders. Once you can rest in that promise, you're ready for the miracle.

## → Connection Point

*Father, I believe you. I receive your promise. I am ready to move forward and parent my kids from a place of confidence and surrender. What a relief it is to know that it's not about me. Thank You for loving them even more than I do. Amen.*

# Like Filtered Coffee
## Nicole O'Dell

*Don't let even one rotten word seep out of your mouths. Instead, offer only fresh words that build others up when they need it most.*
Eph. 4:29a, VOICE

Love a good, strong cup of coffee? Are you the proud possessor of a Starbucks gold-level rewards card? It's a bleary Monday morning and you shuffle into your local coffee shop to buy your favorite concoction. Back in your car, you flip on the news station and reach for the steaming cup. You take one sip and close your eyes as the milky goodness hits your tongue—wait! You sputter and spit a soggy glop back into your cup. Your coffee was brewed without a filter.

Though insignificant in appearance, the filter is necessary. It holds back the bitter grounds and allows those soothing, aromatic drips to flow. Without the filter, there's nothing but a dirty mess of undrinkable grime.

Your words speak life to your teens much like a decadent cuppa brings life to your morning. But if you placed a filter over your mouth for an entire day and let it capture all the negative words you spoke to your tweens and teens, how full would it become?

Teenagers aren't equipped to sift through negativity to find truth. They spit out the good with the bad and miss out on important stuff. We might get angry when it seems they're tuning us out, but how can we blame them? It's on us to make sure we present truth in a palatable way. It's on us to make sure we speak in love. But, we're not in it alone.

The Holy Spirit will be your filter if you allow Him. If you will surrender control of your tongue, He will restrain your fruitless speech and only let seasoned, fruitful words affect those around you.

Is your filter in place today?

## → Connection Point

*Dear God, please forgive my harsh and bitter words. Would you be my filter today? Please convict me of any unkind or negative words so my lips would be free from bitterness and would allow your love to flow. Let my words be life in my teenager's cup today. Amen.*

# A Christian Hamburger
## Nicole O'Dell

*Yes, each of us will give a personal account to God. Rom. 14:12, NLT*

No matter how much work we do to force good behavior, in the end, it's not really about actions. We can coax perfect obedience from our teens, but that doesn't mean their hearts are right. Remember the 70's singer Keith Green? He said, "Going to church doesn't make you a Christian any more than going to McDonalds makes you a hamburger."

We don't just want an obedient child. We want a teenager who walks closely with Jesus. We don't want to make them walk a line in an effort to force righteousness. We want them to chase hard after the righteousness that comes out of intimacy with their Savior.

Resist the urge to focus on individual behaviors and keep the stakes in the spiritual. Work to keep your teen rooted in faith and committed to God's will as a natural response to a relationship with Him.

This type of relationship can only grow with an investment of time. Time in church. Time in the Word. Time in prayer. Then, when the pressure hits, your teen will be armed with the fruit of the Spirit and clothed with the armor of God. Accountability for choices is a powerful motivator. But even more powerful is an intimacy with God that develops choices made in love.

How are you guiding your teenager to spend the time and effort it takes to grow in intimacy with God?

## → Connection Point

*Dear God, please draw my teenager into an intimate relationship with you. Convict and guide my teen into good choices that come from a real love for you. Help me to be an example of that kind of intimate relationship as I parent my teenager. Amen.*

# 4

## Raising Royalty
### J. Alden Hall

*But you are a chosen race, a royal priesthood... 1 Pet. 2:9, ESV*

Have you seen the bumper sticker, "I'm not lost; I'm exploring"?

Your child may think life's a mystery to be searched, but you get frustrated when they steer too far off course. So what do you do?

In ancient times, there lived a wife of a king who struggled terribly raising her son. He was a difficult child. She tried everything to get him to mature. She reasoned, cajoled, encouraged, and threatened. Nothing worked. One day she had an idea. She cut a swath of royal purple and sewed it to her teen's coat.

"What's this for?" The prince examined the patch on the front of his cloak.

"Every time you look at this strip of purple, I want you to remember you are the king's son, so act accordingly."

Sometimes children need to be reminded they're special. That God not only loves them, He has entrusted His world with them. But be cautious, your words alone will not suffice. Teenagers are internally wired to ignore much of what we say, unless we have absolute proof. Instead, go to the authority – the Bible.

Using the word of God to teach, not preach, is one of the most powerful ways you can communicate with your child. So, sew the purple on one of their shirts and wait for the questions. Show them how Jesus says we are a "chosen people, a royal priesthood." Bring them to where He teaches that the kingdom of God is within and like a mustard seed, it's expected to mature into something special.

Let Christ's words take over when yours seem ignored.

Ask yourself, "Is my frustration helping or hurting the situation? Am I forgetting how special my child is?"

## → Connection Point

*Dear God, I long so much for my children to act like they should. Help me to see them through your eyes. Use me. Show me how my actions can reflect who I am in Christ. May I rely more on your words and wisdom, and less on my emotions. Amen.*

# A Mary Parent
## Nicole O'Dell

*"Martha, Martha," the Lord answered, "you are worried and upset about many things, but few things are needed—or indeed only one. Mary has chosen what is better, and it will not be taken away from her." Luke 10:41-42, NIV*

Martha rushed about her work because people were there and needed to be fed. Mary, however, pursued relationship with Jesus. Because of Mary's choice, Martha had to do the work by herself and criticized Mary for not helping. Jesus set things straight by explaining that relationship was the most important thing.

On a spiritual level, this is talking about relationship with Jesus. But what if we applied it to our relationships with our teens? Think of areas where the urgent daily things (housework, church commitments, personal pursuits, or even outside relationships) crowd out relationship time with your teenager.

Mary and Martha are a perfect example of the inner struggle most parents face on a daily basis. On one hand, we want to please people, do well at work, entertain, multi-task, and control many facets of life at one time – all because we believe those are marks of a good steward and a hard worker. On the other hand, we crave rest and good relationships with our family members. The challenge is blending the two into a healthy balance.

Consider asking your teenager what makes you seem distant and inaccessible. Ask for examples when distraction or intense focus has been a hindrance to drawing close to you. Once you know how it's perceived, and which behaviors have the most effect, you can make some changes to find better balance.

## → Connection Point

*Dear Lord, please forgive me for letting the seemingly urgent overshadow relationship with my teens. I want to be a good steward of the tasks in my life, but I know I need to slow down and be more like Mary. I want to rest with my teenager and with you. Please show me where I need to create more balance. Amen.*

# 6
## Keeping up with the Joneses
### *Nicole O'Dell*

*And he said to them, "Take care, and be on your guard against all covetousness, for one's life does not consist in the abundance of his possessions." Luke 12:15, ESV*

One's life does not consist in the abundance of his possessions? Yeah, tell that to the teenager who has watched her BFF buy new clothes every week and get the latest version of the most popular smartphone the minute it's available. Or the boy whose best buddy revs the engine of a new truck pulling into the school parking lot every morning. In those moments, it sure seems like life would be a lot better with some possessions.

So how do we combat covetousness in our teenagers? First, we need to encourage patience and sacrifice by not trying to meet every want our teens have. They need to feel the unmet pang of desire to learn it will eventually pass. If we always jump in to provide for wants, they'll never develop that understanding.

Next, share the truth about your finances. Let your teenagers understand what it takes to keep a family functioning. Teach them about the trappings of debt and explain not going into debt just to meet a want. By teaching responsible money management instead of just saying no, or worse, giving in, you're preparing your teen with lifelong financial values.

Finally, help them develop a work ethic by making them earn spending money. Not only will they have a healthier respect for money, but likely spend far less once they've seen how hard it is to earn.

Over time, your teen will discover possessions aren't making the Joneses happy and that things don't last forever. You'll have taught them to value the blessings in their lives, one of those blessings being the gift of hard work.

## → Connection Point

*Jesus, please help me be a good steward of the blessings you've given? Help me to know when it's good to be generous with my teenager and when I need to use finances as a teaching opportunity. And then, Lord, please help my child learn the truth about the trappings of stuff, and place value on the eternal. Amen.*

Powerline365

# No one said it was Easy
### Nicole O'Dell

*For the righteous falls seven times and rises again, but the wicked stumble in times of calamity. Prov. 24:16, ESV*

Mark Twain once said, "When a child turns thirteen, put him in a barrel and feed him through a hole. When they get to be sixteen, plug up the hole." We nod and chuckle at the thought, grateful someone understands how we feel. It's not easy to parent a teenager.

There are so many things to worry about: their education, their future, their happiness, their health... their faith in God. We want to teach them, but they don't want to hear from us. We want the best for them, but sometimes it seems like they want the opposite. The world current pulls our teens far from us and from truth. And, though we hold on with all our might, it sometimes seems they want to go with that flow.

Allow me to encourage you dear parent, perseverance is credited to you as righteousness. God sees your persistence and rewards it. He knows the cry of your heart and the anguish you feel at times. He offers you comfort through it. Each time you face rejection or anger from your teenager — every time you feel like a failure, He smiles at you and offers His hand of strength and mercy. God is on your side and is grateful that you have chosen to parent in His name.

Keep at it. Your efforts will not return void.

*"Train up a child in the way he should go: and when he is old, he will not depart from it." Prov. 22:6 KJV*

*"For which cause we faint not; but though our outward man perish, yet the inward [man] is renewed day by day." 2 Cor. 4:16 KJV*

## → Connection Point

*Lord, please hold me up when I feel weak as a parent. Shine your face on me and let me feel your approval when I'm down on myself. Walk with me when I feel alone. With you, I know I can do this. Amen.*

# 8

## Instant Prayers
### Cassie Beck

*Be anxious for nothing...let your requests be made known to God; and the peace of God, which surpasses all understanding, will guard your hearts and your minds through Christ Jesus. Phil. 4.6-7, NKJV*

As a parent, there is much you *could* be anxious for. Maybe you can relate to the following example: how to come up with enough money to replace your car engine today, while funding your teens Driver's Ed. Class payment tomorrow, in addition to putting money aside for their college fund, and still keeping all mouths fed. Ah, the juggling act!

According to God's Word, there is *nothing* you *should* be anxious for. Is that even possible? YES! The remedy for your anxieties is prayer and making known *every* need to the Lord. When you do so, you are not guaranteed a joy ride by any means, but you are promised the gift of God's perfect peace in your situation, and God never goes back on a promise.

You can help your teens see God's faithful provision in every situation they face by modeling it yourself. What does this look like fleshed out? Well, it means that whenever you or your teenager expresses a stress or anxiety, an instant prayer is raised up to God, so that right then and there you acknowledge your dependency on Him in the given situation. And keep praying. I Thessalonians 5.17 says, "Pray without ceasing." Pray until you see God's answer. Know that He always answers, and His peace is assured.

When anxieties arise in your home, what does the scenario look like? Are emotions flying high, with voices raised? Is prayer with God's peace at all present? Create a new plan for handling stressors in your family, by making instant verbalized prayer a practice. Post Scriptures around your home such as Philippians 4.6-7 or I Thessalonians 5.16-18 as a reminder of God's desired approach to handling stress, so that God's peace will rule instead of anxiety.

## → Connection Point

*Father, help me cultivate a praying culture in my home so my teens would learn to rely on you in all circumstances. Amen.*

Powerline365

# 9

## Rebel with a Cause
### Nicole O'Dell

*For we are his workmanship, created in Christ Jesus for good works, which God prepared beforehand, that we should walk in them. Eph. 2:10, ESV*

Are you afraid of raising a rebellious teen? We want our teens to make good choices, but it's not up to us. No matter how we try to guide them on a close walk with Jesus, we can't always stop them from breaking rules, behaving destructively, or hanging out with a bad crowd.

Maybe your teen cops a bad attitude, skips a homework assignment, or stays out past curfew. Or perhaps the behaviors are more intense like drinking, getting a tattoo, or having sex. If you see signs of rebellion, consider there might be a reason beyond the obvious. Is your teen dealing with a self-esteem problem?

Our enemy assures us the next thing will make us happy. Losing weight will solve our problems. If only we didn't have _____ cross to bear, then we'd be popular... Finding a boyfriend. Getting a better wardrobe. Those lies and others like them are pelting your teenagers on a moment-by-moment basis. But they're looking for the wrong things in the wrong place. They need you to turn their eyes upward. – *Hot Buttons Image Edition*, 2013

It's easier said than done, right? The key to keeping teenagers rooted in confidence and healthy self-esteem is to praise and reinforce those things God birthed in them. The godly things that make your teenagers unique. Help them focus intentionally on identity in Christ that doesn't leave room for the enemy's questions that lead to doubt and confusion.

*How did God make you special?* Discover what your teenager already possesses and build those nuggets into self-esteem. Once your teens see their special purpose, it's harder to listen to the enemy's lies.

## → Connection Point

*Lord, please help me uncover self-esteem problems in my teenager before they lead to rebellion. Help me to reinforce your plan and purpose for my teen and guide focus from the lie of worthlessness and the arrogance of self-importance. And then please hold my teenager securely in your arms. Confident. Approved. Loved. Amen.*

## Looking in a Soul Mirror
*Nicole O'Dell*

*And I praise you because of the wonderful way you created me. Everything you do is marvelous! Of this I have no doubt. Psalm 139:14, CEV*

When I was a teen, I was uncomfortable being honest about how I felt about myself. That drove a wedge between my parents and I. Even though I felt alone in my struggle, it was difficult to admit feeling inadequate, unloved... ugly. And tweens and teens can barely identify those feelings in the first place, let alone talk about them with Mom or Dad. Dare we actually try to talk to them about those feelings, it reinforces anxiety and pushes them farther away. Or so it seems.

Insecurity gets peppered with peer pressure and becomes the battleground where the enemy destroys truth and lies take over. Lies about self-worth are easier to believe, so that's where teens typically stumble.

It's hard to admit to Mom or Dad the reason for the mistake was to get approval from the popular girl. And what teenage girl is going to admit a date went too far physically because that boy didn't make her feel fat?

Knowing they probably aren't going to come and lay deep, dark feelings at your feet, you must remain educated about what your teens are exposed to and armed with the tools to guide them to truth. Bathe your parenting in prayer and stand watch for the enemy and his lies. Also, turn the focus onto the good qualities already within your teen like kindness, honesty, and compassion, and avoid focusing on outward things like appearance, athleticism, and popularity.

## → Connection Point

*Lord, please give me godly insight into my teenager's feelings of self-worth. Help me to see the areas that might be causing problems before the peer pressure sets in and bad choices are made. And then, please give me the words to say or the steps to take to make a difference in the way my teenager responds to all the challenges. Help me point my teen to you in all things. Amen.*

## Microchip our Teens?
### Nicole O'Dell

*If you then, who are evil, know how to give good gifts to your children, how much more will the heavenly Father give the Holy Spirit to those who ask him! Luke 11:13, ESV*

Sounds extreme, right? But wouldn't it be great if we could implant a little GPS chip into our teenagers without them knowing? We'd know where they're hanging out and when they're on the move every second. It's a safety thing, right? Okay, I admit, it's a bit out there. But you know what? We already have that technology at our disposal. We already have 100% access and insight to our teen's activities and behavior. Even their thoughts.

The Holy Spirit is our GPS.

The Holy Spirit is on watch 24/7, leading, guiding, steering, and protecting our teens if we have surrendered them to God. You see – we can cling to control. We can hover and micromanage every area of our teenager's life. Or we can trust the God who loves our kids even more than we do.

This means, to a certain extent, letting go. It means trusting the work God is doing in the lives of our teens and offering ourselves as a vessel to accomplish that work in His time, not steamrolling them.

It's true the Holy Spirit doesn't give us instant access to the thoughts and activities of our teenager. But if we trust Him, do we really need it? Do we really want it?

My recommendation, if you're struggling with knowing when and how much to let go, is a prayer of surrender when your teenager leaves the house. Saying these words will help focus your energy and alleviate fears as you place your teenagers in the loving arms of their Savior.

## → Connection Point

*Heavenly Father, I surrender my teenager to you. I let go of the plans I have and the fears I cling to. I trust your perfect will and I present myself as a vessel for your work. Please help me to trust you. Thank you for loving my child even more than I do. Amen.*

## Take the Long View
*Valerie Comer*

*The heavens declare the glory of God; the skies proclaim the work of his hands. Day after day they pour forth speech; night after night they reveal knowledge. Psalm 19:1-2, NIV*

We drove far from city lights on a chilly, moonless night and tucked kids into sleeping bags in an open park. Not to sleep, but to experience a meteor shower heralded to be the most spectacular of the decade. And it was.

What better way to spend time as a family? What better venue for reminding our kids of the vastness of creation and the One who made it all? God alone is worthy of our worship and praise, but sometimes we're so busy in the day-to-day we forget to notice. Forget to take the time.

We live in a concrete jungle, sprinting through our days, heads down, focused on the to-do list, aware that the slightest deviation will make someone late for school. Late for practice. Late for dinner.

Hours flash by. Days. Seasons. We're spinning ever faster, but for what purpose?

Think. What is really important in the eternal scheme of things? Relationships between you and your spouse. You, your kids, and God.

Pull out. Spend time together in places unspoiled by humans. Rivers, forests, meadows cloaked in wildflowers or snow. Hike up a mountain trail. Let your teen lead the way. Admire God's creation together, and be amazed at His handiwork.

Can you spend an hour outside this week with your teen, taking the long view? If it's something you don't normally do, they may resist. Keep pushing until they see that it's not a passing fancy, but something you're serious about continuing. And then make sure you do.

## → Connection Point

*Dear Lord, please forgive me for being shortsighted and busy. I need to worship you as creation does, so I can teach my teen to do the same. Let us grow closer to each other and to you. Amen.*

Powerline365
# Does God Speak to Teenagers?
### *Nicole O'Dell*

*And the Lord said to Samuel: "See, I am about to do something in Israel that will make the ears of everyone who hears of it tingle."*
*1 Sam. 3:11, NIV*

Historians say Samuel was around 12 or 13 when the Lord spoke to him. How was it that a child, a teenager, had such a close relationship with God, that of all the people, God spoke to *him*? Samuel knew God because he sought Him. Samuel pursued his Father. But it didn't start there. He'd been raised in the church for service to God and instructed from scripture to find God. And his mama, Hannah, was a pray-er. She was steadfast and devoted to God.

If we, as parents, desire for God speak to our teenagers, we need to ask Him to. Have you thought about praying your teenager would feel the presence of God and hear His voice in such a compelling way it cannot be denied? Pray your teens will experience God's tangible grace and the unmistakable power of the Holy Spirit in their lives.

But we need to teach them to respect God's commands and show Him reverence by modeling it for them. Do your kids see you in hot pursuit of God? Do they see you pour through scriptures and honor Him with your words? Consider carefully where your lifestyle or language might show disrespect to God. Believe me, your teens will pick up on that, and it will ultimately distance them from Him.

Another way to teach your teens to hear God's voice is to tell them about times when you've heard from Him. Share stories when God met your needs and spoke to your heart. Let them see you walk closely with Him.

## → Connection Point

*Dear Lord, would you please make yourself known to my teenager right now? Speak into my teen's heart in a way that it's undeniably you. Let your love and mercy be an overwhelming wave that rushes right over my family. We want to know you more. Amen.*

# 14

## Good Intentions
### *Nicole O'Dell*

*People may be pure in their own eyes, but the LORD examines their motives. Prov. 16:2, NLT*

You mean God can see the truth of my intentions? He knows when I'm grumbling as I carry out my parenting duties? You mean He knows when I'm secretly glad my spouse gets the blame for something I forgot to do? You mean God knows my biggest fear is that people would see into my heart and mind and call me out for my failures? Oops.

Now, we all make mistakes. God knows that. In fact, He allowed us to become imperfect through sin, which entered the world by a mistake. So that's nothing new. And when our errors come from a place of pure intentions, I believe He honors our intentions rather than punishes our mistake. On the flip side, I believe when we do things that look righteous on the outside, but are borne from impure motives like pride or greed, they are not rewarded.

Let this be freeing to you parenting your teens. Do you really think God is powerless to make something good out of your mess? Of course not. He can turn every mistake we make into something beautiful for His purposes. So, trust God to do that. Start your day with a prayerful act of surrender, and move forward with a desire to make Jesus evident to your teenagers. He will honor even the mistakes you make.

## → Connection Point

*Heavenly Father, would you please expose my impure motives? Help me know when I'm doing the right things for the wrong reasons and then get me back on track by filling me with your purpose. Thank you for guiding my steps. Amen.*

# 15

# Half-Full
## *Nicole O'Dell*

> "I am coming to you now, but I say these things while I am still in the world, so that they may have the full measure of my joy within them." John 17:13, NIV

"Just fill it halfway," you say to the waitress as she holds the steaming pot of coffee over your empty cup. Have you ever noticed that servers rarely stop at the half-full mark? They go just over that in an effort to appear generous. And don't you do the same with your guests? You don't want them to feel rushed to leave or like you're not gracious, so you overfill—you'd rather lavish waste on them than have them leave wanting for more.

Our Father pours out His blessings on us in the same way. He'll pour and pour and pour, filling our cup to overflowing. If we let Him.

What if we applied that truth to the struggles in our relationships with our teens? Let's take an area like communication. Many parents of teens lament the lack of good communication with their teenagers. But God's desire is for an open, healthy relationship, and He would love to pour out huge doses of respect, love, humor, and trust. In what way might a parent prevent that from happening? How might they be holding their hand over that proverbial cup? Maybe they stay too busy that they don't give the opportunity for God to work. Maybe they don't listen well when their teenager does talk. Maybe they gave up too soon—before the breakthrough.

This way of reasoning should be applied to every hard task or wrinkle in your relationship with your teens. Ask yourself what God desires to pour over that problem. Then ask yourself how you might be getting in the way of Him doing that.

If your hand is blocking His blessing by something you're doing or not doing, it's time to move into that ready position, expectant for what the Lord will do.

## → Connection Point

*Dear Jesus, forgive me for not realizing how I was blocking the best you had for me and my teens. Help me to see the ways that I prevent my cup from being filled to overflowing with all I need to have the best of you. I stand ready to receive all you have for me. Amen.*

# 16

## Give Life
### *Pastor Jason Lane*

*For as the Father hath life in himself; so hath he given to the Son to have life in himself. John 5:26, KJV*

What little boy doesn't want to be like Daddy? And what dad doesn't want his little boy to be like him? Open a family scrapbook, and you'll see many pictures of little boys trying to be like Dad. Wearing his clothes, carrying around his tools, riding on the lawn mower, etc. You will also find pictures of dads trying to teach their sons by playing the sport he used to play, etc. Dads and sons are a beautiful combination.

Jesus Christ paints the perfect picture of a son being like his dad. Everything Jesus did was a result of what He had seen and heard the Father say. Christ revealed, "...as the Father hath...so hath he given to the Son..." This revelation has such great significance for every believer, for it is through the Son that we have life. In this revelation, we are shown a picture of the importance of being a parent.

Being a parent to a young child who wants to be exactly like you is so rewarding and full of joy. But parenting a teen who now wants to be his own person can cause frustration. Yet it is at this moment, as a parent, that we must learn from the relationship of Christ to His Father. As we are, so will our teenagers be. The life we live, we give to our sons and daughters, so as they grow, they can have their own life.

So we take each moment and each action to think carefully about how this will impact the life of our teens. Will the decision we make lead them to a life full of the blessings of God? Our teens are more like us than we know. The life they will have is the life that we give to them.

## → Connection Point

*Dear Heavenly Father, as you gave to your Son life may you cause me to remember that I give life to my children. Father, may my words and actions please you and reveal eternal life to my children. In the name of your Son, Jesus, I pray. Amen.*

## Legacy
### *Nicole O'Dell*

*But the steadfast love of the Lord is from everlasting to everlasting on those who fear him, and his righteousness to children's children.*
*Psalm 103:17, ESV*

My grandpa was the closest thing to Jesus that ever walked this planet, as far as I'm concerned. One thing I've always said, and always heard others say is, "Harold Carter never said a bad word about another soul." I heard that over and over while he was alive, and countless time since he passed. His legacy.

How do we want our kids to remember us? What do we want our legacy to be? Some things come to mind, but I think I've already ruined my chances for most of them. Might my children say I've never spoken poorly about another person? Yeah, if they're delusional. Maybe they'll say I was selfless and gave of myself 100% of the time. No ... probably not. Might they say I never lost my temper, and they never heard me raise my voice? Well, maybe if they were only talking about today. Then again, there was that incident at breakfast.

So how do we become an example like those mighty servants who've gone before us? Let me suggest just maybe they weren't as perfect as we remember. I'm guessing if I could have my grandmother here, she'd have plenty of stories concerning my grandpa griping about people he worked with or ranting about the guys on the board at the church. But my memory is about what he strived for. What he taught me. No teacher is perfect, but what she teaches, and what she strives for, is how she will be remembered.

And if all else fails, do as I do. When something goes well, I tell my kids, "Implant this moment in your brain, and forget the rest of the week. This is how I want you to remember me." We laugh together and enjoy the moment ... a surefire way to a lasting memory.

## → Connection Point

*Heavenly Father, please help me shed the guilt I feel for the times I mess up. Help them to see through my weaknesses and embrace my intentions. Help me to make good, lasting memories with my teenagers and not let this time slip by. Amen.*

# 18

## Healthy Heartbreak
### Nicole O'Dell

*The LORD is near to the brokenhearted and saves the crushed in spirit. Psalm 34:18, ESV*

I broke off an engagement before Thanksgiving one year. It was a rough breakup for me. It was rough on my parents because they loved him and his family. Looking back, the break-up was the right thing to do, but difficult at the time. Even more, I felt alone during the holidays. I was missing a part of me that had been there "forever."

In the end, I caved. I told my mom I wanted to put things back together and call my ex. She gave a soft smile and a nod. "That's a choice you're going to have to make for yourself. Just be sure you're not reacting because you feel lonely." She understood what I felt and why I wanted the relationship I'd just ended. She also believed it wasn't the best thing for either of us. But she knew I wouldn't receive all of that from her. I needed to make my own mistakes and learn how to deal with heartbreak and loss in my own way.

So I called and rekindled my relationship. I spent the afternoon at his house, and it was nice, but immediately doubted my choice. We both had to go through the initial stages of grief again. If only I'd pushed through and saved us the repeat suffering.

Sometimes our kids deal with pain and we may have to watch as they do something we know isn't quite right. I'm not talking about sinful or clearly wrong or dangerous choices. But those gray areas we know aren't quite the best. Whether it's ending a relationship or a job choice or choosing a college, we have to let them make some mistakes. Let those circumstances lead you to prayer and build your faith. Be sensitive to the Holy Spirit and listen hard for guidance about when it's time to counsel, time to comfort, or time to challenge.

## → Connection Point

*Father God, guide me as a parent and help me know when I'm responding out of fear and control, and when I'm acting as your voice guiding my teen. Please help me be strong when I must step back and let mistakes happen, then use those mistakes to help my teen grow in maturity. Amen.*

# PB & J
### Nicole O'Dell

*A meal of bread and water in contented peace is better than a banquet spiced with quarrels. Prov. 17:1, MSG*

Remember the days when your little five-year-old arrived home from kindergarten just before lunchtime? You'd have a sandwich ready, cut into perfect triangles, not a bit of crust remaining. That eager conversationalist would straddle a stool at the kitchen counter and munch on carrot sticks while sharing every detail about the day.

Are you finding it's not always that simple (or fulfilling!) anymore? Conversations are few and far between, and when they happen, you know full well you're not getting all the details. Now your teenager offers less than a nod, breezing through the kitchen, grabbing a handful of food before rushing out to the next event. The beautiful pot roast, mashed potatoes, salad, and fresh bread you've prepared withers away, ignored. But you long for the days of PB & J.

What's stopping you? Why not greet your teenager at curfew Friday night the way you used to greet that kindergartener? Go back to comfortable basics to reconnect your relationship. No matter what it seems, your kid is never too old for a nice peanut butter and jelly sandwich and cold glass of milk. Trust me, you'll get some sideways looks, and it might seem you've lost your mind, but I'll bet it won't take more than a few minutes for the nostalgia to catch on.

## → Connection Point

*Heavenly Father, Prince of Peace, please bring simplicity and comfort to my home. Remind us of the days of when easy was best and conversation flowed. Help us get back to basics and enjoy the simple things in life. Amen.*

## 20

## Mirror Image
### Laura L. Smith

*For we are God's masterpiece. He has created us anew in Christ Jesus, so we can do the good things He planned for us long ago. Eph. 2:10, NLT*

When you looked in the mirror this morning, what did you see there? Did your daughter hear you spout negativity? Did she hear you say you look fat, you hate your nose, or you've been thinking about Botox?

As early as age one, kids mimic their parents by talking into toy phones, cooking in play kitchens, and pushing plastic mowers around the yard. Our daughters look to us to see how we'll act and react to different situations. If we think *we're* overweight, what do we think about *her* body? If we think *our* nose is too big, what is she to think about *her* nose when everyone says she looks just like her mom?

Eight million people in the U.S. are fighting eating disorders. ABC News reports that 8,000 girls age 13 to 19 had their breasts enlarged last year. Eighty-one percent of ten-year-old girls have dieted at least once. If we are all Christ's masterpieces, then why all this binging and purging and going under the knife?

Helping your daughter feel good about herself starts with you. So, if you have some wrinkles, praise God for the laughter that's etched them on your face. If you're feeling a little heavy, buy some fruits and veggies at the grocery store and prepare them for your family. You'll all be healthier and feel better.

Take a walk to get your heart pumping and invite your daughter along. You'll be amazed by the talks you'll have when you're both soothed by fresh air and the rhythm of footsteps. Eliminate the words "fat" and "diet" from your vocabulary. Train yourself to smile when you pass the mirror. It will take some getting used to, but it will become a habit. And your daughter just might smile at herself more. too.

## → Connection Point

*Dear God, thank You for making me in your glorious image. Please help me stop comparing myself to others and instead hold tight to the fact that you created me exactly how I am. Please help me remind my daughter that she, too, is one of your beautiful creations, your priceless masterpiece. Amen.*

## Take it Back
*Nicole O'Dell*

*He who guards his mouth and his tongue keeps himself from troubles.*
*Prov. 21:23, AMP*

Ever say something to your kids you immediately wished you could unsay? Yeah, me too. How many good things does it take to override one bad? Is that possible? Will this be what my son takes into his adulthood? Will my daughter's self-esteem be forever wrecked because of that comment I made? Those are the questions I ask myself when I mess up.

You too, huh?

Words that fly off our tongues in rash moments can do a lot of damage. We need to keep a tight rein on our mouths. It's so important that God addresses it over and over in scripture. There's power in our spoken words. Power to give life and hope to someone or the power to destroy them.

This is especially important when speaking to our teenagers who are formulating opinions about themselves. Our words can impart security and confidence, helping to shape an expectation of personal success. Or they can rock the foundation of self-esteem and stir up doubt and low expectations.

And when we mess up, because we will, two little words go a long way – I'm sorry. Apologize to your kids when you speak hurtfully. They need to know you're aware of the error. It'll go a long way toward repairing any damage from hurtful words.

## → Connection Point

*Jesus, please help me control my tongue. Help me speak only words of life to my teenagers. When I need to correct or discipline, please give me the grace to do it in a way that encourages growth, rather than stifles your work. Let the things I say impart confidence and hope. Amen.*

# 22

## Use Your Lifeline
### Nicole O'Dell

*The fear of human opinion disables; trusting in God protects you from that. Prov. 29:25, MSG*

When stakes are high, decision-making isn't easy. I get stymied when considering whether to take one of my kids to the ER. I dread that moment when the kid (young or old) jokes with the doc and reality hits – I overreacted. I've taken to polling Facebook friends, and their friends. Should I get an x-ray – pictures posted too, of course – is it normal for lips to turn a slight blue color?

Two out of ten responses are extreme. "Oh no! She's going to die!" Another two of ten go the other direction. "Give her a dose of Benadryl and put her to bed." The rest are in the middle – follow my intuition.

Whose advice do I take? I'll follow the wisdom I sought in the first place. All I really want is reassurance. Someone to back me up if I make a mistake. "Oh, sorry, doc! All my Facebook friends said I should rush her here."

The fear of failure, small or big. If my choice relies on outside advice, somehow it absolves me of the responsibility for the outcome. Maybe rather than spending time polling our friends, we should put time and effort into polling the scriptures.

God gives the best advice because He's been there already. Past, present, and future. He knows not only what will happen, but God knows how He's going to use it for His purposes. He sometimes uses people to bring us wise counsel – even on Facebook. But godly counsel will always agree with and turn us back to the Word of God. Godly counsel focuses on relationship and dependence on Him.

So when parenting your teens, turn to God's word for advice about discipline and expectations. Turn to prayer for guidance on how to react to a situation or teach a truth. Truly, when led by God's wisdom, we can't make a mistake.

## → Connection Point

*Lord, thank you for being my ultimate lifeline. Help me always turn to you when I'm in doubt and need direction. Lead me to people who will give me godly counsel based only on your Word, but tune me to Your voice most of all. Amen.*

Powerline365

# 23
## Righty or Lefty?
*Nicole O'Dell*

*But God's kindness made me what I am, and that kindness was not wasted on me. I Cor. 15:10a, GWT*

The brain has two connected halves known as the left and right hemispheres. They handle different thought processes and styles of behavior. We all use both sides of our brains, but each person has a preference for one side. That preference is coded deep within our DNA.

It's far easier to operate the preferred portion of your brain. Using the other side requires almost double the effort. Think of handwriting. If you're a righty, it's doubly difficult to write with your left hand.

This is also how we get to be numbers or words people. My daughter loves math. That concept doesn't compute with me. Love = Math? Since I'm a creative-type, there's something off about that to me. She's logical, sequential, reasoned. I'm random, creative, and emotional.

We need to consider our teenager's brain preference and adjust expectations accordingly. I can assume my daughter may need extra help with her creative writing homework, but I also know she'll be the one helping my young kids with math in middle school. It's up to me, to us, to support and nurture the preferences ingrained within our kids. God made them that way for a reason.

Is your teenager bored, distracted, unmotivated, moody, disengaged? Is it possible school, work, or other obligations are pushing against natural tendencies and creating frustration? Teens rarely have the insight to say, "Hey, I'm a right-brained person and there are too many left-brained activities in my life. I'm uninspired and checking out." So, we need to protect them. We need to watch their lives don't become so full of who they aren't they lose sight of who they are.

## → Connection Point

*Lord, please show me what it's going to take to inspire my teenager to pursue your will. Help me to embrace our differences and celebrate what makes my teenager special to you and unique to others. Let the differences between us be a source of unity, not division. Amen.*

# 24

## People Pleaser
*Amber Frank*

*Am I now trying to win the approval of human beings, or of God? Or am I trying to please people? If I were still trying to please people, I would not be a servant of Christ. Gal. 1:10, NIV*

I am a people pleaser. As a firstborn, I come by it honestly. I was the good girl when I was growing up, always conscious of what I was doing and whom it might affect. Now, I am not saying this is the worst trait to have as a teen but, after coming to understand Galatians 1:10, it's definitely something I've talked to my teens about.

We need to teach our teens whom they should be pleasing and, as much as we wish it were different, we are not to be first on that list. Parents are in the class of "people" this scripture is talking about. I have witnessed many parents pushing their children into sports, hobbies, or classes just because the parents want to see some kind of achievement or accolades from it.

Often this is done without praying and asking God what it is the child should be doing. It is our responsibility to teach them how to ask God what direction their lives should be headed, and to guide them in *that* direction. God has given our children specific gifts and talents. When our teens are walking in those gifts, they are pleasing the Father.

We all want what's best for our kids. Even the best-intentioned parents can have selfish motives. I know I do sometimes. Who doesn't want to see their kids patted on the back and given the award? Let's be honest — it feels good, doesn't it? Like maybe they are patting our backs, too? It can be hard for a parent to lay aside our hopes and dreams for our children and go with something entirely different. But, we can always trust God; after all He always has the best intentions for us and our children. Remember they are *His* children first.

## → Connection Point

*Heavenly Father, thank you that you are the perfect example of a parent. Help me to focus more on pleasing you and less on pleasing people. Please give me wisdom and discernment in directing my teenagers in the way they are to go. It is in you I place my trust. Amen.*

## The Power of an Apology
### Nicole O'Dell

*Confess your faults one to another, and pray one for another, that ye may be healed.* James 5:16a, KJV

"I'm sorry."

Those two little words hold power. The power to heal relationships. The power to overcome division. The power to right a wrong. But they also have the power to keep us silent. How many times have those words stuck to the tip of your tongue and remained unspoken? Yes, me too.

I used to have such a tough time apologizing because it was like admitting I was wrong. Okay, exactly like it! That was tough for me. But something clicked one day. I realized a sincere apology catapulted a relationship over the offense directly to the good part. Suddenly the apology wasn't a wicked cross to bear, but a treasured balm that soothed the wounds.

So often I'm ready to go toe-to-toe with one of my teens or my husband. But instead of launching into the litany of reasons why I'm right, I just say, "I'm sorry."

Their reaction is almost always the same. First, they rear back a bit in surprise. Their lower jaw snaps shut. Eyebrows furrow as they ponder what just happened. Maybe they consider having one more go at it, so their mouth opens slightly preparing the next argument. But then their face softens in realization it's a happier place on the other side of forgiveness. So they join me there. Peace.

"But if I apologize to my teens, I'm giving them power over me!" Actually, the opposite is true. Our enemy lives in and thrives on division. He dances on our unforgiveness. He parades across our pride. The power comes when we lay down pride and repent for wrong words or actions, surrendering selfishness to God. In that place of humility, the enemy has no power. God can move mightily in our relationships.

## → Connection Point

*Father, please forgive me for the pride that keeps me from admitting when I'm wrong. Help me become more real with my friends and loved ones, especially my teens. And please use my humility to restore my relationships and as a living example to my teens. Amen.*

## What will People Say?
*Nicole O'Dell*

*Obviously, I'm not trying to win the approval of people, but of God. If pleasing people were my goal, I would not be Christ's servant. Gal. 1:10, ESV*

My 14-year old made a photomontage of her sweet friends doing goofy, girly things. She set it to music, uploaded it to Facebook, and tagged all the girls, as well as most of the moms and a few dads. And me. It was really cute, that is until the singer said a bad word! The horror!

Was I worried my daughter was listening to bad music? Nope. Was I afraid she'd gone to the dark side? Nope. Not at all. My first reaction was to fear the other parents would think I let her listen to garbage. My brain went down a rabbit trail, "They'll think that's what we listen to, and that I think it's okay to post it on Facebook. Or worse, they'll think I have no idea what my daughter listens to!"

Well, I quickly grabbed my runaway thoughts and realized I needed to focus on my daughter. I asked why she used that song. She said, "It mostly said the stuff I wanted to say. I figured I could ignore one bad part." Oh, boy. We talked for a long time about how sin is like that. When most of a person's behavior is good, does God overlook the one bad thing? Or does He want us to work on that one bad part, too?

In the end, she chose to change to a more appropriate song. Had people thought badly of me or of her in the meantime? I have no idea. But after correcting my focus, I didn't care. The opportunity to make an impact with my daughter was worth any embarrassment I might have experienced, real or imagined.

Don't be afraid to let your parenting mistakes go public. We're all in this together. If someone can learn, then your error was worth it. God will take all of the messes we make and turn them into something beautiful if we let Him. What weakness have you hidden from view? Is it time to be more vulnerable?

## → Connection Point

*Father, please forgive me for the times I've tried to hide my weaknesses in order to look like the perfect parent. Make me more transparent so others can benefit from what I'm learning. Amen.*

## A Bounced Check
*Nicole O'Dell*

*What good will it be for a man if he gains the whole world, yet forfeits his soul? Matt. 16:26, NIV*

Little kids see Mom and Dad use checks and debit cards, and give no thought to where the money comes from to back up the purchases. They think parents write a check, and then they get to take home a trinket or treasure. Teenagers begin to grasp the value of money, but most don't deal with the struggle to acquire it. They sure know how to spend it, though! But each cashed check or debit transacted depletes the bank account. When the account is empty, the check bounces and penalties are charged.

This cycle is also true for our parenting accounts, especially as it relates to things like peace, joy, and self-control. Kids constantly write checks against our emotional accounts. Bad attitude. Argumentative nature. Failing grades. Deception. Even simple things like not bringing home the band concert details until the day of. Oh, or they us signed up to bring three-dozen cookies. Those are all checks cashed against emotional reserves. What happens when our accounts are depleted?

An empty reserve equals an irrational, tired, and angry parent. It causes arguments and misunderstandings. Resentment builds and expectations go unmet. Hopelessness builds until it zaps all joy.

But there is One who can refill our spiritual accounts to overflowing. If we let go of the checkbook and turn it over to Him, the Holy Spirit will keep our accounts in the black. He has more than enough of whatever we need and stands waiting. Visualize a check ledger with a big deposit of whatever you need today, and then ask Him to provide it.

## → Connection Point

*Jesus, please help me to keep my life balanced. Show me where I'm writing checks I can't cover. Please make a hefty deposit into my emotional accounts so I can be a joyful and confident parent. Amen.*

## Faith to the Fourth
*Wendy Fitzgerald*

> *You have heard me teach things that have been confirmed by many reliable witnesses. Now teach these truths to other trustworthy people who will be able to pass them on to others.*
> 2 Tim. 2:2, NLT

There are four generations of faith mentioned in the above verse: Paul to Timothy, Timothy to trustworthy people, and trustworthy people to others.

I am a sucker for kitchen gadgets! I love them. However, I must confess that some of the gadgets that I "had to have" have never even been used. But there are some items in my kitchen that are heavily used, and my colanders top that list. I have a large one for use while making family meals, one that I inherited from my grandmother's kitchen, and a few hand-held strainers. Each colander has a different design, but they are all used for the same purpose: to strain and filter, allowing liquid, usually water, to flow through.

The benefit of the colander is that the water flows through it. The water purifies as it passes through. Without this function, the washing and cleansing would be ineffective.

In John 4:10, Jesus tells the woman at the well that He is the Living Water. Water flows *into* a pot, but *through* a colander. As parents, our job is to ensure that our faith in Jesus, the Living Water, is poured through us to successive generations. We must, like Paul to Timothy, teach our teenagers what is right. However, teaching them isn't enough. Until they learn to let the love of God flow through them and then begin to teach others how to teach others, our job is not done. Throughout the Bible, discipleship is encouraged because it is the only way that faith will survive!

## → Connection Point

*Father, please help me to pass my faith not only to my children, but also through my children so that future generations will know of Your great love and faithfulness. Help me raise disciples of you who will disciple others. Amen.*

Powerline365

# But for the Grace of God
### Nicole O'Dell

*The secret things belong to the LORD our God, but the things that are revealed belong to us and to our children forever, that we may do all the words of this law. Deut. 29:29, ESV*

When I dealt with the reality of my teen pregnancy, I had a tough conversation with a pastor and his wife. I worked for their church near the Bible college I attended. A great job for wonderful people. But I messed up. I was afraid to tell the pastor's wife ... like I'd let her down the most. But she gave a soft smile and squeezed my hand, "But for the grace of God, there Pastor Jody and I go."

Oh my. Realization flooded my understanding. We have *all* sinned. I knew that verse and truth. I'd never seen it applied in a real-life situation as it affected me in that moment. She shared that she and her future husband had engaged in the same sin. They just hadn't gotten caught. *We have all sinned.*

These truths about grace we believe, but have a difficult time employing, can apply to our parenting. What sin have you not been forgiven of? Think of the woman caught in adultery. Jesus said, "You who are without sin, cast the first stone." Who had the right under those conditions? Only Jesus. Yet He didn't condemn. But for the grace of God. Now offer your teenager the same grace you've been shown.

Should you overlook bad behavior and choices? Of course not. Treat those as God deals with them – teaching moments, not defining moments. As inspiration and a call to higher living, not condemnation and a path to punishment. Use them for instruction. Discipline. Freedom.

How many times have we caught our teens in their sins? How many times have we not? It doesn't matter. God chooses to reveal and keep hidden what He wishes according to His purposes alone.

## → Connection Point

*Father God, thank you for your forgiveness in my life. Please help me to extend just a fraction of grace and forgiveness to my teenager. Help me to live as an example of your grace and favor in my teenager's life so that through my actions you will be revealed. Amen.*

## It is Well with my Soul
*Nicole O'Dell*

*When peace like a river attendeth my way*
*When sorrows like sea billows roll*
*Whatever my lot, Thou has taught me to say*
*It is well; it is well, with my soul.*

A familiar hymn, but do you know the story behind it? Horatio Spafford had lost everything in the Chicago fire and then lost his wife and four daughters at sea. He penned that hymn as he sailed from America to Europe after learning the news about his family. We cannot imagine the pain he felt. A writer for Choose NOW Ministries, Dori Powledge Phillips, received a phone call at work one day that her husband and four youngest children were killed in a car accident on the way to school. Dori's world shattered in a matter of moments. She, like Horatio Spafford, chose to praise God through it all.

It is well with my soul.

What are you enduring? Hopefully nothing as tragic as those two stories, but I would hazard a guess you have your own set of trials. Would you consider involving your teenagers in your struggle? Let them know what's causing pain. Talk to them about how it feels to lose a job or what it feels like to watch the bottom dropping out of your finances. Let them know you're worried about your ailing mother or father. Let them see you weep and cry out to Jesus.

Hiding the realities of the world will not prepare them to rely on God. Show them no matter what you're going through, you turn to Jesus. Explain it's not easy to face trials, but rather a daily choice to surrender to God in faith.

## → Connection Point

*Holy Spirit, guide and show me what I should share with my teenagers. Let me know what is safe to talk about and how to use my own struggles as teaching opportunities for them. And while I'm pointing toward you, help me make sure my actions stay true to my calling. Let me be an example of strong faith in you. Amen.*

# 31

## Run your own Race
### Nicole O'Dell

*I have fought the good fight, I have finished the race, I have kept the faith. 2 Timothy 4:7, ESV*

A young woman began running her first 10K race side-by-side with her dad. Excited to test her limits, she looked ahead at the course like a racehorse at the starting gate. They began to run, and it soon became apparent they had different needs. She needed to run faster in order to maintain her endurance on the hills, and he needed to run at a slower and more even pace to even hope to finish. They decided to separate so they could run their own races more effectively and arrive at the finish line their own way.

Although she'd wanted to finish with her dad, this young lady crossed the line well ahead of him. Proud of her accomplishment and reveling in the moment, something was missing. The moment, in her mind, was one she'd share with her dad.

She ran back the way she'd already come, hoping to find her determined, but likely weakened, father. When she met him, she smiled and finished his race with him.

Parents, your teenagers will outrun you one day. This is a good thing. It means you've raised them well, inspired independence, and nurtured ambition. Be proud to step aside as they blow past you in life's races. Keep running your own race at your pace, as a steady example of faithful endurance. One day they'll realize your encouraging presence beside them is worth every gold medal.

## → Connection Point

*Lord, give me the strength I need to finish my race, and the wisdom I need to run it well. Help me to encourage my teens to pass by as they embark on their own course, and then unite us at the finish line. Amen.*

## Give Them a Work
*Pastor Jason Lane*

*Jesus answered and said unto them, "This is the work of God, that ye believe on him whom he hath sent." John 6:29, KJV*

My son Isaiah is preparing to enter high school. Just the other night we went to an open house for a high school we're considering. I was amazed at how things are so different from when I was that age. One of the first questions they asked Isaiah was to define his chosen career path. But my son's biggest concerns to that point had been what to eat when hungry or what game to play when he was bored. Now he was suddenly being asked to make a decision that could impact the rest of his life?

I asked him what he thought he would say. He threw his hands in the air and said, "Dad, I don't know!" His response was not merely the typical avoidance tactic of a teen; it was his honest answer. His honesty left me, the all-confident dad, scared and wondering. Was he supposed to have this all figured out already? Had I somehow failed by not steering him to a confirmed vision for his future?

The followers of Christ asked Him, "What shall we do, that we might work the works of God?" His response to them is equally a direction for us as parents. "This is the work of God, that ye believe on him whom he hath sent." We are to give our children work and that work is to believe on Jesus. Believing on Christ is the greatest thing our teens can do. And imparting that faith to them is our number one charge.

We can't make our children believe, but we can reveal how our beliefs truly impact our lives. We can let them see our faith lived out in daily circumstances. And we can let them see our hunger for more of Him.

## → Connection Point

Dear Heavenly Father, thank You for giving Your Son a work. I praise you for His work on Calvary and for Your Word that gives me faith. I ask you to help me to reveal my faith to my family, so I may give my children the work of believing in Your Son. Amen.

## Parenting Recipe
*Nicole O'Dell*

*Preach the word; be ready in season and out of season; reprove, rebuke, and exhort, with complete patience and teaching. 2 Tim. 4:2, ESV*

Do you have a favorite recipe? What goes into it to make it really special? One of my favorite things to make is my "world-famous" chili. World-famous is in quotes because it's a title my kids awarded, not because my chili has received any global celebration, in case you were wondering.

Two ingredients that go into my chili might make you grimace. Logically it doesn't even make sense. One of those ingredients makes the chili spicier, even though that ingredient has no heat properties itself. But those two ingredients blend to accent the spice of the chili and make it easier to take. In fact, finicky children will eat it without complaint — and ask for seconds.

It's the perfect recipe.

What can we put into our parenting to simulate the effect on our teens as those secret ingredients have in my chili? Do we have something that adds flavor and zing, but also offsets the spice to make it easier to swallow?

Exhortation is that ingredient. Some definitions of the word exhort include: strongly urge, encourage, influence by words or advice, persuade. Notice exhortation is not criticism; it's a call to improvement. Yet along with it comes the expectation of success. It's different than criticism, which carries an element of despair and discourages the teen. Exhortation expects and assumes the recipient will succeed in the challenge and thrive in the call to improvement.

## → Connection Point

*Father, please help me season my words with enough flavor that they leave no bitterness. Help me to encourage my teens to live better and strive for more without making them feel criticized. Love them through me. Call them to yourself through me. Amen.*

## Checkmate
*Nicole O'Dell*

*... so that Satan will not outsmart us. For we are familiar with his evil schemes.* 2 Cor. 2:11, NLT

I stink at chess. There, I said it. I don't like it, and I'm not good at it. It's maddening to think ahead and guess the other person's move. Statistics and a master chess player would know when he places a piece his opponent is likely to respond with a certain move. They can plan three or four steps ahead in that way. For me that's way too unknown. There's nothing I can control.

I can set it up the way I want to, but I realize I'm not the only one with a strategy. My opponent is working up a plan, too.

In parenting our teenagers, we have to be aware our opponent is cooking a devastating scheme while we're working for the win. He's not going to step back and accept defeat easily. He knows all the right moves and has practiced them time and time again. The only way to victory over our ultimate opponent is to know our Master so well it doesn't matter what move the enemy makes.

You don't have to gamble on what temptation he'll throw at your teenagers. What obstacle he'll put in their path. What danger they'll be in. All you need to worry about is your Master's plan. If you trust Him, God will tell you the next move and relieve you of the burden of trying to read your enemy's mind. It doesn't matter what the enemy thinks because victory is sure.

## → Connection Point

*Thank you, Lord, for promising ultimate victory! Help me not to try to see so far into the future that I miss out on what you have for me to learn today. In your Holy Name, I pray against the enemy's schemes. May they have no victory in my home. Amen.*

## From the Back
### Nicole O'Dell

*Start children off on the way they should go, and even when they are old they will not turn from it. Prov. 22:6, NIV*

When they're babies, we coax those first few steps out of them as we cheer them on from the front. But once they catch on, it seems we're always watching from behind. Their first tottering steps take them away from us as they pursue a toy. The toy turns into a bicycle and we watch as they ride away.

"I'll be back before curfew!" The door slams as we race for a hug. Too late. We watch as the car drives away. Before we know it, prom night arrives. They pose for a few pictures, and then drive away waving out the window.

Not long after, we watch proudly as they process into the high school gymnasium to accept their diploma. Then the day comes when they walk a different aisle. We strain for the last glimpse as after the pastor declares the two, "man and wife." Then they float out of the church and sail off for a new life.

We parent, pray, press on, and pray some more. Then we take our places in the cheering section and watch, always from the back, as our kids journey on. Those milestones represents a lot of work and even heartache. But it's the smiles they wore that will fill our memories. And when they grin in pride and shout, "I did it!" We'll nod along, "Yes, you did."

## → Connection Point

*Lord, would you remind me every day my children are not rushing away from me, they are rushing toward something. Would you remind me that I want what they want, which is what you want. Would you help me guide them toward the beauty you planned for their future? Never let me hold them back out of fear or selfishness or personal ambition. Let me parent in freedom and confidence, empowered by you. Amen.*

## Greetings of Love
*Shannon Deitz*

*Greet one another with the kiss of love. Peace to all of you who are in Christ. 1 Pet. 5:14, NIV*

Bailey is a yellow Labrador retriever with a special talent: jumping. Upon our arrival home she goes from 0–100, jumping straight up and down as if the concrete is a trampoline. It's difficult to be annoyed with a heartwarming greeting filled with such great abounding joy. The love of a pet is so simple and pure. No matter how long the day or what troubles and tribulations we are suffering, when we see Bailey jump, ears flopping and tongue hanging, for that moment we remember there is always room for joy.

I've often considered how I greet those I love in my life, especially my children. When they walk through the door, do I greet them with arms opened wide and appreciation in my heart?

When my children were younger, I knew that if I smiled at them, they'd smile back. If I laughed, they'd laugh. If I cried, they'd furrow their eyebrows and pat my shoulder. It didn't take long in Parenting 101 to realize I needed a smile on my face and a joyful greeting in my heart whether it was the first greeting of the morning, a connection after a nap, or a reunion after a long day at work.

Dogs and young kids are fairly similar. They exist to be loved. Teenagers appear to grow out of this need…but it's a deflection. They throw up defense mechanisms to guard against disappointment, but they need you just the same. They want to know they are noticed and welcomed into a loving environment. Just as we long to be greeted by the Lord, to know when we come face to face we might hear, *"Well done, good and faithful servant! You have been faithful with a few things; I will put you in charge of many things. Come and share your master's happiness!"* Matthew 25:23 (NIV).

## → Connection Point

*Father, help me to appreciate those I love, to greet them with an abounding love, and to offer security and confidence to my children. Amen.*

# 37

Powerline365

## Journeying Alone
### Nicole O'Dell

*I will never leave you nor forsake you. Heb. 13:5b, ESV*

Are you parenting alone? Maybe you're a single parent or a parent whose partner isn't present. Maybe you're feeling alone because your spouse isn't a believer, so you're shouldering the spiritual responsibilities yourself.

I want you to know your circumstances aren't too big for God.

Financial burdens have you worried about the future? Not too big for God. Do you fear the choices your teenager is making will lead to long-lasting consequences? Not too big for God. Are you worried about your employment situation? Not too big for God.

The key here is surrender. Any doubt or fear you feel stems from a place of unbelief. If I were speaking publicly right now I'd repeat that line. It's so important to know, without some level of unbelief, there'd be no fear. If you truly believe God's promises, then you believe He will complete the work He began in your teenager. If you believe in God's Word, then you know He will restore the damage the enemy has caused. If you really believe in God's plan for you, then you expect, without doubt, He will take what your enemy meant for bad and turn it around for good. And if you believe the Lord, then you know you're never alone. Ever.

This is not meant as a condemnation. Unbelief expressed in the form of doubt or fears are normal human conditions. But when we hold our fears up against the promises of God, we're left with one action. Surrender.

## → Connection Point

*Lord, help me, please. Help me believe with every fiber of my being that your word is true and your promises will never go unfulfilled. Help me cling to those promises as I parent my teenagers in confidence. Empower me. Embolden me. And please restore the joy that has been swallowed by fear. Thank You. Amen*

## Powered Up
*Nicole O'Dell*

*When I am afraid, I will put my trust in you. Psalm 56:3, ESV*

Cell phones, texting, and social media access present confusing decisions for many parents. Privacy is important, but how much is too much? Teenagers need space, but how much is too much? Texting isn't bad, but how much is too much?

The first step in parenting teens in today's touchscreen climate is to setting ground rules. The most important rule is that you should have all access, all the time. If your teenagers have social media accounts, you should have the passwords. If they send text messages, you should be able to check them at will –and do so randomly. You wouldn't give a group of teens complete privacy in person, so why when an electronic device is involved? Especially since technology affords a sense of anonymity that might lead to things they wouldn't normally do.

Some dangerous behavior red flags:
- Hides cell phone when you come in the room.
- Won't leave phone unattended – ever.
- Changes passwords regularly.
- Has chunks of deleted text messages.

Be on guard because these behaviors are cause for concern. That said, trust is important. The goal of setting boundaries is to give your teenager room to prove trustworthiness while ensuring safety. As long as there are no red flags, be open and trusting with your teen. If you have reason to think something is amiss, stay calm. Pray for guidance, and then approach your teenager with logic and openness. The goal should always be to reinforce boundaries, grow from mistakes, and restore trust.

## → Connection Point

*Dear Jesus, it's really hard to make good decisions about things that change so fast. Technology confuses and scares me. Help me to be wise and keep my kids safe. Please protect them and show me what I need so I can do my part. Thank you for loving them even more than I do. Amen.*

## Spilled Milk
### Nicole O'Dell

*Brothers, I do not consider that I have made it my own. But one thing I do: forgetting what lies behind and straining forward to what lies ahead... Phil. 3:13, ESV*

Don't cry over spilled milk. I see that well known piece of advice lived out every day in the lives of my preschoolers. They spill something – they cry. It's a simple but endless cycle. I tell them not to cry, but I do hope they'll eventually learn reaching across the table is a sure way to knock over a glass. Or if they don't sit flat on their seat and eat properly, they'll tip something over. Or if they try wrestling their brother at the dining room table, something is bound to spill. One day they'll learn – right?

The same thing is true for our teenagers. We don't want them dissolving in a fit of tears over mistakes, but we do want them to learn. We hope that the consequences of bad choices will leave a lasting impression so next time they'll make a different choice.

Preschoolers, teenagers, and parents – we're in the same boat, whether we like it or not. It doesn't help to look back on our parenting mistakes and cry about them, but we do need to identify and repent, and then learn from them. I'll admit most of my parenting mistakes have to do with losing my cool, not being available when I was needed, and being too busy to enjoy the moments. I can cry and beat myself up, or I can learn and move on.

What are some things you have regretted as a parent? Let's leave our regrets in the past and do things differently next time.

## → Connection Point

*Lord, thank you for your unending forgiveness. Now please help me to forgive myself. Help me see my mistakes and learn – and then let them go. Let my mistakes be a growth point in my parenting and an example to my teens. Amen.*

# 40

## Training for Ultimate Success
### Dori Powledge Phillips

*Train up a child in the way he should go: and when he is old, he will not depart from it. Prov. 22:6, KJV*

The moment we lay eyes on our beautiful newborn, aspirations of greatness run wild and the possibilities are limitless. Of course we never dream about the hiccups or the trials of life, though they certainly will come. During these seasons, we must stand firm on the Word of God and fight the fight of faith. Our teens are watching how we respond in good times and bad, and we are training them in the way they should go, whether we realize it or not.

As a mother of eight, four boys and four girls (six born to me and two by marriage), I can say without a doubt that I have some parenting regrets peppered throughout the years. I thank God for His amazing grace which covers a multitude of my mistakes. But in Christ, as we are led by His Spirit, the good will *always* outweigh the bad if we let it.

In 2005 an incredibly tragic car accident took my husband and four youngest children to Heaven. Our four older children (18, 17, 16, and 14) experienced great pain and devastation, and even some rebellion. My husband and I were not perfect parents, but we had trained our children in the way they should go. It was the ultimate test.

I stood on the Word of God and fought for my children in prayer. The Word always works. Today, now all in their early twenties, my children are living free in Christ, healed, recovered, and restored. They held to their childhood training and are living God-filled successful lives. In spite of life's circumstances or trials—good and bad—standing on the Word of God will always work and, ultimately, our children will not depart from it. And this is true success.

Have you let guilt keep you from training your children with the Word of God? If so, you are only a moment away from releasing those feelings and trusting the Lord with their futures.

## → Connection Point

*Lord, I thank you that because of Jesus' sacrifice on the cross, I am not guilty. I lay all guilt and shame at your feet and trust that your grace is truly sufficient for our lives. Help me to see where my children need daily guidance. I thank you and trust you. Amen.*

## Teenage Talents
### Nicole O'Dell

*For to everyone who has will more be given, and he will have an abundance. But from the one who has not, even what he has will be taken away. Matt. 24:19, ESV*

Have you heard the parable of the talents? Three men were given talents according to his own ability. One was given five. He invested them and built a return of five more. One was given two. He also earned a full return on his investment with two additional to show the master. But the man who was only given one buried it. He didn't want his master to return and find it squandered. The first two were praised for their business sense, but the third man was chastised for wastefulness.

Your teenager is very much like those talents. How are you investing your efforts into your teenager? How are you raising your teen to bring profit to the Kingdom of God? There's a little secret about teenagers: they want to be useful. They believe everyone else thinks they have nothing to offer so they sulk, or hide, or avoid. In reality, when they know someone believes in them and has use for them, teens thrive.

Are you raising an evangelist unafraid to talk about Jesus? Are you raising a worker willing to help those in need? Are you raising a generous heart that blesses the Kingdom with financial gain? When we're intentional about how we pour into our teens so they'll overflow and bring glory to God, then we're gaining traction with the next generation.

We have the choice to "get by", barely make it, through the teen years and hope they do well as adults. Or we can parent victoriously by raising our teens to take charge of their talents and make their Master proud.

## → Connection Point

*Dear Jesus, please help me see your vision for the future and help me invest in my teenager, reaping dividends for the Kingdom of God. Show me what to focus on, and help me to train and guide my teenager into whatever role you have called. Amen.*

# Good Fences
## Nicole O'Dell

*Be self-controlled and alert. Your enemy the devil prowls around like a roaring lion looking for someone to devour. I Pet. 5:8, NIV*

I am not a dog-owner, nor, due to my allergies, a dog-lover. But I agreed to dog-sit for a very old, very sleepy, hypoallergenic dog, plus I had a fenced-in backyard. Perfect scenario.

When they arrived, they opened the car door and let the dog out, unleashed. He followed at their heels as we went through the garage, through the kitchen, and then out to the fenced-in yard where the doggie did his business. Taking care of that pooch would be a breeze.

Doggie was napping near the window, and I needed to put the garbage out, so I opened the garage door. Well, that dog jumped up and bolted through the open door as if he'd been shot from a cannon. He ran out of the garage, around the house, past the yard and onto the highway where he was instantly hit by a pick-up truck and killed.

I was stunned. I beat myself up for weeks. Months. I couldn't think of what I should have done differently. Maybe I shouldn't have opened the door. But he had been sleeping, the owners hadn't warned against him running or provided a leash, he had shown no indication of energy exertion to that point...and we had a really great fence. The problem was that he had chosen to circumvent the fence and go his own way.

We construct protective boundaries—spiritual fences—around our families, but how do we make sure our teenagers stay within them? For starters, be sure your fence posts include open communication, respect, encouragement, and security. Make the zone within the constraints of your borders a place of comfort. Talk openly about what's on the other side, sharing both the desires and the dangers that lurk beyond.

Challenge: Ask your teenager what triggers the impulse to bolt beyond the boundaries. You may be surprised at what you hear.

## → Connection Point

*Father, help me build a solid fence around my home that will protect the unity in my family and keep my teens secure in your plan. Help my teenagers to always be on guard against the temptations and lies of the enemy that lure them to the other side of the fence. Amen.*

# Mission Statement
## Nicole O'Dell

*...what does the LORD require of you but to do justly, to love mercy, and to walk humbly with your God? Micah 6:8b, NKJV*

That's a pretty good mission statement, if you ask me. Guess whose mission statement this is: "To inspire and nurture the human spirit – one person, one cup, and one neighborhood at a time." If you guessed Starbucks, you got it right.

To create a good mission statement, first identify your passion, purpose, and plan. The Starbucks website expands on their mission statement. They aim to bless people with good coffee and community. Their purpose is to inspire and nurture. And their plan is to do it consistently, one bit at a time.

Do you have a family mission statement?

**What is your family's passion**? What motivates and inspires you? What draws you closer in unity with God and each other? Identify your passion because that can help you figure out your purpose.

**What is your purpose as a family?** When you understand what God has for you as a family, it's much easier to work together to achieve that purpose. What burden has God laid on your hearts? What calling do you feel? Whatever God has birthed in you is there for a reason. Now you need a plan.

**What is your plan?** Once you know your passion and you've identified your purpose, you can begin to construct a plan. All plans should be held loosely so God has room to redirect as needed, but they should have enough structure to keep everyone moving forward.

**Challenge**: Sit down with your teens this week and work on your mission statement. Ask them what they see as a driving passion and purpose for your family, then work together to construct a plan that will help you achieve it. Start with broad descriptions and narrow it down to a catchy one-liner that you can each memorize.

## → Connection Point

*Father, thank You for calling my family to you. Thank you for instilling godly passion and for giving us a purpose. Now, will you help us make a plan? Help us devise and then live out a mission statement that reflects your heart in us. Amen.*

## Three To-Do's of Parenting
### Bethany Jett

*I planted, Apollos watered, but God gave the growth. So neither he who plants nor he who waters is anything, but only God who gives the growth. I Cor. 3:6-7, ESV*

From the moment people learned we were having a baby they said, "Train a child in the way he should go, and when he is old, he will not depart from it" or some variation or translation of Proverbs 22:6.

Then fear whispered: But what if our child does depart? What if we train biblically, but our sweet baby grows up and becomes an atheist, an agnostic, or a Buddhist? We have friends who grew up in the church and turned away. What's to keep our child from doing the same? The thought of not having control of our unborn baby's salvation was sobering. Once we held that baby, it was frightening.

It is by the grace of God that this semi-control-freak, constant-planner, non-risk-taker mom basks in peace over her children's salvation. After years of working with teenagers in ministry and doing life with parents who had reason to fear for the path their child was taking, I learned an important lesson I'd seemed to miss every time I read 1 Corinthians.

I may be the planter. I may be the water-er, but I am not the grower. I am nothing. God is everything. My responsibility to my children and to others, is to either plant or water the word of God. The result of the planting and watering, good or bad, is not up to me.

Plant and water. Plant and water. Plant and water.

Perhaps the Proverbs verse and the 1 Corinthians verse should be put together. One is a promise and one is the how-to. Train a child in the way he should go...by planting and watering. Three to-do's of parenting: train, plant, and water.

Most important is the last part. Only God gives the growth. May we plant and water the best we possibly can so that God can give incredible increase to any "seeds" we encounter, including our own.

## → Connection Point

*Dear Lord, I give my children's future into your hands. Help me to do my best in training them and to trust you for the growth of those seeds in their lives. In Jesus' name, amen.*

## In Your Past
### Nicole O'Dell

*You intended to harm me, but God intended it for good to accomplish what is now being done, the saving of many lives. Gen. 50:20, NIV*

As a speaker, I'm often in the position of talking about my past while my kids are in the room. The first time I faced that concern, I realized they needed to hear it from me first. I didn't want them to be surprised or embarrassed in public, and I didn't want them to have burning questions they couldn't ask until later.

So, first I told them God has a plan even for our mistakes. His desire is that the mistakes we make will be used for His purposes one day. And I told them each one of us is called to be a minister of the Gospel, so we have to be ready to share. I invited them to join me in the mission of using my past to help parents and teens.

When they saw that letting the information out can be used by God, they saw it's a way of partnering with me. It became exciting for them as God took what could have been a source of shame and turned it into fuel for their fire.

I sense your cringe from here. You thought you could leave that stuff back there, forgotten. Yes, you can. But that doesn't mean you should. Not only will your parenting have much greater effect if you share from your own life, but so will your witness for Christ.

In order to begin the sharing process it's important to teach kids that no one is perfect. When they understand you're coming at your parenting from practical knowledge, not perfection, they grow more comfortable and you gain credibility.

Take a chance. Open up to your teenagers in ways you haven't before. Let them take ownership of some of the truths of your past so you can step out together and use them for God's glory.

## → Connection Point

*Father, please help be more comfortable sharing the truth about my life. Use the mistakes I made for the good of my children and the kingdom of God. I can't do that unless I'm honest. Please help me share openly and honestly. Go before me to prepare my kids' hearts to receive what I have to share with them. Amen.*

## Three Stranded
### Nicole O'Dell

*And though a man might prevail against one who is alone, two will withstand him—a threefold cord is not quickly broken. Ecc. 4:12, ESV*

Married Christian parents will usually say they believe that God wants them to be united, but often they live like they prefer to go it alone. "If you want something done right, you have to do it yourself!" Right?

That line of thinking...and living...is the direct opposite of God's plan. Oh, I can hear it now, "I can't wait around for my spouse to get on board with what's clearly the best plan!" You know what? I get it. In fact, I've been there. In fact, I'm often still there. And I know from experience that it comes from a well-meaning place. But it's still wrong.

Partnering with a spouse creates strength in unity that can stand against the world. Ecclesiastes 4:12 explains two people working together can withstand the things that come against them. Even more so can those who are partnered together with each other and with God as a three-strand cord.

God joins two people together in the covenant bond of marriage because He intends to mature them into a full package, together. When not partnered, those two individuals are only working with half of the strengths God has given them. They're locked out of the fullness of what He planned to develop in them. Rather than battling and fighting against partnership, why not join with your spouse as one unit, together with God, to take on the world together?

## → Connection Point

*Father, please forgive me for my sometimes controlling ways and for dismissing the partnership of my husband so that I can "just do it myself." Help me to join together with my husband and you as a three-strand cord that cannot be easily broken. Amen.*

Powerline365

# When They're Different
### Nicole O'Dell

*"For I know the plans I have for you," says the LORD. "They are plans for good and not for disaster, to give you a future and a hope." Jer. 29:11, NLT*

My daughter is almost 17. As I look back over this year, I'm amazed at all she's accomplished and experienced. She obtained her driver's license. Went to her first prom. Landed her first job. Paid her first real bill in the form of car insurance. Achieved a scholastic honor that only one student receives each year per school. Joined the National Honor Society. All the while, she's dealt with a chronic illness.

Rewind to my son who is now 22 and serving in the Air Force. It was very different with him at the same age. He was content being home. He didn't want to bother with a car because he wasn't interested in paying for insurance. He didn't try very hard to get a job, because he loved his video games. He charmed his way into everyone's good graces and stayed there by flying under the radar most of the time, keeping good grades, and staying out of trouble. He was a completely different teenager than my daughter. Yet they're both headed in the same direction: adulthood. And they're both arriving there gracefully in their own way.

Your kids are going to do things differently than each other and differently than you did...which can make it difficult to relate to them. It's important to let go of expectations and provide wide enough boundaries that they have room to be themselves.

My son is now doing amazing things in the Air Force. If you had asked me when he was 17 if he would be so successful, I would have laughed and said, "Sure, if he can play video games for a living." Well, that's exactly what he's doing. Very expensive, very secret...video games. Who knew?

## → Connection Point

*Lord, my plans are not part of this equation. My expectations are clearly not the driving force in raising my kids well. My prayer is that they serve you and love you and trust you. If those things are in place then they will be secure in your will. Please draw them to you in all they do. Amen.*

# Armed and Dangerous
## Takiela Bynum

*The tongue has the power of life and death, and those who love it will eat its fruit. Prov. 8:21, NIV*

Words can kill or heal. They can selfishly rob or sacrificially give, destroy without mercy or edify with grace. Our verbal expressions can be sweet and decadent or bitter and foul. As seeds are planted, so comes the harvest, and what is grown is determined by what is sown.

Like bullets from a gun, so are words from the tongue. Once fired, the damage resulting from it cannot be undone. Physical assault with a deadly weapon can have fatal consequences, but most people don't realize that verbal assault can be just as deadly. Verbal assault with a deadly weapon (the tongue) can lead to not only emotional, but spiritual assassination as well.

As parents, youth group leaders, etc. we play vital roles in the lives of teens. We are a powerful influence, but unfortunately we are not the only one. In most cases, we are outnumbered by legions of tactics and schemes trying to pull our teens' hearts away from God. We may be small in numbers but, through God, we have the power to claim our teens for the Lord and do so victoriously!

I'd like to challenge you to be intentional in regards to speaking life and hope into the lives of your teen. Mark your calendar every day when you speak words that will heal and uplift your teen...in spite of their behavior that day. This will help you develop the habit of speaking hope into their lives. It may take time to see the results of your powerful healing words. Don't give up, because in due season, you'll reap what you sow.

## → Connection Point

*Father God, I ask your forgiveness for words I've spoken that hurt my children. Please help me to consciously choose words of life, words of healing, words of hope even when it's hard. Especially then. May the Word dwell in me richly and be evident. Amen.*

## Because I Said So
### Nicole O'Dell

*Slaves, obey your earthly masters with respect and fear, and with sincerity of heart, just as you would obey Christ. Obey them not only to win their favor when their eye is on you, but like slaves of Christ, doing the will of God from your heart. Eph. 6:5-6, NIV*

When you were a kid, didn't you despise it when your parent forced you to apologize to your sibling? It drove me nuts. So much so that I vowed never to do it to my kids. An apology has to be sincere, right? Forcing it accomplishes nothing. Right?

Well, here we are, decades later, and you probably think I gave in to the pressure and now force my own kids to, "Tell your sister you're sorry!" Nope. I held out—but I can't say that I held out for sincerity. No, if my kids argue, I make them hug for one minute. If that doesn't work, I take a picture of them hugging. If THAT doesn't work, I post the picture on Facebook. Well, I can honestly say it's never gotten to that last point, but they know it's next on the list and it terrifies them. Bet they wish I'd just make them apologize.

Do we want our kids to obey us just because we force them to? Of course not. But if you're like me, you'll take what you can get. Isn't it that way with God? He's given us every reason to trust Him and to be obedient to His calling on us as parents, in the way we serve our families and interact with others. He wants us to be unswerving in our dedication to His will and our pursuit of his plan. But, in the end, if the best we can do on a particularly tough day is to do it just because He says so, well, that's okay too.

What is He asking of you today? How can you turn your begrudging sense of duty into a power-packed pursuit of God's best?

## → Connection Point

*Dear God, some days I just don't feel the zing. I can barely get through. Thank you for taking my obedient sacrifice just the same. Please turn my eyes upon you so all the negativity can turn to energy and I can be that power-parent you've called me to be. Amen.*

## The Finish Line
*Nicole O'Dell*

*And let us run with perseverance the race marked out for us, fixing our eyes on Jesus, the pioneer and perfecter of faith. For the joy set before him he endured the cross, scorning its shame, and sat down at the right hand of the throne of God. Heb. 12:1b-2 NIV*

Long-distance runners are trained to settle into a comfortable speed. Their bodies move mechanically to the point where they might even forget those middle miles because they've tuned out the race and are thinking about something else. Their bodies are working, but their brains have shifted gears.

But then they see that finish line ahead in the distance and their brains shift back in tandem with their bodies. They have one more chance to ramp up the speed and gain a few extra seconds. Somehow they muster up the adrenaline and pump up the speed enough to get over that finish line.

Many times, parents do the same thing. They get to the middle school and high school years and settle into autopilot. They stop worrying about little things like the dangers of crossing the street or falling off the slide. Their eyes shift to something else as their teens function on their own.

Parenting on autopilot.

But then that finish line appears. Maybe graduation day looms on the horizon. Is there one more shot to make an impact before it's time to let go for real? Panic might even set in. They do a quick scurry and try to fix the wrongs or reverse the lessons they've been teaching their kids by their own lifestyles. But really, whatever is in place is there. The job has been done.

Are you operating on parenting autopilot right now? How can you find the adrenaline to make the surge now rather than waiting for the finish line?

## → Connection Point

*Heavenly Father, please show me where I need to kick myself into high gear as a parent. Help me to treat every day like it's the finish line. Help me to finish strong, empowered and invigorated as a parent. Amen.*

Powerline365

# A Series of Fortunate Events
### Nicole O'Dell

*...we also rejoice in our sufferings, because we know that suffering produces perseverance; perseverance, character; and character, hope. Rom. 5: 3-4, NIV*

*Lemony Snicket.* The very sound of that name elicits a sense of impending doom. With a name like that, Lemony Snicket is definitely the most likely storyteller for *A Series of Unfortunate Events*, in which terrifying and unimaginable things happening to sweet, little—albeit very resourceful—children. Mr. Snicket weaves his stories from one dramatic misfortune to the next disastrous catastrophe. Just when it seems likely that the innocents will catch a break because anything short of a picnic in the park would barely even be believable, the next earth-shattering calamity occurs. But, the children keep plodding along with hope reigning in their hearts.

So it is for the Christian parent. We aren't promised life will be rosy at every turn. We aren't promised our teens will get straight A's or never get into big trouble. We aren't promised something catastrophic or life-altering will never happen. In fact, we're warned by Jesus that this life is fraught with calamity, trial, and testing of every kind.

But, unlike the Beaudelaire children in Lemony Snicket's stories, followers of Jesus Christ have a reason for hope. We're instructed to take joy in our struggles because it's only through those trials that we can be molded and shaped according to God's will. When you suffer, you learn to withstand hardship. It's through the development of that longsuffering that your character is strengthened.

When life seems to be one unfortunate event after another, take a moment to be grateful for the growth that is happening in your heart and mind as a result of your experiences. Look for the teaching opportunity within your hardship. After all, you can only teach it to your teens once you've learned it yourself.

## → Connection Point

*Dear Jesus, help me see life's unfortunate events as opportunities. Teach me to persevere and thrive through the testing. Develop a hope in me that will withstand every trial and be an example to my teenagers. Amen.*

## Getting Past the Anger
*Brenda Yoder, MA*

*He who has ears to hear, let him hear. Mark 4:9 ESV*

"*I hate you!*" she screamed at me more times than I cared to count. Morning after morning on our way to school we had shouting matches. *Why wouldn't she just listen to me?* My middle schooler seemed to have one mode and it was **against me.**

I slipped into my friend's classroom. As a teacher in my daughter's school, there were days I had to compose myself either from anger or tears between morning fights with my daughter and facing teenagers all day in my classroom. There were few people I could talk to about my daughter's hatred and my anger and not risk judgment. Roberta was one person I could trust to not judge either me or my daughter when I spewed the details of the ugliness of our fights.

"*Even though she's pushing you away, she still needs you,*" my friend said. Even though she didn't have children yet, she was wise beyond her years, growing up in a large family as a preacher's kid. She often showed me my daughter's perspectives based on her own feelings growing up. The words she offered this day were new to me, but they gave me hope.

They also proved true as I learned to parent through the lens of not taking the *I hate you's!* personally. As I've learned to understand teens better from parenting, teaching, and counseling them, I've learned her words are true. Even though your teen is pushing you away, they still want and need you. Don't quit in your pursuit of your teenager's heart. That's what your enemy wants you to do. He wants division in your home. He fosters hate. Instead, be the light of God's love that will drown out the hate.

## → Connection Point

*Father, help us to hear what our teens are saying even when our feelings are hurt or we are wrestling with objectivity. Let your words be what we hear in times of conflict. Thank you. Amen.*

## A Day in the Life
*Nicole O'Dell*

*So be careful how you live. Don't live like fools, but like those who are wise. Make the most of every opportunity in these evil days. Don't act thoughtlessly, but understand what the Lord wants you to do. Eph. 5:15-17, NLT*

Have you ever read a blog post or an article that describes "a day in the life of" someone you don't know? Reading about where they drink their coffee in the morning, what kind of exercise they do, what they do at the office...that information draws you in and helps you understand that person, maybe even empathize a bit.

Have you ever considered what a day in the life of your teenagers looks like? Do you know what happens when your teens arrive at school? Where do they hang out before the bell rings? Which class is first...second? How is the journey from class to class? What about lunch? Where do they sit and with whom? These are details most teens wouldn't think about sharing and most parents wouldn't even ask for. But if you have that information, it's easier to visualize where they are throughout the day and to pray for them with specifics.

If you're interested in a day in the life of a celebrity or a co-worker, why not seek that level of information from your teenager. Make it an event. Go to dinner or for a long walk and drive them crazy with your questions. Even take it a step further and go with them on a discreet walk through their school one afternoon. Let them show you the steps they take as they move throughout their day.

It may seem like its overdoing it, but can you really overdo the love and attention you pay your teenagers? They might not understand exactly why you're doing it, but they'll lay their head on their pillow that night feeling embraced and confident that you're interested in every detail of their lives.

## → Connection Point

*Jesus, I can't be there with my teenagers as they take their every step throughout their days. But you can. I have a hard time even visualizing what they see and experience on a daily basis. But you don't. Would you give me godly insight into the days in the lives of my teens? Help me understand what it's like to be them. Amen.*

## Lipstick on a Pig
### *Nicole O'Dell*

*Ask, and it will be given to you; seek, and you will find; knock, and it will be opened to you. Matt. 7:7, ESV*

I've always loved that visual, but never as much as I have since my husband and I bought an old Victorian home to rehab. Sometimes I think about buying new curtains or hanging a picture, but it all feels like I'm just putting lipstick on a pig. Until we fix the foundational issues like repairing the plaster or replacing the window frames or ripping out the floors, there's no point in decorating. No matter how much make-up we put on it, there's still a pig underneath.

This is also true with our parent-teen relationships. We often gloss over important issues by taking the path of least resistance and then moving on. Are there hurts or questions or fears that your teenagers are dealing with that need to be rooted out? Or discipline issues that need more digging rather than punishment?

For example: maybe you walked in the room and caught your teenager making out with his girlfriend or her boyfriend. Your gut reaction might be to punish that behavior and make it more difficult for it to happen again. Maybe you change curfew or make more rules about where they're allowed to be in the house. But, really, that's just putting lipstick on that pig. That's doing nothing to get to the heart of why that behavior happened in the first place.

Definitely set more boundaries and get tighter on your supervision, but while you're doing that be sure you fix the foundational issues that may go unaddressed. Ask questions, search scripture, and pray together. Those are the best ways to attack the foundations of these hot button issues that you'll face with your teenagers.

## → Connection Point

*Dear Jesus help me have your wisdom to see what needs to be addressed and what can be passed over. I don't want to make big issues out of things that are unimportant, but I don't want to miss out on the teaching opportunities You give me. With Your godly wisdom and insight, help me to reach my teenagers and steer them to healthy choices. Amen.*

Powerline365

## Take the Mystery Out
*Nicole O'Dell*

*No temptation has overtaken you that is not common to man. God is faithful, and he will not let you be tempted beyond your ability, but with the temptation he will also provide the way of escape, that you may be able to endure it. 1 Cor. 10:13, ESV*

Sometimes teenagers make bad choices out of simple curiosity. Parents can help prepare their teens by imparting concern for God's will, giving them the tools they need to succeed; and walking them through the process of making good choices.

What's in it for your teen to make good choices? Are you parenting with a because-I-said-so mentality? Teenagers need to see both the temporal and eternal value of doing the right thing. It takes consistent and effective communication in order to impart that kind of understanding.

Our teens also need certain tools in order to stand up in the face of peer pressure and temptation. They need a growing understanding of God's Word and His will. They need a mentor or someone with whom they can talk openly. And they need options. If you make a rule against something, offer an "instead" in its place. A redirection gives them something else to turn to.

It's vital that you have the conversations and prepare your teens to make the hard choices—willing to withstand and endure persecution for the sake of Christ. It's only through that preparation that they'll be able to stand in the face of temptation and peer pressure and say no. And they won't just say no, they'll know why they're saying it.

\*\*\*My Hot Buttons books provide scripts and a communication method that enables parents to have those tough talks about life's Hot Button issues. You can check them out at www.hotbuttonsite.com.

## → Connection Point

*Dear God, thank You for having all the answers to the mysteries of sin and faith figured out. Help me use your truth to expose my teens to just enough reality that sin and exploration become unappealing. Then help me teach them to find answers and direction in your Word. Amen.*

## Heard That One Before
*Cara Putman*

*Go over before the ark of the L*ORD *your God into the middle of the Jordan. Each of you is to take up a stone on his shoulder, according to the number of the tribes of the Israelites, to serve as a sign among you. In the future, when your children ask you, "What do these stones mean?" Josh. 4:5-6, NIV*

The other day I spoke at a woman's retreat, and my teenager turned to me with a smile when I finished. "I've heard that one before." *That one* was an exhortation based on these verses. God told Joshua and the Israelites as they were finally prepared to move into the Promised Land after the 40-year detour in the wilderness to collect stones and remember what God was doing. Why? Because someday their children would ask why the stones were there. And in that asking, the parents would have an opportunity to teach their children about how God had been and continued to be active in their lives. I love that!

I want my kids to see and understand that God is living, breathing, and active in our lives. Several years ago, it looked like a once-in-a-lifetime opportunity to teach overseas might disappear mere months before our flight departed. My husband and I prayed and asked friends to pray, because we wanted to know if God was in this opportunity. A couple weeks later, the funding was back in place, and we were able to go. That was one of the times we were very intentional about letting the kids into the process. We even quip that it's one of the times God killed a cow for us. He owns the cattle on a 1000 hills, after all.

Do you look back as parents, as a family? Do you note and celebrate the times that God intervenes in your lives? Do you share those with your family? If not, I encourage you to start that practice. You could physically write a word or two on a rock and collect those moments. Or you could collect them in a journal. However, you choose to do it, I urge you to remember what God has done, memorialize it in some way, and then share those times and events with your kids.

## → Connection Point

*Lord, please help me teach my kids that you're in everything we do and in every opportunity we have. Help me hold my plans loosely as I lean into you, and let my teenagers learn from that example. Amen.*

## Dealing with Change
### Nicole O'Dell

*For we are God's masterpiece. He has created us anew in Christ Jesus, so we can do the good things he planned for us long ago.*
*Eph. 2:10, NLT*

Change is part of life. Relocating to a new home or town. Starting a new job. Attending a new church. Some of us handle change well, and some of us fight it with every fiber of our being. I'm actually a change lover. I look forward to variety. I need it, really. I get bored easily and want a new challenge pretty regularly. But I have friends and family members who mourn the thought that change may come one day. They resist it even before it happens. They love the familiar.

Both personalities are good. Whichever side you fall on, or any blend of the two, is exactly who God made you to be and he has His good reasons for making us that way. But your teenager may deal with change differently then you do. When you face something major, consider how your teen may see it. Ask lots of questions like these:

- What excites you most about this upcoming change?
- What excites you the least about this upcoming change?
- How can we make this transition easier or better for you?
- How can we make this transition better for the whole family?

Giving your teens the opportunity to have a voice into how they feel and how things happen goes a long way toward helping them cope with change. It's when they feel like circumstances are spiraling out of control and they have no power over their own lives that they build resentment and fear. When you hear them out and validate their concerns with real acceptance and practical application, they will trust you more. They will be able to move forward confidently, empowered to be true to themselves while embracing the newness that God has brought into their lives.

## → Connection Point

*Lord, we're facing change, and I know it won't be the last time. Please help me validate my teenager's fears and concerns about it. Give me wisdom into unique ways I can address every concern. Please meet them where they are and comfort their hearts? Amen.*

## The Art of Letting Go
*Nicole O'Dell*

*Forgetting what is behind and straining toward what is ahead, I press on toward the goal to win the prize for which God has called me heavenward in Christ Jesus. Phil. 3:13b-14, NIV*

Once upon a time we looked into the cherub-like face of our infant and dreamed of perfection. What were all those other parents always crowing about? If their kid made bad choices or did poorly in school, it had to be the parent's fault. Looking at that sweet baby, we knew there was no way that would happen to us. We'd be there every step of the way. We'd find a way to convince our angel that we knew best. And our child would always follow our advice because of the perfect relationship we'd have had all those years.

You finished laughing?

Yeah, we've all been that starry-eyed parent of a newborn, but it doesn't take long to figure out that things don't always go as planned. How are you at letting go of your ideals?

There are some things you need to know that might help make the process a bit easier:

**You can't control your teen's choices.** You can advise. You can set boundaries. You can have expectations. But ultimately, it's their choice. You can't own their choices.

**Choices have consequences.** Consequences need to be swift and consistent. Your teenager needs to see that discipline is not just your way of getting revenge, but rather a matter-of-fact part of life. Cause and effect.

**God has a plan.** Choices and consequences, even the ones that seem devastating, may have lasting effects, but their impact fades away as maturity and resolve take over. You need to allow that process so God can be glorified and even use the hard stuff for His good.

What ideals are you holding on to that are making it difficult for you to let go and trust God?

## → Connection Point

*Dear God, I love my teenager and want the very best for that special soul. Please help me trust you even when things look gloomy. Help me let go of my ideals and trust in your plans. Amen.*

## Great Expectations
*Nicole O'Dell*

*No, O people, the LORD has told you what is good, and this is what he requires of you: to do what is right, to love mercy, and to walk humbly with your God. Micah 6:8, NLT*

The expectations that plague me come from three main sources. There are the expectations I put on myself based on what I think I should be able to handle: clean house, bills paid, healthy meals, and good relationships. Encompassed within those things are other traits that look at work ethic, honesty, and perseverance. There are also outside expectations I assume others have—those almost always come from playing the comparison game. What kind of house does she live in? What kind of car does she drive? Where is her family going on vacation this year? What kind of clothes do her kids wear? And those kinds of perceived expectations almost always lead to disappointment.

Then there are the expectations God has for us. We are to do what's right. We should love mercy—both the giving and receiving of it. And we need to walk in meekness as a humble servant. When we parent in the pattern that Micah 6:8 provides, we are teaching by example, we are showing grace to our teens and others, and we are humble and gracious as we walk with Jesus. Those are the only expectations we need to concern ourselves with—the rest will follow as an outpouring of that love.

It's only when we can set aside our own expectations of ourselves and what we think others want of us, looking at ourselves through God's eyes, that we can truly fulfill the plan He has for us as the parents of these teenagers with whom we've been entrusted.

Misguided expectations breed disunity. There's no place for disunity in your family or in your relationship with God.

## → Connection Point

*Jesus, please help me to do the right things in accordance with the expectations you have for me, not what I perceive as righteous. Help me to embrace the mercy you've shown me, and to show it to my teenagers. And please walk with me and lead me into humility. Amen.*

## Plan Now or Pay Later
*Steve Repak, CFP®*

*Good planning and hard work lead to prosperity,
but hasty shortcuts lead to poverty. Prov. 21:5, NLT*

There is a saying that people who fail to plan, plan to fail. To tell you the truth, most people spend more time planning for a vacation then they do for their finances or their budgets.

God never promised life would be easy or fair. So, as Christians we need to be prepared for anything that the destroyer may have in store for us. And we need to prepare our teenagers to face the same things in their own lives. The same financial pitfalls we've experienced, they will too. The same struggles we've had with employment, debt, and medical bills—they'll face those things too.

Financially speaking, you should plan on having at least 3-6 months of your non-discretionary spending in a safe, liquid account that is separate from your checking account. A FDIC insured money market account would be an example of what you could put this emergency savings in. If you currently don't have that much saved up, it will take hard work and some sacrifices on your part but, if you will make a commitment now, in no time you will reach your goals and won't have to pay for it later. And when I say you won't have to pay for it later, I mean you won't have to use a credit card to bail yourself out of an emergency!

With that principle in place in your own life, you can guide your teenagers to do the same thing. Give some, save some, spend some. Set them up for a healthy financial future.

## → Connection Point

*Heavenly Father, I trust that you will always provide for all of my needs. But please help me to be proactive by planning for an unexpected emergency instead of being reactive, which could harm my financial health. And please help me teach the same principles to my teens. Amen.*

## Are you BFFs?
*Nicole O'Dell*

*No discipline seems pleasant at the time, but painful. Later on, however, it produces a harvest of righteousness and peace for those who have been trained by it. Heb. 12:11, NIV*

Many studies have shown that teens act like they want their parents to be their friends, but in reality, they are crying out for leadership, boundaries, and parents who are in control.

Are you becoming your teenager's friend more than parent? If you are, you need to make some changes right away. One easy way to set things on better footing is to adjust the way you speak. If you take on the language and attitude of an authority figure, your teen will respond. Maybe a bit negatively at first, but in the end, the reaction will be healthy and positive.

For example, if your teen's grades are slipping and you say, "I wish you'd turn off that music when you study," you might hear, "I think better with it on." The door shuts and the music gets louder.

If one of my kids acted that way toward me, I would open the door and remove the stereo along with any other electronic distractions. Overreaction? Some might think so, but it's the knowledge that I *would* react that way that keeps my kids from pushing me. Shutting a door in my face? No way. As parents, we don't *wish* for things; we *require* them. "You're studying right now. Please turn the music off." It's not a suggestion.

Mom and Dad, if you're allowing that level of disrespect, you're being walked all over, and you must take charge. Show you're not afraid of upsetting your teens by speaking in loving declarations that leave no room for negotiation. Be the parent who is worthy of the respect you deserve. You will be friends one day, but, if respect is earned now, it will never fade.

## → Connection Point

*Lord, please help me to be the parent you've called me to be. Help me stay consistent with discipline and expectations in order to raised these teens into the godly people you have called them to be. Please show me where to draw loving but firm lines and then give me the strength I need to stay strong. Amen.*

## Politically Correct
*Nicole O'Dell*

> But in your hearts honor Christ the Lord as holy, always being prepared to make a defense to anyone who asks you for a reason for the hope that is in you; yet do it with gentleness and respect.
> I Pet. 3:15, ESV

Politically correct. People use that term as though being politically correct is a positive character trait. Like it's better to be that, than to be confident enough to defend a belief system. To be honest, I'm tired of it. There was nothing politically correct about Jesus. In fact, He was the opposite of politically correct; He corrected the politics.

Are we raising teenagers to be concerned about politics and diplomacy? Or are we raising teenagers who are willing to take a stand and defend righteousness whatever the cost?

Now, I'm not advocating rudeness or disdain for people who disagree. I'm not saying teenagers should be taught to reject other people for their beliefs or ideas. In fact, by doing that, they risk defeating their message regardless of its content. Instead, we need to train our kids to defend the gospel. But to do that, they have to understand it. They have to know the basics and be able to defend it with support from the Word of God.

It's only when they're equipped and confident of their knowledge that they'll be able to stand strong. They will be able to look peer pressure and temptation square in the face and brandish truth like a sword. With that kind of confidence comes a quiet calm, exuding strength. Arm them with that so they will not only be able to defend the gospel to others, but they will cling to it themselves.

## → Connection Point

*Heavenly Father, please take me to your Word and show me what my teenagers need to know. Help me prepare them for the testing they'll face on their path. You know what lies ahead, so please give me your wisdom to know what they'll need in their arsenal. Amen.*

## Treat the Truth
*Nicole O'Dell*

*Whoever can be trusted with very little can also be trusted with much, and whoever is dishonest with very little will also be dishonest with much. Luke 16:10, NIV*

Your palms begin to sweat. Your stomach clenches. Your voice quakes as words stutter from your lips. At least that's how it was for me when I first started lying. The first time I lied, I was miserable and confessed immediately. The next time, I was able to make it through most of the day before I confessed to my parents, but there was no way I could sleep that night. The third or fourth time, it took a few days before I came clean. But soon I was desensitized to the guilt and began to get away with it every time. I got so good at it as a teenager that I began to wonder what the truth really was.

It wasn't until I finally surrendered my life to the Lord that He softened my heart toward my sin. I craved *His* truth, so I knew it was important to give others *my* truth. Big and small.

Let me go out on a limb and say that your teenager has lied to you. I will further guess that it will happen again. The key is to continue to speak life into your teen. The goal is to raise teenagers with a passion to pursue God. When they understand that His truth requires theirs, perhaps honesty will take on a new meaning for them, too.

Another way to elicit honesty in your teen is to make sure you're living it fully yourself. Do you make excuses for breaking plans with friends? Do your teenagers hear you on the phone with bill collectors uttering all sorts of half-truths? Do they hear you fibbing to your spouse about how much you spent on something or when you'll be home? Those things may seem inconsequential to the big picture, but the impact your honesty has on your teenager can affect the way they treat the truth.

## → Connection Point

*Dear Lord, please help me impart truth to my teens. Help me inspire them to live honestly and forthright in all their dealings and relationships. And let me live as an example of this. Please forgive me for times I failed, and help me to move forward from this place in truth. Amen*

## The Recipe of your Teenager
### Sherri Wilson Johnson

*Remove the dross from the silver, and a silversmith can produce a vessel. Prov. 25:4, NIV*

Have you ever tried to make a cake without all the ingredients? You improvise, and the results may be tasty — but not quite what you intended. I tried to make a cinnamon crumb cake one night. Instead of using butter, I used margarine. Instead of a crumbly cinnamon-y filling inside the cake, I got a cinnamon swirl. A few days later, I made the cake with butter. The difference wasn't in the taste as much as in how it looked and felt.

Very few cake ingredients are tasty by themselves. No one wants to eat a spoonful of shortening, drink a cup of oil, or suck down a raw egg. Sugar and salt are flavorful, but you wouldn't eat them by themselves in large quantities. And cinnamon doesn't have near the flavor alone as it does when it's mixed with sugar.

Raising each child requires a unique recipe. Some ingredients might be the same but they get applied differently. You may have to substitute some items with others, and depending on the degree of challenge, some aren't particularly palatable. Sometimes we try to make the mix better or take shortcuts. However, this never results in the finished product intended by the Master Chef.

By nature, we only want to experience the good things in life. We expect a perfect cake no matter where we make substitutions. We want to make up the recipe as we go and still have a perfect outcome.

Teens are unpredictable. The only way we'll succeed at parenting them is to use God's ingredients: prayer, wise instruction, and love. Our teens are unique and created for unique purposes. The experiences we go through with them fashion us all into who we are meant to be. When we allow God to teach us and to sift away the undesirable ingredients, He polishes us into beautiful masterpieces.

## → Connection Point

Lord, help me to be a good parent. Help me to use the right ingredients with my teenager, even the ones that don't taste so good going down, like discipline. I know you have plans for my teen and for me, and I can't wait to see how the recipe turns out. Amen.

## Heartbreak Ridge
*Nicole O'Dell*

*The LORD is close to the brokenhearted; he rescues those whose spirits are crushed. Psalm 34:18, ESV*

I made a pretty severe parenting mistake by letting my daughter enter into a "dating" relationship when she was still in middle school. It was nothing outside of school, nothing public, nothing at all, really. But she saw it differently. To her it was everything. It took over her heart and her mind for a while. She began to pull away, and I didn't really know why it was happening at that time.

When that "relationship" ended, as it was bound to do, she suffered greatly. She didn't know how to handle the loss. She didn't know how to refocus her energies. I had no idea it had gone so far, but I needed to do some repair work.

We spent a lot of time talking about realistic expectations. We talked about what she could have done to avoid growing so attached. We talked about what God would want out of a future dating relationship and how it could affect her one-day marriage. And we agreed that she would put dating and relationship energy on hold for several years.

Heartbreak is a big educator. It's impossible to explain the magnitude of pain accompanying it. They must experience it themselves. Now that my daughter is nearing 17, she is much more guarded with her heart. She learned early on, and then made a personal choice to not let herself go there again until she's ready to be in a permanent relationship.

I'm sorry she had the struggle she did, but I'm not sure my words alone could've ever achieved such a result. When it happens, I encourage you to let heartbreak do its job.

## → Connection Point

*Lord, I don't want to make mistakes, and I don't want my teenager to suffer for them. But if my teenager suffers heartbreak, help me to allow it to teach your lessons. Help me back off and let it happen if it needs to, and then give me the words to say in accordance with whatever you're trying to teach. Amen.*

## Compromise
### *Nicole O'Dell*

*So whoever knows the right thing to do and fails to do it, for him it is sin. James 4:17, ESV*

What are the important rules in your home about dating, curfew, chores, homework, respect, etc.? Which have been stretched by compromise for the sake of keeping peace? If you find you've allowed your expectations to be tailored by your teenager's complaints, you've surrendered the power, and you must take it back.

From the time my kids were all teeny, tiny babies, I had them sleeping through the night by simple consistency. My preemie triplets slept twelve hours a night by the time they were five months old. This is because I reacted the exact same loving way each and every time they needed my attention. I lavished my love and constant attention on them by day and then parsed it out on my terms at night—meeting their needs, but adding few extra bonuses. After a short time, they realized that the night was different than the day and the reward of getting me into their room wasn't worth the effort, so they just went back to sleep.

Teenagers are human beings, too. If they can depend on you giving in after thirty minutes of arguing and door slamming, you'd better believe they'll push it to that point. But if they come to realize you're never going to give in to any amount of arguing, and that, on the contrary, a bad attitude will only make things worse for them, eventually they'll tire of the fruitless battle of wills.

Satan wants your teen to rebel against you and push your boundaries. But God wants you to set firm boundaries and maintain consistent discipline and control over your household. Whose plan do you want to carry out in your home?

## → Connection Point

*Compromise. Inconsistent. Weak. Please, Lord, let those words never describe my parenting. Help me to be so confident in my discipline that my teenagers never consider challenging me. But when they do, allow me the foresight to respond swiftly and prove I will do what it takes to raise them in a way that is always pleasing to you. Amen.*

Powerline365

# Spring has Sprung
### Nicole O'Dell

*There is a time for everything, and a season for every activity under the heavens. Ecc. 3:1, NIV*

Green leaves. Fresh air. Gentle breeze. I'm from the Midwest so spring brings with it a sense of accomplishment and freedom. We made it through the long, hard winter, and now we're free to explore and breathe. That might sound dramatic, but until you've experienced a Midwest winter...

I feel the same way about fall. Fall, to me, is also about new life. A new school year. A new grade. New opportunities. The approach of the holiday season. The air smells different, but it's fresh in a different way. Burning leaves and spiced pumpkin. Apple cider and hot chili. In many ways, I actually prefer fall over spring.

Both of those seasons of firsts lead into something harsh. Spring, in my neck the woods, opens into summer. A hot, humid, suffocating summer. Fall opens into Chicago's wintry conditions with freezing slush, sleet, and blizzards. And no matter how hard it was the year before, I'm always looking to escape into a different season. Every winter, I long for summer. Every summer, I long for winter.

Your teenagers go through seasons just like those. Moments of fresh newness and awakening...followed by testing and trials. It's important that in the seasons of birth and renewal you're planting and preparing your teenager for the trials that lie ahead. And then, rather than always looking for the escape from the season, stand still and let God teach you both.

## → Connection Point

*Father, would you open my eyes to the seasons of life? Help me recognize opportunity for renewal and the need for preparation at each stage of my teenager's life. Please involve me in whatever it is you're doing or teaching through the harsh seasons. Amen.*

## Teachable Moments
### Jill Hart

*Hold on to instruction, do not let it go; guard it well, for it is your life. Prov. 4:13, NIV*

Do you ever find yourself waffling back and forth about how to spend your time? There are so many options: washing a few loads of laundry, working a few extra hours, or spending extra time with family.

Too often it's the time with family that gets put off. I know how important time with my kids is, but if they aren't demanding my attention, it's easy to say to myself that I will make time for them later.

Not long ago, my daughter asked if I would let her paint my nails. She is a blossoming nail-art fashionista, so it would be fun to let her spice up my boring fingernails. But I also knew that it was not going to be a short process, and I had several household chores to finish.

I was faced with a choice. Take time to sit and spend with my daughter or continue rushing around the house trying to get things done. Many days I would have chosen the latter, but on this day I chose to sit and relax with my daughter.

We sat there somewhat quietly as she concentrated on getting the nail design just right and then she began telling me about something going on between her and a friend. It wasn't something major, but it was a big deal to her.

As I sat and listened to her share her heart, I realized that she would never have shared that with me had I not chosen to spend that one-on-one time with her. It was a reminder to me that even though she's growing up and doesn't often seek me out to spend time with her, she still does enjoy it (at times).

She still needs me.

Where are you in this process? Can you carve out some quiet time for your teen this week? Sit together and let them to do the talking.

## → Connection Point

*Dear God, please forgive me for when I have put off time with my children in favor of chores or other busy-work. Please help me to remember they need my attention, possibly now more than ever. Help me to be a listener, a sounding board, and someone they can trust with their hurts and fears. Amen.*

## False Advertising
### Nicole O'Dell

*I remember your genuine faith, for you share the faith that first filled your grandmother Lois and your mother, Eunice. And I know that same faith continues strong in you. 2 Tim. 1:5, NLT*

You're pouring over the menu at a restaurant, but you can't decide what to eat. You thought you wanted a steak, but that picture of a succulent burger and seasoned fries on page two looks amazing. You can't resist that dinner, so you place your order. When the waitress returns with your order, you groan at the sight of the sloppy plate with its stale, soggy fries and a lopsided burger with wilted lettuce and a slice of cheese that isn't even melted. And the bread! Not a single buttery nook or cranny in sight.

Do you engage in false advertising like that? Super joyful and exuberant in public, the picture of a perfect parent, employee, leader, Christian. But in private, you grumble and complain about hardships or relationships. Do you pace your home, worried about finances and stressed about your job, but then turn on your super-faith when the phone rings or someone shows up at the door? Do you sit in church proud of your family, happy to be there, engaged in the service, but then go home and disengage from the family and return to brooding and sulking?

The surest way to lose your teenagers' trust is to practice false advertising. If they see you living as two different people, or even more depending on where you are, they'll begin to wonder which is the real you. Authenticity, even when it's imperfect, fosters trust and builds relationships. This is true in your parenting as well as in every connection you make.

In what ways are you engaging in false advertising? What can you do to put a stop to the façade?

## → Connection Point

*Lord, please forgive me for the times when I have cared more about what people think than the authentic message I'm sending my teens. Help me to live so that they see you in me at all times, and let that be an inspiration to carry the faith into the next generation. Amen.*

# 70

## Bully or Bullied?
*Nicole O'Dell*

*If anyone stirs up strife, it is not from me; whoever stirs up strife with you shall fall because of you. Isa. 54:15, ESV*

I was part of a women's Bible study group when a woman asked for prayer for her teenager who was being bullied at the Christian school she attended. This mom described incidents when her daughter experienced verbal bullying and even some physical events. The women expressed outrage that the school could let that go on. The associate pastor's wife said, "I can't understand how a Christian parent could raise a teenager who would treat people that way."

The mom raised her gaze. "I wasn't going to do this here, but I guess you should know, it's your daughter who is doing this to mine."

Though her shock was evident, the pastor's wife didn't deny the possibility. She calmly replied, "I had no idea anything like this was happening. Let's talk after this meeting and make a plan to fix it."

It's hard enough to watch your child deal with a bully, but what if your teenager *is* the bully? When we realize that our kids have mistreated another (and it's common even among Christian kids), we have a lot of work to do.

> There's often an emotional disconnect that prevents the bully from feeling compassion, and it's difficult to elicit a regretful or sorrowful response. We may need to eradicate an entitlement attitude in order to make the bully aware of the problems and to help them toward a balanced acceptance of self and appreciation of others. (Hot Buttons Bullying Edition)

That's just a fancy way of saying that bullies are suffering and we need to make them care about the way others feel. If you discover your teen is mistreating someone else, you need to act swiftly. Ask questions to uncover the root cause, seek godly counsel and prayer, and persist until there is healing both for your teenager and any others involved.

## → Connection Point

*Dear God, I can't imagine that this could apply to my family, but please open my eyes to anything I need to see. Prepare me to accept truth so I can parent effectively, and please instill a loving, compassionate spirit within my teenager. Amen.*

Powerline365

## The Enemy's Lies
*Nicole O'Dell*

*Even before he made the world, God loved us and chose us in Christ to be holy and without fault in his eyes. Eph. 1:4, NLT*

I recently spoke at a youth conference I also attended when I was a teen. As I looked out on the faces, I remembered sitting in those same seats feeling pulled by the Holy Spirit to surrender to God, while I also heard deafening shouts of all the reasons why I wasn't good enough. I was sure that the enemy was telling the same lies to each one of them. They were going to either listen to the truth or to the lie.

There are three things that lead to a decision: emotions, intellect, and will. The emotions create desire, the intellect asks questions, and the will drives action. When our emotions begin to move toward a decision, our intellect puts on the breaks. *Are you sure? Is this for you? What if you fail?* The brain overpowers the emotions, but if a person pushes past the intellect, they still have one final hurdle. The will. *Are you willing to take that final step?*

I handed out slips of paper and asked the teens to identify the one thing that kept them from going all in with God. Once they wrote on the slip, they were to bring it up to the front. I would have liked to burn them in a grand, symbolic gesture, but the hotel didn't quite see it my way. So instead, I had them trade their slip of paper for a piece of candy. Symbolic of trading the bad for the good. *The lie for the truth.*

The lies they wrote, though different for each person, each described the same misunderstanding of God's grace. They hadn't grasped that He loved them passionately just as they were at that moment. That He chose them. That He craved their companionship.

How are you imparting that kind of understanding to your teens? Do they see God as a powerful judge waiting for them to mess up, or as a loving Father, eager for relationship? Help them trade the lies they've been hearing for the truth of what God has in store for them.

## → Connection Point

*Dear Jesus, please help me and my teens believe what you say about us. Make me aware of any specific lies the enemy is using against my teenagers. And help me raise them to be confident that they are forgiven, worthy, and loved. Amen.*

## Forgive Yourself
*Amy Joob*

*As far as the east is from the west, so far has He removed our transgressions from us. Psalm 103:12, NIV*

You lose your temper. You slip and utter a four-letter word. You forget an appointment or birthday. You fall off your diet and eat a half a bag of potato chips. You wish you could hit the rewind button and start all over. And the regret piles on. "If only I hadn't..." and then you beat yourself up over it. We've all been there! I feel your pain.

So maybe you did mess up...again. It's all right. Welcome to the human race! Whether you are a Christian or not, you will have your moments of failure and defeat. (For all have sinned and fall short of the glory of God. Romans 3:34, NIV) When you fail, you only need to acknowledge it, ask God to forgive you (and perhaps ask your loved one to forgive you, too), and it is finished.

Now's the hard part. Letting go. If you continue to beat yourself up, you're saying what Jesus did for you on the cross is not enough. He took the punishment for your sin, so you don't need to punish yourself. You need to receive the gift of His forgiveness and forgive yourself, too.

Ephesians 2:8-9 says we are saved by the grace of God, which is received through faith. It's a gift from God, and it has nothing to do with anything we say or do. He designed it that way so it's very clear it is His grace or unmerited favor that brings salvation and forgiveness. There is nothing we can do to earn it.

None of us enjoys blowing it, but the good news is we have a Savior who stands with arms open wide, ready to forgive and to receive us back. And once we ask for and receive His forgiveness, we need to do ourselves a favor and let ourselves off the hook.

Forgive yourself. He has already forgiven and forgotten it...so why shouldn't you? And remember, if you can't forgive yourself, your teenager will begin to harbor guilt and shame, as well.

## → Connection Point

*Father, I ask you to forgive me for messing up today. I thank you for forgiving my sins. I pray your mercies would flow into and through my life. Help me to forgive myself and those who have hurt me. And please help me be an example of Your grace in my home. Amen.*

# Sin's Erosion
## Nicole O'Dell

*That which has been is that which will be, and that which has been done is that which will be done.*
*So there is nothing new under the sun. Ecc. 1:9, NASB*

The ocean's tide is affected by the magnetic pull of the moon. Or some such scientific thing that people smarter than me know much more about. But it is a great example of how things stay the same even while constantly changing. The tide waxes and wanes, and beats at the shoreline only to recede again, changing the landscape with each attack.

In Ecclesiastes, we're told there is nothing new under the sun. And even though it seems like society gets worse and pressures increase, the fact is, sin is the same now as it has been for all generations. Sin, like the tide, comes in and out with pressure, temptation, and empty promises. It works irreversible changes on the heart, and adapts to the changes it encounters on each return.

Your teenagers are being sold a lie that times have changed and tolerance should make them more adaptable. They are being told that you can't relate because it wasn't like this when you were young. But we know that's simply not the truth. Are you willing to take a stand and enforce the unchanging, inflexible, completely intolerant principles of God's Word? Are you willing to hold your teenagers to those standards regardless of the pressures of this society and the lies the enemy tells?

Rather than being their friend, you need to help your teenager become a friend of God and an enemy of the world. It's time to stand firm against the erosion powers of sin. No matter how unpopular it feels.

## → Connection Point

*Father, please give me the strength to battle the tide of sin that seeks to erode my life and my teenagers' lives. Please help me combat the lies of the enemy with Your truth. Amen.*

# Tread Water
## Nicole O'Dell

*With the crowd dispersed, he climbed the mountain so he could be by himself and pray. He stayed there alone, late into the night.*
Matt. 14:23, MSG

A long-time competitive swimmer, I trained as a lifeguard when I was in high school. It was difficult training but it led to the best summer job a teenager could ever hope to have. The lifeguard test contained many challenging components, not the least of which was treading water.

Treading water is a tactic employed before a swimmer's strength fails or when a rescuer needs to conserve energy and wait for help, sometimes even while supporting a resistant or unconscious victim. No advancement is made during that time, but the gentle arm and leg movements keep them above water and strength is conserved or regained for when the swim continues.

As parents, sometimes the journey gets overwhelming, and it feels like we may be drowning—slowly losing strength as the waters of fear and inadequacy overtake us. Treading water for a time may be the best choice. Maybe no great forward gains are made during that time, but a conscious choice to do nothing new, take no large steps, address no big issues, and just rest, can be exactly what is needed to re-energize the weary parent.

Tread water for a few days or weeks if necessary. Spend your time in prayer and let the Holy Spirit renew your spirit and body so that you can begin the journey once again, renewed, invigorated. He will be faithful to restore your energy and sharpen your skills. Just as a rescuer would be ineffective without treading water, a parent cannot be effective without rest.

## → Connection Point

*Jesus, please renew me and re-energize me as a parent and as a believer. Through rest and prayer, please strengthen me and return me to the vigor I once felt. Thank you for the renewing power of the Holy Spirit. Amen.*

# Raging Bull
## *Nicole O'Dell*

*Live in me. Make your home in me just as I do in you. In the same way that a branch can't bear grapes by itself but only by being joined to the vine, you can't bear fruit unless you are joined with me. John 15:4, NASB*

My favorite roller coaster, *Raging Bull*, is 202 feet tall and is the world's first hyper-twister roller coaster. At its fastest, it travels 73 miles per hour, and the entire time it feels like a bull trying to throw his rider.

I will usually wait the extra time to ride in the front car so I can savor my favorite part. After the slow 20-story climb, the front car crests the mountaintop and hesitates for just a moment before tipping forward for the plunge down the 65-degree drop into the underground abyss. My husband and I grab hands and scream during the gut-dropping, life-flashing, exhilarating moments of terrifying joy.

From the very beginning, parenting is just like that rollercoaster ride. Pregnancy is a long uphill climb—we want it over, yet we feel trepidation at what lies on the other side. Birth and those first tender months and years can be like that exciting descent. But uphill climbs toward milestones are constantly sprinkled throughout life's journey as we parent our children toward adulthood, battling that raging bull all the way. We must enjoy the climb, savor the anticipation and eagerly await the next hill we will face.

But, who fills the empty seat beside you as you climb the hills and dive to the valleys of life? Whose hand do you grab as you crest the hill and prepare for your ride? Many times, the empty seat might be filled with friends, family members, and co-workers as you seek their advice and lean on them for support. But as you ride the rollercoaster of parenting teens, make Jesus your constant companion. The ride will leave you breathless.

## → Connection Point

*Jesus, forgive me for not always making room for you beside me. Please be my constant companion, and remind me that the climb to the top is just as exciting as the fast descent. Help me to savor every moment. Amen.*

## Chaotic Whisper
### Nicole O'Dell

*A hurricane wind ripped through the mountains and shattered the rocks before God, but God wasn't to be found in the wind; after the wind an earthquake, but God wasn't in the earthquake; and after the earthquake fire, but God wasn't in the fire; and after the fire a gentle and quiet whisper. I Kings 19:11-12, MSG*

Good ol' Elijah was so desperate to find God. He searched for Him in all the places you might expect the Almighty Lord of the universe to inhabit. Elijah looked in the hurricane winds...wasn't there. Then in the earthquake and the fire...wasn't there.

He expected the One True God would require all the forces of the universe to sustain His presence. In truth though, The Lord could be found in none of those things. And it wasn't until the chaos abated that His presence could be felt and His voice heard as a quiet, gentle whisper.

Do you find yourself a slave to inaction because you're waiting for the wrong thing to shout at you? Sure, it would be so much easier and clearer if God shouted parenting instructions with hurricane force volume, or if He consumed wrong decisions and sin with mighty flames. It would be great if He steered our actions with a tornado and forced His will upon us and our teens like a tsunami.

But that's not the way He works. He won't compete with the chaos and noise we allow into our lives, so He waits for our striving to cease, and then speaks to us gently once we are quieted. He moves upon our spirits and waits for us to listen to and obey His gentle prodding. That's how we grow in relationship with Him and learn His character.

This week, practice quieting yourself before God. Let Him speak to you in His still, small voice. And help your teenagers sit still and listen to the things God would say to them in the quietness.

## → Connection Point

*Sovereign, Almighty God of the Universe, help me hear your gentle whisper over the chaos of life. Guide me with your still, small voice, and give me the patience to quiet my longing heart in your presence. Amen.*

Powerline365

# Connection
### Nicole O'Dell

*But seek first his kingdom and his righteousness, and all these things will be given to you as well. Matt. 6:33, NIV*

We talk a lot about making and losing connection with our teenagers. In fact, that's the whole point of this devotional series. I believe connecting is such an important aspect in every parent/teen relationship that it's a priority every single day with my kids.

Here's what I do:

When my girls wake up in the morning, they aren't allowed to turn on cell phones or check social media accounts. They don't get on Facebook or post anything to Instagram. They spend time getting ready for their day, including a daily devotion.

I worked with them to pick appropriate books that would speak to where they are in their walk and are appropriate for their age group. On their own, they read the devotion and have quiet time with God. I don't tell them how long or what it needs to consist of. I'm leading them to the Word. The rest is between them and the Holy Spirit.

They have to come and tell me about their devotion. They describe it, and tell me about the scripture, and then we find the application to their lives.

Only after that are they allowed access to the outside world. Cell phones, friends, the school day. Whatever it is. The connection between child and God must be made first, and then the connection between child and parent. Only then are they allowed to connect with everything else.

This isn't a control issue; it's a priority issue. God. Family. Friends. Isn't that how it's supposed to be? Let's model that for our kids by living priorities ourselves and by helping them structure their daily focus accordingly.

## → Connection Point

*Father, please help me as I establish appropriate structure to my teenagers connecting points. Help me be an example of proper communication with you, healthy connections with them, and an ongoing desire to connect others with You as well. Amen.*

# Trophy Scars
## Nicole O'Dell

*Not only so, but we also rejoice in our sufferings, because we know that suffering produces perseverance; perseverance, character; and character, hope. And hope does not disappoint us, because God has poured out his love into our hearts by the Holy Spirit, whom he has given us. Rom. 5:3-5, NIV*

Three Caesarean sections, several other surgeries, a million various burns, cuts, and scrapes. I'm pretty scarred. We all have scars on our bodies, and each tells its own story of bravery, carelessness, or illness. Some of those stories are funny to retell, but other scars stir up painful memories.

Physical scars are sometimes-painful reminders of things we've endured, but perhaps the most difficult scars we bear are the ones we can't see. Rejection. Disappointment. Regret. Grief. Failure.

As a parent of teens, what wounds are you suffering right now?

It's important to address those wounds before they cause relationship-damaging scars. You can do that by dealing with injury when it happens. When arguments or misunderstandings take place, work toward clarity and forgiveness before the wound closes. When division sets in, race toward unity before the gash is too great to repair.

Whatever the cause of them, those scars are an opportunity. They give you a chance to let God work in your relationship, showing you where you need to focus your attention. They also become building blocks to better communication and trust in the future. And they can be markers that testify to the great things God has done.

A scar is a mark of remembrance; it has already completed its healing. We need to let Jesus turn the open wounds in our families into trophy scars that celebrate His restoration mercies.

## → Connection Point

*Jesus, thank you for healing the wounds of my past. Please show me the injuries in my relationships with my teens and help me use them as opportunities for You to work in us. Then help me expose the scars so You can use them to reach others. Amen.*

## Watch the Invisible
### Wendy Fitzgerald

*It was by faith that Moses left the land of Egypt, not fearing the king's anger. He kept right on going because he kept his eyes on the one who is invisible. Heb. 11:27, NLT*

*So we don't look at the troubles we can see now; rather, we fix our gaze on things that cannot be seen. For the things we see now will soon be gone, but the things we cannot see will last forever. 2 Cor. 4:18, NLT*

I slammed the door and started the car. How could I have wasted the last three hours on a conversation that had nothing to do with Algebra? We were now even more behind schedule, and my precious, planned time was gone. With nothing to show for it.

As a working, homeschooling mom, I felt like a failure. And then it hit me! We had just spent the past three hours discussing, debating, and searching God's Word. My son had challenged me with an issue about his faith, and we had wrestled until the problem was settled. Invisible faith-building had displaced the visible, tangible algebra assignment at hand. In the grand scheme of things, we had spent our time on what was right and worthy.

As parents, it is easy to get caught up in the things that are visible and pressing in the lives of our teens. We focus on grades, sports, jobs, responsibilities, church functions, and other things that offer obvious, measurable results, and we forget that often the most important issues that need our attention are invisible. Don't lose heart or focus. What is seen lasts only for a short time, while what is invisible, lasts for eternity.

## → Connection Point

*Father, give me wisdom to be available for conversations about you, and give me patience to communicate in a way that my teenager will hear my voice. Help me to be more concerned with the eternal than the immediate. Amen.*

# 80

## Bear Fruit
*Nicole O'Dell*

*But the Spirit produces the fruit of love, joy, peace, patience, kindness, goodness, faithfulness, gentleness, self-control. There is no law that says these things are wrong. Gal. 5:22-23, NCV*

We bought an apple tree a few weeks ago, and we planted it as soon as we got home. My littles thought they'd get to pick an apple from it the next day. Imagine their disappointment to learn that not only would they not get an apple from their tree any time soon, it would probably be a year or more before it produced fruit. And then when it did produce apples, it would only be for a little while. The rest of the year, though, the tree would be growing, getting nourishment from the sun, soaking water up through the roots, and waiting for the fruit to fully ripen.

Picked too soon, the apples would be dry and bitter, too late and they'd be overripe and mushy.

We are constantly on watch for proof (fruit) of the lessons we've taught our teens. We want to see that they've applied our advice and are growing as they make good choices. But, just like fruit trees, sometimes that growth is happening below the surface. Just like the tree is preparing for the time it blooms and reveals its fruit, so are our teenagers.

Sometimes we grow impatient when we don't see immediate results. But growth comes in stages, and each stage must have the time it needs to perfect its work. If we rush any part of it just to get to the fruit faster, we will be disappointed in the results.

Just like the apples on the tree, our teenager's growth requires cultivation and patience. They must soak up the light of the Father, they need to be nourished from the Word of God, and they need the gift of time while we allow the Holy Spirit to work in them. If we keep them rooted in Christ, they will bear good fruit.

## → Connection Point

*Jesus, please work within my teenager to develop fruit that will bring glory to you. Help me exercise patience during the seasons when it seems like nothing is happening. Teach me to prune and cultivate the work You're already doing with my teens. Amen.*

## An Unlikely Disciple
### Nicole O'Dell

*But I tell you to love your enemies and pray for anyone who mistreats you. Matt. 5:44, CEV*

I used to think Peter was a bad choice for a disciple of Jesus Christ. He was rash. He wasn't always faithful. He had a bad temper. He didn't really understand everything Jesus said. In short, he was just an average, hotheaded person.

Then I realized I'm just like Peter. Suddenly, rather than questioning Jesus' choice in His unlikely disciple, I was so grateful that He saw something in Peter that I wouldn't have seen. Maybe, just maybe, He'd see something worthwhile in me.

What qualities do you see in your teenager that would make an unlikely disciple? Do you live with a teen who leaves the cap off the toothpaste no matter how many times you tell her not to? Or one who ignores curfew when it suits him? Or one who has a sarcastic quip ready for everything you say? Sometimes it's really difficult to imagine there's potential for that teenager to make a great impact on the Kingdom of God.

Satan knew Peter was going to have a big impact on the body of Christ, so he tried many times to get him off course by using Peter's greatest weaknesses. It was in making mistakes related to his weaknesses that Peter grew into a hero of the faith. When your teenager struggles with immaturity and makes mistakes outside of God's will, surrender it to God and trust that Peter-like growth is right around the corner.

## → Connection Point

*Lord, help me to see what you see in my teenager. Help me to appreciate the qualities that make my teen the most likely disciple of all. And please use me to turn weaknesses into strengths in both of our lives. Amen.*

## A Table before You
*Nicole O'Dell*

*You prepare a table before me in the presence of my enemies; You anoint my head with oil; My cup runs over. Ps. 23:5, NKJV*

"We must tell them that there is no pit so deep that God's love is not deeper still." Corrie ten Boom said to her beloved sister, Betsie, just before Betsie died in a Nazi concentration camp in 1944.

Corrie and Betsie were sentenced to the most squalid, flea-infested barracks at Ravensbruck prison. Corrie struggled with her faith over the conditions, but Betsie gave thanks anyway. Corrie later realized the fleas kept the guards away, enabling them to hold worship services. Horrid conditions kept them safe from abuse. Fleas became a blessing in the midst of their hell on earth.

Those nighttime worship services were a banquet table the Lord laid before them in the presence of evil. Enemies surrounded them. They suffered pain and endured misery most of us will never know. Yet, God's faithful presence brought beauty amidst the mire. Corrie ten Boom learned she couldn't fully understand the majesty of heaven until measured against the backdrop of hell. Hell manifested in the concentration camps, the conditions, and at the hands of the guards. But heaven was revealed in the table the Lord laid before her in the very presence of those enemies. Here we are, generations later, talking about her example.

What conditions do you face right now? How are you preparing a table for your family in the midst of enemies? Job loss? Divorce? Illness? Do your teens see you praising God anyway? Turn what your enemy meant for evil into something great so generations later, they'll be talking about your example.

## → Connection Point

*Lord, forgive me for the times I've grumbled and complained about my circumstances in front of my teenagers. Forgive me for letting them see my fear or lack of faith. Renew in me a heart of faith that praises you in all things. Help me to know you have a plan even for the fleas in my life. And then help me to impart that truth to my teens in my words and actions. Amen.*

# Knowing and Loving
## *Cassie Beck*

*The Lord directs the steps of the godly. He delights in every detail of their lives. Though they stumble, they will never fall, for the Lord holds them by the hand. Ps. 37.23-24, NLT*

A teenage girl floundered in her identity and purpose, as most teens do. She worried that a God who loved a billion other human beings walking the Earth could not possibly know her, let alone love her. Yet, one unforgettable day, her earthly father looked deep into her eyes and discerned her struggle. He knew. Without hesitation, that girl's father spoke truth into her life.

"God delights in you, my love."

*Psalm 73.23-26,* "Yet I am always with you; you hold me by my right hand. You guide me with your counsel, and afterward you will take me into glory. Whom have I in heaven but you? And earth has nothing I desire besides you. My flesh and my heart may fail, but God is the strength of my heart and my portion forever."

She couldn't hold back the tears as her father reminded her of God's love for her. And with the power only God's Word holds, her perspective and outlook on life was transformed as she embraced a renewed passion to become the woman God created her to be.

Inside every heart lies a desire to be known and loved. Your teens long to feel securely loved by you, despite those moments when you can't live peaceably in the same room. Become a student of your teens, discern how they best receive love, learn to understand their strengths, and know how to encourage them in their weakness. You may not have every answer, but God's Word does!

## → Connection Point

- What is your teen's love language? Words of affirmation, physical touch, acts of service, gifts, or quality time?
- Are you showing them love in a way that is most meaningful to them personally?
- Do you know where your teen is at right now? In what ways can you speak God's Word into his or her life?

## Cleanest Car on the Block
*Nicole O'Dell*

*Whoever can be trusted with very little can also be trusted with much, and whoever is dishonest with very little will also be dishonest with much. Luke 16:10, NIV*

My pastor often says that the inside of a person's car is indicative of the state of his checkbook, and the state of his checkbook is an indicator of the health of his relationship with God. In other words, if you don't have order and control in the small areas of life, it's unlikely there will be order in the big stuff.

The first time I heard my pastor say that, I cleaned out my car. The second time I heard him say that, I cleaned it out again. By the third time, I realized that my messy car was just a symptom of a disordered life. And my teenagers were watching.

Are your teens watching you scramble through your day from one activity to the next, or are they learning to schedule carefully and allow time for rest? Are they watching you shoot up arrow prayers when you're in need, or are they learning to press in to the throne on a daily basis, seeking relationship not response? Are they learning to juggle finances in hopes there's enough to pay the bills, or are they learning to live within a well-planned budget with a focus on giving?

Faithfulness over the little things paves the way for greater opportunity. Your teens will naturally gravitate to the same level of faithfulness you have over the big and small things in your life. Moving beyond that is possible, but it will be a hurdle for them to overcome. Why not set your teens up for more by modeling the behaviors of one who can handle the big and the small?

God wants us to surrender everything to Him—our commitments, our emotions, our finances, and our allegiances. It's only then, in a state of surrender, that we will prove faithful in all things.

## → Connection Point

*Dear God, I want to be a good example of faithfulness in all things. Will you please show me the areas of my life that are lacking? Help me find order and balance in the small things, so you can trust me in the large things. Amen.*

# Not Yet
## Nicole O'Dell

*Delight yourself in the Lord, and He will give you the desires of your heart. Psalm 37:4, NASB*

I always send my teenagers to prayer when they have a worry or a need. I tell them to turn to Jesus even when there's something they want. But what about the times when He says *no* or *not yet*? Does that mean my advice backfired?

When God says no or doesn't allow something into our lives that seems good, it means He's got something better in store. And when He chooses not to spare us from something that seems bad, it means He wants us to learn from it.

As for the *not yet*, at times that's an even greater lesson to learn. Patience. Waiting for His timing to receive the good stuff and to be freed from the hard stuff—wow, that can be hard sometimes. As parents, we need to embrace God's lessons of no and not yet, understanding that He always wants the best for our teenagers, even more than we do, but sometimes takes a circuitous route to get there. Are we on board with His plan? Or do we just want it our way?

Psalm 37:4 teaches that God will grant the desires of your heart, but the first part of that verse assumes that your desires line up with His.

Our Father takes no delight in the things of the world, which will all wither and die. His desire is for us to be witnesses for Him, to live right, and raise our children in His Word. If those are things that we truly desire, will He not grant us the desires of our hearts and let us see people brought into the Kingdom? Will we not have a life rich in spiritual growth and children who honor His name? Maybe not in our timing, but we prefer it in His timing, don't we?

## → Connection Point

*Lord, help me to see where my desires for myself and my teens are not in line with your will, and where the things I chase after in life are only and always according to your perfect will. I believe you will grant me the desires of my heart, because I want nothing more than what you will. Amen.*

## The Five Pillars of Parenting
*Nicole O'Dell*

*The counsel of the LORD stands forever, the plans of His heart from generation to generation. Psalm 33:11, NASB*

If you're like most Christian parents of teens, you have the best of intentions. You care about your kids. You're willing to do what it takes. If only there were a checklist you could follow that would give you the specifics of successful parenting.

Well, I don't exactly have a checklist, but I'll share with you what I believe are the five pillars of powerful parenting. If you focus on these five things, you'll see great results.

**1. Time.** "Quantity time doesn't matter, only quality time does." Have you heard that one? Yeah, don't believe it. Your kids are ranking themselves as a priority in your life based on the amount of time you spend with and on them. Yes, quality time does matter, but so does quantity.

**2. Communication.** It opens the doors to all sorts of growth and healing. Without it, you'll go backwards in your relationship. Even when your teenagers seem to shut you out, press on. They want to see how hard you'll fight for them. So don't give up!

**3. Example.** Teenagers claim to resent parents who say one thing, but do another. Don't be a do-as-I-say parent. Live as an example of the Christ-filled life you want your teens to have.

**4. Consistency.** Basic parenting, all the way back to potty-training, requires consistency. Follow through on your discipline and stick with your commitments like family dinners and daily devotions.

**5. Prayer.** Pray with and for your kids daily. Hearing your name lifted in prayer and knowing that your parents are trusting in God are powerful ways to instill faith and security in your teens.

## → Connection Point

*Dear God, thank you for prescribing your best practices for parenting. Help me to remember these five pillars on a daily basis, and then give me the strength to carry out the work I need to do. Draw these teens closer to me and to yourself. Amen.*

Powerline365

## We Need a Good Shepherd
### Janet Sketchley

*I am the gate; whoever enters through me will be saved. They will come in and go out, and find pasture. John 10:9, NIV*

*What if I get it wrong, Lord?* Anxiety is a long-time and not-loved companion, especially for parents. Fear and what-ifs sabotage us, but prayerful trust in our Savior's care brings courage. I start my day by committing my husband, sons and sons' girlfriends to the Lord, asking His care on our comings-in and our goings-out.

You and I can't be everywhere, and our teens need to find their way into adulthood. They don't want us shepherding them, even though they need it. They're going to follow their own choices.

We do our best to raise our children, but so much of the time we're guessing — or reacting. By the time they're teens, our influence is like the precious drops remaining in a lotion bottle. The instructions would read "apply sparingly and in times of greatest need."

It comforts me to remember we have a good Shepherd who leads us. He can help us recognize when to speak and when to listen...and when to let go. Which battles to choose and which to avoid.

I have a good Shepherd. That truth makes all the difference, and it has a twin: My children have a good Shepherd too. Jesus is even more invested than we are in growing our teens into responsible, Christ-following adults. He sees the long view and is not frightened by hiccups and detours in the here and now. Let's allow this to fill our prayers with confidence, no matter what we see today.

In times of anxiety we can say, this child whom I love, Jesus loves him/her more. My good Shepherd knows my pain and fear, and He has a plan. He is my child's Shepherd too, and although I can't see how it will work out, I choose to trust Him.

## → Connection Point

- If I fully trusted Jesus to shepherd my children, how would that change my words and actions? My attitude?
- Am I afraid that Jesus won't be enough to grow my children into godly adults?
- If I let Him help me with this fear, how might that change my prayers as a parent?

# 88

## Bullied in Pursuit of Popularity
### Nicole O'Dell
*Excerpted from Hot Buttons Bullying Edition*

*"You shall love your neighbor as yourself." There is no other commandment greater than these. Mark 12:31, NKJV*

It's often the pursuit of popularity that causes someone to submit to bullying, or it's the desperation to hold on to a social status that leads to bullying others. And that same desire can lead teenagers to making bad choices in response to peer pressure in hopes of winning the favor of someone cooler or more popular. In all of those examples, it's a self-image problem that drives the behavior.

So, if we aren't to encourage our teens to chase after popularity, how do we steer them toward a life rich with relationships and fulfillment? After all, having friends is important. Isn't it?

Popularity is a state of mind, and each individual can decide not to grant that kind of power to others, whether as a result of intentional peer pressure and bullying. Why let someone else decide one's worth? Why submit to someone else's arbitrary standards?

When our tweens and teens ask themselves those questions, and when they are able to see themselves the way God does and reject the cost that comes with the chase for popularity in favor of building their self-worth and remaining true to themselves, they will find fulfillment.

We definitely don't want to pull them so far back that they are alone or cast out of having a good middle school or high school experience. Somewhere in the middle is where the healthy place exists.

We want to encourage our kids to find their own way to a fulfilling life filled with good, godly friends. This is an intentional choice and it goes against what society preaches and what the bullies might want. Because, in that place, our kids are untouchable. If they have no desire to fight for position or approval, then peer pressure loses its sting.

## → Connection Point

*This is a tough one, Lord. I want my teens to have friends and be popular, but I don't want them to make bad choices or suffer bullying in the process. Help them to stay strong in the face of peer pressure and to love you more than they love the world. And please convict them to show kindness and love in all circumstances. Amen.*

## Celebrate Marriage
### Nicole O'Dell

*Marriage should be honored by all, and the marriage bed kept pure.*
*Heb. 13:4, NIV*

The Bible teaches that sex outside of marriage is dangerous and destructive. But it depicts marital union as joyous and mind-blowing. The Bible warns against pre-marital sex, but there's much more biblical content that shows the physical union in a marriage is ordained and celebrated by God.

Christian parents spend a lot of time railing at teenagers what they shouldn't be doing. So much is forbidden, sinful, and dangerous that teens often feel unnatural about their feelings and desires. Teenage relationships become testing grounds as our young people try to make sense of why they feel like they do if it's so wrong. They wonder if there's something wrong with them, so they pull away from Mom and Dad on the topic of sexuality.

I wonder if we—both churches and parents—would be more successful in raising pure teens if we spent as much time raving about the beauty of the marital bed as admonishing them to reject any hints of sexuality at all. If we spoke of the wondrous nature of human love in God's divine plan and shared openly about what lay in store for them upon marriage, might our teens yearn for that and decide to wait for it and protect it at all costs?

What if we took the mystery out of sex and treated it more as a prize than as taboo?

What if we fanned the flames of desire for the miracle of sex within marriage rather than dousing them in an effort to turn off something natural God planted within human beings? Even teenagers.

## → Connection Point

*Dear God, please help me know how to best handle my teenagers on the issue of sex. Help me inspire them to remain pure until their marriage, and give me the wisdom to answer their questions and guard against any temptation that arises. Amen.*

## Clanging Bell
*Nicole O'Dell*

*If I speak in the tongues of men or of angels, but do not have love, I am only a resounding gong or a clanging cymbal. If I have the gift of prophecy and can fathom all mysteries and all knowledge, and if I have a faith that can move mountains, but do not have love, I am nothing. 1 Cor. 13:1-2, NIV*

I've spent a lot of my life studying the Bible. I love finding new ways to look at Scripture, and I've been known to enjoy a friendly debate now and then. That feeling of unearthing a nugget of truth hidden deep within the passages and nestled among the history and tradition is invigorating to me. But as I've hurt people with my earnestness and turned them off in my zeal, I've learned that knowledge spewed without love just sounds hollow.

The knowledge of the *content* of the Bible without a grasp on the intent—the love—and without giving it the proper *context,* will never get through to our teenagers. We can speak to teens about ancient customs and the true meaning of a Greek word until we turn blue. But if we don't lovingly apply it in a way that makes sense to them, we've done nothing more than sound like a clanging bell that rings in their heads while they roll their eyes.

We can be right, but that doesn't mean we'll get through to them.

And teenagers have an amazing radar system. They can tell if you've really taken the Scriptures to heart and applied them to your own life, or if you're just trying to do your spiritual duty. They can tell if you're preaching out of control and fear, or if you're reaching out to them out of love and concern.

Make sure your teenagers see you soaking up God's Word and applying it your own life. Let the Bible be a natural part of the discussions you and your teens have about the choices they will make. Truth will be much sweeter to their ears if it comes to them that way.

## → Connection Point

*Thank you, Lord, for reminding me that your Word brings life and joy. It's not a rulebook of doom. Help me impart a love for Scripture and a drive to know You more to my teenagers by my own example and teaching. Soften their hearts toward your Word. Amen.*

# Framed Treasures
## *Debi Lee*

> *Fix these words of mine in your hearts and minds; tie them as symbols on your hands and bind them on your foreheads. Teach them to your children, talking about them when you sit at home and when you walk along the road, when you lie down and when you get up. Write them on the doorframes of your houses and on your gates, so that your days and the days of your children may be many in the land that the LORD swore to give your forefathers, as many as the days that the heavens are above the earth.* Deut. 11:18-21, NIV

One day while reading my Bible, those verses jumped out at me and that little, familiar voice spoke to me as it so often does when I'm in the Word. "You live in a nice home. There are pretty pictures and wall hangings everywhere. Sure, they're nice, but what good are they? They have no significance."

Hmm. Ok.

I knew what I needed to do. From that time on, little by little, I began replacing decorations. I hung a scripture over the doorpost, and framed verses on the walls...even over the guestroom toilet! My husband and teenagers probably thought I was weird, but I knew what God had spoken to my heart.

It was fun, and I was pleasantly surprised at how many very pretty items I found. Some teenage friends came in the house one day, looked around and asked, "How come you guys have Bible verses and stuff everywhere?" Bam! Success! At least in my mind it was.

Although those verse were written as commands to the Israelites a long time ago, do you think it has significance to us today?

What are some things you can do to promote the Word of God in your home?

## → Connection Point

*Lord, Thank you for the gentle reminders you give us to bring you into our everyday lives. May the walls of our homes and the words of our mouths bring glory to you always. Amen.*

## Cyber Check
*Nicole O'Dell*

*All things are lawful for me, but not all things are helpful...but I will not be enslaved by anything. I Cor. 6:12, ESV*

I'm going to assume that you closely monitor your teens' Internet activity. If not, you might want to check out *Hot Buttons Internet Edition*. Are you watching for signs of cyber addition? Here are some warning signs that hint at a dangerous connection with the Internet:

- Routinely loses track of time on these sites
- Has less in-person time with people in favor of computer time
- Shows anxiety if not near a computer
- Stays up late perusing social networking sites without permission
- Thinks about social networking, even when not near a computer
- Talks about online people as though they're a real-life friend

If your child exhibits some of these danger signs, you need to consider how much time and access your child has to the Internet. Set a time limit and establish boundaries, consider turning off all electronics one or two evenings a week and hanging out together. Establish a reward system where your kids earn computer time only after other activities are enjoyed.

Or you can take it a step farther and try an extended unplugged period—a sort of cyber fast. A week? A month? A summer? Do whatever you think will be enough to make an impact.

For many families it makes a lot of sense to unplug on school nights. With sports, youth group activities, music practice, homework, chores, and meals, there's not much time for anything else anyway, and this presents the opportunity for reading to make a comeback.

Ultimately, the goal is to protect our teens from outside influences and the dangers that lurk around every cyber corner, and to bring the focus back home where we can make the biggest impact of all.

## → Connection Point

*Jesus, please protect my teens from the evil that exists through the vehicle of the Internet. Give me the wisdom I need to set safe and reasonable boundaries, and then help me regain the hearts of my teens so they thrive within our cyber limits. Amen.*

**Powerline365**

# Your Teen's Spiritual Gifts
*Nicole O'Dell*

*We have different gifts, according to the grace given to each of us. If your gift is prophesying, then prophesy in accordance with your faith; if it is serving, then serve; if it is teaching, then teach; if it is to encourage, then give encouragement; if it is giving, then give generously; if it is to lead, do it diligently; if it is to show mercy, do it cheerfully. Rom. 12:6-8, NIV*

A spiritual gift isn't necessarily a person's biggest talent. It's not a job or a title. Spiritual gifts are certain traits that help a person achieve things for God that wouldn't be possible without help from Him.

Teenagers can't have spiritual gifts. They're too young!

Oh, no. Don't be deceived. Spiritual gifts are simply that: gifts. They aren't earned like Boy Scout badges or by doing time in the choir. They aren't bestowed upon the oldest or most holy. They are simply gifts that Jesus gives to help believers partner with Him in His work. Your teen has spiritual gifts, but you may need to help unearth them.

First, pray with your teen and ask God to reveal any special qualities and callings. Next, allow your teenager the space to work out those gifts in the real world. Involve a trusted advisor to help steer the growth. Next, in order to better understand the gifts, read these scriptures with your teenager:

*Romans 12:6-8*
*1 Corinthians 12:6-10*
*1 Corinthians 12:28*
*1 Corinthians 12:29-30*
*Ephesians 4:11*
*1 Peter 4:11*

What spiritual gifts do you see in your teen? How can you call them out?

## → Connection Point

*Dear Jesus, thank you so much for using us in what you do. Please empower my teen to search for the spiritual gifts you've placed beneath the surface and help me to nurture those gifts. Amen.*

## Hands of Success
*Valerie Comer*

*Make it your goal to live a quiet life, minding your own business and working with your hands, just as we instructed you before.*
*I Thes. 4:11, NLT*

In a society obsessed with higher education and money, success is defined by where you vacation, whether you have a corner office, how big your house is, how many cars are in your garage...and how clean your hands are.

Say what?

Not only clean in the sense of no illegal dealings, but literally. A mechanic's hands may have oil in the pores; a miner's may have coal dust. A working man—or woman—may not have hands white and soft, but often calloused and scarred with dirt embedded beneath chipped nails. Marked as a working man or woman.

What is the life you've envisioned for your teens once they're out on their own? Do you want them to have a better life than you had? More money, more success? It's natural to desire an easy life for our kids, but there is no cookie-cutter solution. God has a unique plan for each person, and He's given aptitudes and passions for different things for each of us and our children.

What is your teen's true interest? Cultivate that before the Lord. Pray with him or her for God's career directions. And if your teen chooses a future without a corner office, without a guarantee of wealth, remember there is no shame in working with one's hands to create an honest living.

The only clean hands lifted up in God's Word are the ones in Psalm 24:3-4 (NLT): "Who may climb the mountain of the LORD? Who may stand in his holy place? Only those whose hands and hearts are pure, who do not worship idols and never tell lies."

## → Connection Point

Dear Jesus, I'm sorry for the times I've put physically clean hands above those that are spiritually clean. Please teach me, so I can teach my kids, that leading a simple life in obedience to you is to be cherished far above the world's definition of success. Thank you that you embraced scarred hands on my behalf. In your name, amen.

## 95

Powerline365

## Being Praise
### Nicole O'Dell

*I praise you because I am fearfully and wonderfully made; your works are wonderful, I know that full well. Ps. 139:14, NIV*

I have six kids and every one of them thrives on praise. Who doesn't, really? The best way to grow is to know what you've done right and then do it again, plus some.

But your teens need a different kind of praise from you. They hunger for the kind of praise that tells them they are awesome regardless of what they do. They need you to be the person in their corner who claps and shots encouragement no matter what.

Is your praise based on "doing" or based on "being"?
- "You're the best player on the team!" Doing.
- "WOW! Look at those grades. You're so smart." Doing.
- "You did this or that so well!" Doing.

While good and valid points, those things all praise your teenager for works. What if you flipped it around and said things like this:
- "I love your heart for the underdog. You're so compassionate." Being.
- "You are so special to me. God made you so perfect, just the way you are." Being.

While it's important to praise our children for doing good things, there is great danger in allowing all of our praise to be focused on what our child is *doing* while neglecting the importance of their *being*. Our words must reflect to our children that they are God's workmanship, precious and valuable to us apart from their actions, because they are God's creation, fearfully and wonderfully made.

What a gift it is to be freed from a value that is based on what we do, and into the value that comes entirely because of who we are, sons and daughters of a King. In the same light, our children are valuable because they are *our* sons and daughters, reflecting our image, and most importantly, made in the image of an Almighty God.

## → Connection Point

*Lord, thank You for loving me for who I am, not what I do. Please help me show that same grace to my teens. Help me speak truth and life into their lives by celebrating who they are. Amen.*

## Take the Mystery Out
### Nicole O'Dell

*No temptation has overtaken you that is not common to man. God is faithful, and he will not let you be tempted beyond your ability, but with the temptation he will also provide the way of escape, that you may be able to endure it. 1 Cor. 10:13, ESV*

Sometimes teenagers make bad choices out of simple curiosity. Parents can help prepare their teens by imparting concern for God's will, giving them the tools they need to succeed, and walking them through the process of making good decisions.

What's in it for your teen to make good choices? Are you parenting with a because-I-said-so mentality? Teenagers need to see both the temporal and eternal value of doing the right thing. It takes consistent and effective communication in order to impart that kind of understanding.

Our teens also need certain tools in order to stand up in the face of peer pressure and temptation. They need a growing understanding of God's Word and His will. They need a mentor or someone with whom they can talk openly. And they need options. If you make a rule against something, offer an "instead" in its place. A redirection gives them something else to turn to.

Teens need to be armed with the tools necessary to make the hard choices—willing to withstand and endure persecution for the sake of Christ. And they need to be prepared with the words and tools they need to keep themselves safe in the battle against temptation and to even use those incidents as a means of sharing God's love with others.

What can you do today to prepare your teen for a peer-pressure battle? Are you willing to be pro-active instead of reactive?

## → Connection Point

*Dear God, please forgive me for my get-through-the-day mentality. Help me to seize every opportunity you give me to prepare my teens for what lies ahead, and then please give me the wisdom I need to be effective. Amen.*

Powerline365

# Bring Back the Cleavers
## Nicole O'Dell

*What has been will be again, what has been done will be done again; there is nothing new under the sun. Ecc. 1:9, NIV*

The days of dating the way it was portrayed on the hit television show *Leave it to Beaver* are over. Parents no longer have the ability to act as gatekeeper when an interest develops among their teens, with such easy access through means like the Internet, cell phones, and even in-person access at a host of activities.

When it comes to those all-encompassing boy-girl relationships, we don't have the luxury of waiting until a boy calls our daughter, assuming that will be her first signal that he's interested in her. We can't pretend that a no-dating-before-sixteen rule means there won't be anything going on in our son's love life that we're unaware of. In fact, these days, it's best to face facts fast.

Dating isn't a black-and-white sin issue. But it is a platform that allows temptation to build to the potential of poor choices. Choices about sexual activity, educational focus, marital decisions, faith-based commitments, and more. The prep work must be done now . . . the sooner, the better.

But even though this society feels as though it's on hyper-drive in every way, we're told in Scripture that there's nothing new. That human nature is the same now as it was then. And also that God's expectations are the same now as they ever were. So, it's up to us as parents to keep a tight rein on who has access to our teens. We need to be willing to say no when an unhealthy interest develops. And we need to prepare our kids for the temptations of sin that can arise with the platform of dating.

## → Connection Point

*Dear God, please help me do the prep work I need to do to ensure my teens are equipped to make good choices as they consider dating. Help me set boundaries and stand my ground. Birth a desire for righteousness with my teenagers that will precede any dating decisions, sexual choices, and commitments for the future. Amen.*

## Don't Steal the Struggle
### Brenda Yoder, MA

*...we also glory in our sufferings, because we know that suffering produces perseverance; perseverance, character; and character, hope. Rom. 5:3-4, NIV*

"*I do so much better when you and dad aren't with me. I figured it out.*" My son had just received his driver's license and was referring to learning to drive the stick-shift car we bought him. The first time his dad took him out for a driving lesson, my son was discouraged. "It's useless," he said, having stalled the car ten times.

But here he was a few weeks later, license in hand, learning how to release the clutch and shift gears on his own. He told me he was more relaxed without his dad beside him. It just clicked with him.

From this conversation, I realized that kids learn things, perhaps better, when we're not hovering over them telling them what to do. It was a lesson in the growing up process, that adolescence is for releasing our children to their future, their intellect, and their choices that will guide their life. It's about letting them figure it out after we've taught them well. It's about trusting them and who God is in their lives.

This conversation was eye-opening for me. I'm challenged to take my hands off my kids at the right time to allow them to learn and grow. Do you struggle with that? How can you know when it's just the right time to help your teen figure it out by releasing them to their own abilities?

## → Connection Point

*Dear Lord, equip us to let our children learn. Help us to not steal the struggle so they can become the person you've created them to be. Amen.*

## Majority Vote
### Nicole O'Dell

*The fear of human opinion disables; trusting in God protects you from that. Prov. 29:25, MSG*

Are you parenting by majority vote? Does your teenager see you get on the phone with all your friends every time you have to make a parenting move? Do you wait until your weekend golf game with the guys to decide what to do about your son and his latest problems? Do you poll the man behind you in the checkout lane and your entire list of Facebook friends in hopes of gaining some wisdom?

Maybe you're desperate for help and really want to know what other people have done and what the results were. There is wisdom in learning from others. Or maybe you're subconsciously looking for a way to pass the buck if something goes wrong. But, "They told me to do it that way!" is not a parenting scapegoat.

Parenting by poll risks worldly influence and denies the power of God to lead you through the truth in His Word and with guidance from the Holy Spirit. Furthermore, when your teenagers notice that you run to everyone but God for help with your parenting, they will learn to do the same thing in important areas of their own lives. *Why would they turn to a God you don't trust or, at best, rank as second place to the advice of your friends?*

Are you modeling trust in God by turning to Him with your parenting needs? Let your teenager see and hear you praying for divine guidance in all things. Imagine the reaction when your teen hears you pray, "Almighty God, help me know how to discipline that kid of mine who keeps coming in late." Maybe that tardy teen will make it home before curfew next time. And, just maybe, he'll do the same and turn to God with his own decisions.

## → Connection Point

*Lord, thank you for the amazing, godly friends you've placed in my life, but help me to always turn to you first when I am in doubt and need parenting direction. Please help me to be an example of good relationship priorities and to show my teens what it means to have complete faith in You. Amen.*

## Planks and Specks
### Nicole O'Dell

*You hypocrite, first take the log out of your own eye, and then you will see clearly to take the speck out of your brother's eye.*
Matt. 7:5, NASB

Can you list some times you've messed up and then been forgiven by others? Boy, I can sure come up with some doozies. Times I've said the wrong thing and hurt someone's feelings. Times I've lied to spare myself while getting someone else in trouble. Times I've not done the right thing because the personal cost was too great. I'm sure you have some examples of your own.

Whenever I'm having a tough time getting past my teenager's latest offenses, all it takes is a quick look at my own. When I allow the Holy Spirit to show me how much I've been forgiven and when I realize how richly I am still loved, it helps me to let go of my anger and embrace my teen. Imperfections and all.

But I'm not God!

Believe me, I get it. It's not easy to forgive those who have committed a painful wrong against you and are truly guilty. It's not easy to ignore a snotty attitude or to forgive a recurring offense or hateful words. The problem is that unforgiveness drives a wedge between you and your teen and between you and God. Your free and open walk with a loving Savior is difficult when your spirit is harboring unforgiveness, which God cannot abide.

You might be training your teens to confess their sins to God. You've talked about His grace and forgiveness and His healing and restorative mercies. But are you modeling those traits yourself? What offenses are you clinging to that need to be forgiven once and for all?

Now's the time to take a chance. Forgiveness is a step away. God has forgiven your sins, past, present, and future—now it's time to pass that on to your teens and others.

## → Connection Point

*Thank you, Jesus, for your forgiveness. Thank you for covering my sins and my parenting failures. Let me show grace to my children so they will trust me with their sins and believe in your mercy as evidenced through my actions. Amen.*

## Something about Sex
*Nicole O'Dell*

*Run from sexual sin! No other sin so clearly affects the body as this one does. For sexual immorality is a sin against your own body.*
*I Cor. 6:18, NLT*

There's just something about sex. Outside of the covenant of marriage, it's the most insidious sin that gets ahold of our teens and tears them away from God. I can't think of another teenage sin or stronghold that carries on into adulthood and doesn't let go to the degree that sex does. It's much easier to let go and move on from other choices than from the one that requires heart, mind, and body.

God intended sexual intimacy for marriage. Anything outside of that will leave teenagers feeing soiled, dirty, and used up. The enemy uses those lies to keep kids rooted in the wrong crowd and in their own bad choices, searching, longing for connection and completion.

Prevention by purity is the very best plan, but what if it's too late for that? Maybe you know (or fear) your teenager has already had sex. Statistically that will be the case for over half of the parents reading this. On which side of those stats do you fall? Are you sure?

Really search your heart on this is because if your teen has had sex or some level of sexual impurity, healing must take place before the wound festers and leads to more sin and self-doubt. If it isn't dealt with, it will be a lasting reminder of regret, shame, and loss. The great part is that we serve a God who forgives and restores. He can heal the empty places in your teen's heart and mind. He will bring wholeness.

If your teens have not had sex, launch a purity campaign in your home. Make it part of your conversations, your Bible study, your personal sharing, and your prayer time. Your teens will roll their eyes every time you raise the issue in prayer. They will run the other way when they see you coming with the Bible. But I guarantee they will thank you on their wedding day.

## → Connection Point

*Father, if there is any sin or heartache in my teen's life that I need to see, I want to know. Please help me be the parent you've called me to be in this area of sexual sin. Please give my teens a heart for purity, and give me the wisdom to guide them to it. Amen.*

## Small Beginnings
### Cara Putman

*Do not despise these small beginnings, for the Lord rejoices to see the work begin, to see the plumb line in Zerubbabel's hand.*
Zech. 4:10, NLT

Life is filled with small beginnings. A tiny newborn grows into an adult. A seed planted in a garden develops into a towering tomato plant. An entry-level job evolves into a more satisfying and challenging career. With this consistent pattern appearing in so many areas of our lives, why aren't we more comfortable with those small beginnings?

Recently, my husband and I have had to work with one of our children on a character issue. I'd love to see full and complete turnaround in this area, but the reality is that it is a moment-by-moment process of coaching and guiding him into new patterns and choices.

Our oldest daughter is a competitive gymnast. If as an eight-year-old she'd decided the skills the coaches asked her to master were too elementary, today she wouldn't be performing a handful of skills that you see in Olympic-level routines. The small beginnings lead to more.

But we have to start.

So often we choose never to start because we think the work is too hard, too menial, too small. There have been times in my life where God has held this verse up to me and pounded it into my spirit. Do not despise the day of small beginnings. Without a beginning, there can be no growth. Without a beginning, there can be no movement. Without a beginning, there can be no foundation to build on.

So let's commit today to appreciating the small beginnings in our children's lives and coaching them to see and appreciate them.

## → Connection Point

*Father, help me nurture my kids through a lifetime of small beginnings in a way that will turn them into the men and women of God You have called them to be. And please let me never model dissatisfaction with the small beginnings in my own life, but rather to always appreciate the blessings that come from them. Amen.*

# 103

Powerline365

## Don't Play with Fire
### Nicole O'Dell

> The proverbs of Solomon, son of David, king of Israel: for attaining wisdom and discipline; for understanding words of insight.
> Prov. 1:1-2, NIV

Don't run with scissors, don't play with fire, and don't throw a ball in the house. Those are all pieces of wisdom that parents have been handing down through the generations. The book of Proverbs is referred to as the *book of wisdom because* Solomon was given both spiritual and practical wisdom from God and then handed it down to us through his writings.

When parenting teens, it's good to consider where you're getting your wisdom. Are you relying on your own logic and past experiences, or are you learning from God's Word and the leading of the Holy Spirit? Imagine if Solomon relied solely on himself, and Proverbs was a book of his best tips rather than wisdom right from God's heart to ours.

Secondly, how are you passing on your wisdom to your teenagers? The Bible is full of direction, parables, prophecies, and other means of getting the point across. God knows that we receive things in different ways, at different times, for different reasons. And He is creative enough to get through to us in the way we need.

Are you reaching out to your teens in every way possible rather than just handing down the law and acting as an enforcer or, the opposite, letting go and hoping nothing bad happens?

Wisdom is being able to discern the things that produce good results and also understanding what causes negative results.

Wisdom is linked with instructions. Once we know His will, it is up to us to follow it. This is especially true when parenting teens.

## → Connection Point

*Jesus, please give me a new dose of your wisdom so I can reach my teens in the way that's most effective for them. Help me be consistent in my response to your guidance, and please make them receptive to my efforts even when I mess it up. Amen.*

# 104

## For Their Good
### Nicole O'Dell

*And we know that to them that love God all things work together for good, even to them that are called according to his purpose.*
Rom. 8:28, ASV

It's so difficult to watch your kids go through tough stuff. When they first learned to walk, it was painful to watch them bump into things or trip and fall. Bike riding brought a whole new set of bumps and bruises. Those early years of team sports taught them they wouldn't always win. That was a tough lesson, but a necessary one, we knew.

Then middle school hit and with it came the battle for popularity and approval—a battle they wouldn't always win and will continue to fight through high school and beyond. Those painful moments give us the opportunity to teach them about the guarantee of God's approval. That's about the time when the stakes change and we learn that heartache can no longer be covered with a Band-Aid. In fact, doing that will only make it worse.

We need to use the hard times in our teenagers' lives to teach them important lessons from God and so the glory of God will be shown in them. Consider the man who had been blind his whole life. That sure was a hardship! The people wondered if his blindness was due to his sin or his parents' sin. Jesus taught them, "Neither this man or his parents sinned, but this happened so that the work of God might be displayed in his life" (John 9:2-3). And then He healed the man.

Sometimes things happen to our teenagers (friendship struggles, bullying, break-ups, rejection, failure...), and we want to make it all better. But God's response to us is the same as it was about the man's blindness, sometimes He allows our teenagers to suffer so the work of God will be shown in their lives.

There is no better thing than to see God's hand moving in the lives of our teens, even when it's painful. Trust Him to be at work even when a Band-Aid seems like a quicker fix.

## → Connection Point

*Father, help me to trust more. Help me to see your hand at work and to let go of my control. Work Your will in my teenager's life so your glory might be displayed for all to see. Amen.*

# GenHIM
## Nicole O'Dell

*Don't copy the behavior and customs of this world, but let God transform you into a new person by changing the way you think. Then you will learn to know God's will for you, which is good and pleasing and perfect.* Rom. 12:2, NLT

Generation X, Y, Z? The whole idea of labeling a generation irritates me. I'm not going to shove my teenagers into a box just because some sociologists think the generation, as a group, feels certain ways or exhibits certain patterns of work ethic or ambition.

Make it GenHIM. Help shape your pre-teens and teenagers into godly young adults with their hearts set on what God wants for them and the work ethic to chase after that.

Don't let them believe they're lazy. My sixteen-year old has two jobs because she sees the value of hard work and knows if she wants things, she's going to have to earn them. Fight the lie that they don't care about anyone but themselves. Encourage the spirit of camaraderie, patriotism, and selflessness. My son knew from a young age that he wanted to join the Air Force. He's now 23, has been serving for three years in an intelligence field, and intends to make it a career.

Arm your teenagers with the belief that they can do anything they feel called to do, but equip them with the truth that they have to do the work to go after it. It starts now. Ask yourself:

- How can I help my teenagers value hard work?
- How has laziness or entitlement attitudes crept into my home?
- What is something I can do this week to encourage a mindset of putting others first?

Help your teens blaze their own trail in this Generation-Whatever. Instead of listening to the world and putting limits on their ambition, help them chase hard after GenHIM.

## → Connection Point

*Jesus, I reject the stereotypes that this social climate wishes to force on my teenagers. I see they are only a lie of the enemy who wants to make young people powerless for God. Help me teach my kids the value of hard work and give them a passion to chase after whatever it is you have for them to do. Amen.*

## Relationship to Last
*Bethany Jett*

*How good and pleasant it is when God's people live together in unity! Ps. 133:1, NIV*

Once kids reach their early teens, the dynamic changes from instructional to conversational teaching. It's a beautiful thing. When this shift happens, and your child begins speaking in more adult-like terms, with opinions and rationale, a deeper relationship forms. How do you stay relevant and remain the parental figure? How much friendship is appropriate?

Many of the students we've had in youth group come from broken homes and have had absentee or uninvolved parents. Those kids flocked to other families where real boundaries existed. Teens want parents, not friends. After more than a decade working with teenagers, I assure you that the coolest parent is overwhelmingly one who acts like a parent.

What are some ways to stay relevant and involved?
- Read popular books together
- See movies together
- Host dinners, cook-outs, game nights, or sleepovers
- Be available when it's easy, and especially when it's difficult
- Let your teens see you interact with their friends.

Stay interested in what's going on in their world, be involved in their interests, and get to know their friends. Allowing your teen the freedom to be themselves within your boundaries is a great way to build a foundation for a relationship that will last.

## → Connection Point

*Jesus, please help me set appropriate boundaries and follow through with the discipline my teenager needs. Help me to know what I need to do to build a strong relationship that will last through time without striving too hard to be my teen's friend. And please protect our communication and guard our hearts so that misunderstanding and conflict have no part in our relationship. Amen.*

## Not at Home
### Nicole O'Dell

*He has made everything beautiful in its time. He has also set eternity in the human heart; yet no one can fathom what God has done from beginning to end. Ecc. 3:11, NIV*

My grandfather was as close to a personification of Jesus as a man can be on this earth. My papaw served his family, his friends, and his church with his whole heart. It's because of him that I can even partly understand how God loves me so sacrificially and unconditionally. The day my grandpa died was like all of his other days. He had spent it on a ladder painting his church. Then he came home, went to sleep, and woke up in the presence of God.

His brothers often said he was a different sort of boy...when the others where cussing and causing trouble, he was quietly singing, "This world is not my home. I'm just a-passing through. My treasures are laid up somewhere beyond the blue."

We spend so much time teaching our kids how to live right, do well in school, be good to their friends, etc. I wonder, sometimes, if by spending so much time doing that, we put too much focus on this life. If we turned their eyes onto Jesus and really taught them and lived in display of the truth that this world is not our home, would better choices and selflessness naturally follow that understanding? Do we worry too much about the actions that we lose sight of the motivation?

I'm under no delusions that my grandfather thought that way because someone told him to. I believe the Holy Spirit birthed eternity in him in a special way. And I believe it's possible for each of us and for our children to shift our focus and long for God's presence in such a way that the things of this world grow strangely dim.

## → Connection Point

*Jesus, the thought of eternity with you is so difficult for me to grasp—how much more so must it be for my kids? Would you please impart a new level of understanding in them (and in me!) so they will long for your presence in such a way that makes them a stranger in this land? Let them win the war with their flesh and embrace the victory they find iou. Please shape our home—our conversations, actions, and goals—into a place that points to eternity in all ways. Amen.*

## Choose NOW
### Nicole O'Dell

*...guard the deposit entrusted to you. Avoid the irreverent babble and contradictions of what is falsely called knowledge,*
*1 Tim. 6:20, ESV*

The "deposit entrusted to you" is the truth you have been shown. Timothy was warned (as an example for all of us) to guard that truth. And we, as parents, must guard it in our homes at all costs.

In this age of Universalism, tolerance, and moral relativism, it would seem there is no immutable truth. More than ever in history, the young minds of the upcoming generation are assaulted with innumerable false teachings and misdirections, sinful and worldly views of faith and doctrine, and the ideal that all truth is relative to the individual and it's hateful to say otherwise.

Parents, how are you guarding the truth in your home? Do you celebrate worldly ideals by the entertainment you seek? Do you encourage tolerance by your friendships and those you allow your teens to have? Do you embrace Universalism by staying quiet in the face of anti-Jesus teachings? *Note: when people say they believe in God, ask them how they feel about Jesus. You'll find out exactly where they stand.*

Ask yourself questions like:
- Today, how have I taught/shown my teens that Jesus is Lord of our lives and our home?
- How can I guard against false teaching and ungodly tolerance?
- How can I reinforce God's authority in our home?

This isn't something you can wait to worry about tomorrow. Joshua 24:15 says (paraphrased), "If serving the Lord seems undesirable to you, then go ahead and serve a false God if you choose. But as for me and my family, we will serve the Lord." Choose NOW.

## → Connection Point

*Father, as for me and my family, we choose YOU. Please help me to reinforce truth in my family, and help me to arm my teens with the tools they need to defend it. Please protect my family and our home that no false teachings or watered-down versions of truth would sneak past my watchful eyes. Amen.*

## Clear Margins
### Nicole O'Dell

*For anyone who enters God's rest also rests from his own work, just as God did from his. Let us, therefore, make every effort to enter that rest, so that no one will fall by following their example of disobedience. Heb. 4:10-11, NIV*

Parenting toddlers is nonstop. You can't take your eyes off of them for a moment because they can get hurt or break something. Then in the elementary and pre-teen years, the bulk of parenting time is spent carpooling and volunteering at school. But in the teen years, the needs pop out of nowhere. Just when you think you'll get a bit of a break, the phone rings... you know what happens next. You're suddenly putting out a proverbial fire or meeting some need. No break.

The margin of a sheet of paper is meant for notes, additions, and corrections. It's there for the afterthought — not for the initial effort. It's for the first draft, but then other ideas or research needs to be added in the middle of a paragraph. Where would all of that extra and important stuff go without a margin? God wants us to plan rest in our schedule, to leave our margins free of clutter in order to accommodate those last minute things that arise in the lives of our teenagers.

Hebrews references the eternal rest we'll have with Christ, but it's still great advice for this life. Let's parent with clean margins so we can respond to our teenager's needs and to God's direction. Does your life have a clean margin? Is there room in your life for the plans God has for you?

## → Connection Point

*Lord, please help me clear the junk that clutters the margins of my days and mind. Help me to keep my margins free so your plans, and the needs of my kids, can be top priority in my life. Let me not be so busily focused on my own agenda that I miss yours. Amen.*

## Almost Perfect Love
*Sara Goff*

*God is love. Whoever lives in love lives in God, and God in them. This is how love is made complete among us so that we will have confidence on the day of judgment: In this world we are like Jesus. There is no fear in love. John 4:16-18, NIV*

The other night I was putting my five-year-old son to bed and for the first time when I told him I loved him, he didn't say it back. I sat on the side of his bed, stroking his moppy blond hair and waited for the words, *I love you, too, Mommy.* But they didn't come. He wasn't asleep. I thought of excuses: maybe he's too tired, maybe he's thinking of something else, or...maybe I'd done something wrong.

Fear gripped my heart. Am I losing him already? He's not even a teenager yet! I considered asking him if he loved me back. But what if he says no? Or yes, but he didn't mean it? But something inside me said to let it go. I kissed his soft cheek, told him that God loved him even more, and quietly left his bedroom.

God loves us every minute of every day. How often do we stop to appreciate His love? How often do we tell Him we love Him back? It feels good to reciprocate His love, but actually that's not what He expects. His love is perfect; He asks for nothing in return. Our love will never be perfect.

If my love for my children, my spouse, my friends is riddled with expectations and insecurities, then it is far from perfect. My goal is to love completely, through God, without fear. As my boys grow up, that may become more of a challenge, which is why saying *I love you* should be the norm around the house now. I know teenagers are naturally shy about expressing their feelings, and they may even reject love for reasons they can't explain. That's okay. All they need to do is hear it, and in this way our love for them will be almost perfect.

### → Connection Point

*Dear God, I forget to trust in your love when I crave affirmation from others. Help me to strive for your perfect love and then to show it to my kids so they, too, will know your unfailing, perfect love. Amen.*

Powerline365

## Comfortable Inadequacy
*Nicole O'Dell*

*Praise God, the Father of our Lord Jesus Christ! The Father is a merciful God, who always gives us comfort. He comforts us when we are in trouble, so that we can share that same comfort with others in trouble. 2 Cor. 1:3-4, CEV*

I'm a new Christian.
I'm a single parent.
I've made a lot of mistakes.
I've got nothing to offer.

Knowing you're in charge of your teenager's spiritual upbringing, it's easy to beat yourself up over the inadequacies you see in yourself. We all have them, and we all have to fight hard not to let them slow us down. You might identify with that list, or maybe you've got a different one that runs through your mind, and feel like you're not the best one for the job. After all, how can you hold your teen accountable for something you got wrong yourself?

The truth is, none of those things, no inadequacy you feel, is a surprise to God—yet He still called you to be your teenagers' parent. Mistakes, insecurities, failures, and all. Was that because there was no one better in line for the job? Or was it because He had plans for how to best use your past for the betterment of your teenager's future?

He will comfort you in your weakness and then empower you to use the lessons of your past as you parent your teens. If you let Him.

Look back with gratitude on the things you've gone through as its purpose in your parenting begins to unfold. It may be hard to see past the fear to the outcome, but one day you'll look back and see how your vulnerability led to more open dialogue, honesty, and trust between you and your teens. And your teenagers will learn more about God's grace and forgiveness as they see the evidence of it in your life.

## → Connection Point

*Jesus, please help me shed my insecurities so I can parent my teenagers in confidence. Please show me what you've got in mind, and then let me partner with you in leading them in to a closer walk with you. I give you everything I've got—it's yours to use however you see fit, and I'll hold nothing back. Amen.*

## Trash Talk
### Nicole O'Dell

*Indeed, I count everything as loss because of the surpassing worth of knowing Christ Jesus my Lord. For his sake I have suffered the loss of all things and count them as rubbish, in order that I may gain Christ. Philippians 3:8, ESV*

A fancy vacation. A bigger house. A new car. Everyone else seems to have no trouble getting all of those things for themselves and their own families. Especially if Facebook is any indicator. Maybe it's time to work some extra hours, get a second job, or even take out a loan so you and your family can have some of the finer things in life.

Right?

According to the Word of God, if we are chasing hard after God and have our sights set on Him and His will for us and our families, all of the glittery things of the world will seem like garbage in comparison. There's nothing inherently wrong with any of those things, but they can't drive our decision-making or lead us into a situation that costs too much. We are to live as though none of that matters.

And it's not just about getting it right for ourselves. We have eyes on us, watching what we do, and deciding what to value in their lives based on what we elevate in our own. We need to measure worth on an eternal scale and place little importance on the things that won't last.

Here are some important questions to ask yourself:
- Do I have a healthy relationship with material things?
- Do I cling to possessions and clamor for more, more, more?
- Am I teaching my teens the importance of giving?

If you can place the perspective of value in the proper light, your teenagers will learn to seek eternal gains over earthly pleasures.

## → Connection Point

*Father, thank you for all of the wonderful blessings you have given us as a family. Help me to be thankful for each blessing rather than always looking for the next big thing. Help me teach my teens to value the things that you do and to place little importance on any earthly possession. Amen.*

## Bread and Water
### Nicole O'Dell

*A meal of bread and water in contented peace is better than a banquet spiced with quarrels. Prov. 17:1, MSG*

You spend hours making the perfect pan of lasagna, cook it just right, and pull it out of the oven with enough time for the layers to settle and the cheese to harden just right. You slice a big piece for each family member, serve up a bowl of fresh mixed-green salad, and add a hunk of buttery garlic bread to the plate. You call the family in for dinner.

The kids come to the table bickering and pushing each other. Another is staring at her cell phone, and another one has his nose in a book. Someone even has the nerve to complain about what you've served. You no longer feel like eating your beautiful meal, right? All that work and the anticipation of blessing your family with a great meal and a good time of togetherness—out the window.

Proverbs 17 says that it would be much better for a family to dine on bread and water in peace, than to have a huge feast if everyone was fighting and unhappy. But the disconnect is often in the expectations. They are often self-centered and, left to their own devices, will often develop an entitlement attitude and a complaining spirit. It's our job to teach them the value of someone else's love offering. We have to teach them gratefulness.

Next time, instead of spending time on an elaborate meal, call your family to the dinner table but provide only a loaf of bread and a pitcher of water. Share the scripture above and talk about what it means. Use the shock value of the "dinner" to make your point. But don't back down. Let the bread and water stand as that night's fare (trust me, everyone will survive the night), and let the lesson really grab hold. It's time to get back to basics before expectations override civility and family relationships suffer.

## → Connection Point

*Dear God, please forgive me for letting a spirit of entitlement creep into my home. Please help me to nip it right now and allow gratitude, generosity, and servanthood to rise up in its place. Please help me teach the hard lessons that need to be taught in order to take us to a new level as a family. Amen.*

# 114

## Winter's Promise
### Amber Frank

*For I consider that the sufferings of this present time are not worth comparing with the glory that is to be revealed to us. Rom. 8:18 ESV*

It's been a long, cold, snowy winter here in the Midwest. More snow and cold than we have had in our area in a long time. And, well, let's just say it has made *some* of us more than a little grumpy, itching for warm weather so we can get out and do something. We had two days this week when the temperature crept past 60 degrees, but then, there it comes again. Snow, cold, wind. When I saw that weather forecast I just about cried.

It has been a hard winter for me, emotionally, physically, and spiritually. Dealing with my hormones and two teenager's hormones has been a challenge to say the least. So it was this morning as I was taking my kids to school, again fighting ice and partially snow blocked streets that God showed me something. I turned the corner to head back to our house and glanced up at the bare trees. The sunlight was streaming through, and I saw the most beautiful landscape before me.

The storm two nights before had poured a little freezing drizzle on the trees. They were glistening, shining so beautifully in the sunlight. It was in that moment of reveling at God's creation when He reminded me that all hard times with our children have beautiful moments in them, and they won't last forever. Even in this never-ending winter there were times of beauty and fun. We just have to take the time to look for them. As you go through the teen years, daily take time to look, and you may have to look hard, but really look for those few, brief moments of beauty. Just like in a long hard winter, they will be there, shining as the SON reflects off of them.

## → Connection Point

*Father, raising teenagers is tough, not just on the teenagers, but especially on me. Help me to see those beautiful moments in the midst of the chaos and struggles, and to remember that someday in the all too near future, we will look back on these days and miss them. Amen.*

Powerline365

## Handwritten Treasure
### Nicole O'Dell

*Let love and faithfulness never leave you; bind them around your neck, write them on the tablet of your heart. Prov. 3: 3 NIV*

I searched my house for blank paper the other day. None in the scrap note pile by the microwave. None in the pile with my schoolbooks. None in my secret drawer everyone forgets is at the bottom of the dining buffet. Ah ha! The printer tray. Hopefully no crayon-wielding five-year olds found the printer-tray stash before I did. Yes! There were a few sheets left, which I snatched. Who'd have thought paper would feel like contraband in a house with seven people?

That caused a thought. When is last time you wrote your teenager a letter? Has your teenager ever actually received a letter from anyone? With emails, text messages, and all forms of social media, letter writing is a dying art form and something your teen may never come to appreciate. But something about reading handwritten words gives them more impact. It feels purposeful, intentional. Why would someone take the time to write the words if they didn't actually mean them? How much more meaningful would it be to see a handwritten note signed, "I love you, Mom" than to receive a text with the sign off: *I <3 u!*

Why don't you try it this week? Write your teenager a letter explaining some of the things you love most about your relationship. Then end it with an invitation to hang out doing something special this weekend. My guess is a year from now you'll find that letter tucked under a pile of socks, hidden in the back of a drawer. A treasure.

## → Connection Point

*Dear Jesus, thank you for reminding me that my teenager needs to hear from me in many ways. Help me to write love on the tablet of their hearts—let my words be treasures. Amen.*

## Quirky Kids
*Nicole O'Dell*

*You made all the delicate, inner parts of my body and knit me together in my mother's womb. Thank you for making me so wonderfully complex! Your workmanship is marvelous—how well I know it. Ps. 139:13-14, NLT*

My little brother was quirky. So much so he used to bring sardines in his school lunch! When he'd open those little cans, other students would grab their brown bags and slide as far away as they could get, noses wrinkled in disgust. I give my mom a lot of credit for not forcing him to leave the kippers at home for an after-school snack and sending a more normal school lunch.

In a youth culture that demands conformity, how do you ensure that your quirky kid is happy and well adjusted? How do you allow for personal creativity and the development of unique qualities without setting them up for being picked on or worse?

Other than showing nothing but complete love and acceptance yourself, confirm that your child is comfortable. This is most important. Many quirky teens are perfectly happy on the fringe of what others deem as normal. They march to the beat of their own drummer, and they prefer it that way. Be careful you don't impose your own societal expectations or popularity rules on your teens when they are doing just fine the way they are.

Watch out for red flags like sadness, isolation, or potential bullying and intervene when necessary. Again, though, don't mistake solitude for loneliness or normal teenage disagreements for bullying. Let them be themselves and seek solitude if they want it, and allow them to work out their own conflicts within normal limits.

Be careful not to show concern about a perceived weakness or quirky or unique style. Don't send the message to your wonderfully unique child that you're in any way dissatisfied with God's creation.

## → Connection Point

*Dear Jesus, thank you for my creative and unique teens. Please help me learn how to encourage individuality. Let me never use my own insecurities to impose expectations on them. Please continue to mold my kids into exactly the people You created them to be. Amen.*

## Ready...Set...Go!
### *Nicole O'Dell*

*Do you not know that in a race all the runners run, but only one receives the prize? So run that you may obtain it. I Cor. 9:24, ESV*

I've already shared the story about the time I ran my first 10K race with my dad, but I've got a little more to say about that event. We started off just fine—the weather was perfect and it was so nice to be out there doing it together. Soon it became apparent I needed to run faster in order to get up over the hills more quickly or I'd not finish well, but he needed to run at a slower pace to even have a hope of finishing at all. We found that we were too worried about each other's needs that we weren't focused on what we needed to do to finish our own course. We decided to separate so we could run our own races more effectively.

Even though, at the start of the day, I'd intended to finish with my dad, I gave in to wisdom and crossed the finish line well ahead of him.

It is important to run your own parenting race, at your own pace. It's also good to notice the needs of other parents and to be an encouragement to them as they run theirs. Try not to compare yourself too closely with others, but be open to the times and places where your journeys intersect.

Parenting teens is hard, and we're all at different stages on our own courses. You can learn from those who have gone before, and you can have the privilege of running with those who come behind. Avoid the trap of comparison that only leads to feelings of inadequacy and disappointment. Keep your eyes on the finish line and take the time to celebrate your successes.

## → Connection Point

*Dear Lord, give me the strength I need to finish my own race, and the wisdom I need to run it well. Help me not to compare myself to other parents or my teens to theirs. Let me keep my eyes securely locked on the finish line You've set before me. And please help me to be an encouragement to others along the way. Amen.*

## Straight Talk about Porn
### Vicki Tiede

*Consider it pure joy, my brothers, whenever you face trials of many kinds, because you know that the testing of your faith develops perseverance. Perseverance must finish its work so that you may be mature and complete, not lacking anything. James 1:2-4, NIV*

Your teens have no need to seek out pornography, because *it* finds *them*. Multiple studies report that more than seventy percent of teenagers have accidentally stumbled upon Internet pornography. Because kids are literally growing up with this technology, parents are becoming desensitized. When kids are able to access the Internet when they are alone, without parental supervision and interaction – in their bedrooms, then it's only a matter of time before they see porn.

You know what's heartbreaking? For far too long the church and many parents have been silent about sex. That silence has been misinterpreted by many (including youth) that the Bible (specifically the gospel) has nothing to say about it. I probably don't have to tell you that the silence of the church has been masked by the loud, emphatic, persistent voice of the world proclaiming that sex is about ME!

Parents, it's time to speak up. Talk about God's design for sex within the bonds of marriage. Talk about pornography and the temptation it is. Tell them that pornography and sex within marriage are completely different things. There is no measure of equality between illegitimate, selfish sex, and wholesome sex within marriage.

If your kid were in a burning building and you had an opportunity to save him/her, you would do it without hesitation. Likewise, Satan and porn producers have a target in mind and it's your children! If they can capture the mind of a child, they often have them for a lifetime. You have a responsibility to tell them the truth and save them from the snares of the enemy.

## → Connection Point

Father, I hate that my kids are exposed to these things. Help me find the right words to say to teach them about the dangers of porn and the beauty of sex within your boundaries. Prepare their hearts to reject any unclean thing and make them passionate about purity, not willing to trade Your plan for anything. Amen.

Powerline365

## Physical vs. Mental
*Nicole O'Dell*

*There is a time for everything, and a season for every activity under the heavens. Ecc. 3:1, NIV*

The physical and emotional changes as kids approach the teen years often occur simultaneously, but not always. Think of the girls whose bodies develop before their brains catch up. Or the boys whose voices change and faces break out with acne before they hit five-feet tall.

*Puberty* is physical. Maturing bodies transform. *Adolescence*, however, brings more emotional and mental changes. Even though the physical adjustments suggest emotional changes are imminent, they don't always go right along the same path or speed.

The first time I wore a bra to school in fifth grade I was so embarrassed, yet somehow excited. I felt grown-up. I felt like a sixth-grader! Until I stood at the pencil sharpener and felt all eyes on me. I just knew the boys were snickering at the strap visible through my shirt. I was sure the girls would spend recess whispering comparisons of their bodies to mine. My eyes stung as I no longer felt mature — I wanted the ground to swallow me up.

In truth, no one noticed. At least they never let on that they did. The day ended and the weekend came. All was well... until Monday when four girls showed up sporting brand new bras. Copycats!

Parents – watch closely and respond appropriately to the physical and emotional changes even if they aren't happening at the same rate. Just because your tween's body advances into the teen years, doesn't mean her mind has. Just because a boy has a man's body and a man's voice, that doesn't mean his head has caught up with the expectations and responsibilities of being a man. If we keep our eyes and hearts open to our teens and pre-teens needs, we'll be better able to help through the coming changes.

## → Connection Point

*Father, please help me guide my kids through these years of physical and emotional change. Help me know when and how to respond without rushing them. All in your time... in your ways. Amen.*

## Lies Vs. Truth
*Nicole O'Dell*

> *For our struggle is not against flesh and blood, but against the rulers, against the authorities, against the powers of this dark world and against the spiritual forces of evil in the heavenly realms.*
> Eph. 6:12, NIV

Parents, we're at war. Not with our teens, but for them. Our enemy pelts them with doubt, insecurity, peer pressure, and fear, and no matter how much we try, how hard we work, or how much we pray, we can't stop his efforts. We're told in Ephesians that our struggle isn't against other people and their schemes; it's against spiritual forces of evil that work against us and our teens.

Even though we can't prevent our enemy from working against us, we can use God's Word and His truth as the weapons of our warfare. And we can win that war. In fact, that's the plan.

When Satan shoots lies at our teens, throw truth in the path.
- Your teen feels insecure — point out the interesting and unique qualities others see.
- Your teen feels uncool — look at what Kingdom cool really is.
- Your teen feels unattractive — talk about inner beauty and the light that shines from within.
- Your teen feels unworthy — look at the way God values them.

It's no secret we all battle insecurity and doubt from time to time. But it's our job as parents to combat the lies the enemy throws at our teens with the truth of God's Word. What does HE say about them?

Remember, we aren't fighting against other people. We're fighting against Satan who longs to keeps our teenagers embroiled in self-doubt and personal struggles.

We're at war, friends! Not with our kids...for them.

## → Connection Point

*Dear God, I'm mad. I'm so angry that my efforts are attacked at every turn by an unseen enemy who seeks to destroy all you've done for and in my family. But I am so thankful for truth and for your word. Thank you for handing me the parenting victory. Now, would you please help me grab that victory and move in it with confidence? Help me combat the lies with the truth. Amen.*

## The Big Picture
### Nicole O'Dell

*Do not let any unwholesome talk come out of your mouths, but only what is helpful for building others up according to their needs, that it may benefit those who listen. Eph. 4:29, NIV*

"That's not how we load the dishes."
"Your room is a mess!"
"Come on, snap out of it."
"Don't complain if I ask you to do something."
"When is the last time you read your Bible?"
"Stop picking on your siblings!"

It's really easy to slip into a pattern that can feel like over-criticism to your teens. Now, I know your goal isn't to push them down or discourage them. You really want to see them making responsible choices and to have a good attitude while doing it. But sometimes it can all just be a bit much to take and eventually, they'll tune you out.

Looking at the list above, ask yourself which of those are absolutely necessary to point out. It's much more important to choose your battles and win the ones that need to be won. Bible study and kindness toward others are major issues—don't ignore those. But some of the other things will work themselves out in time—mood-related issues are often due to hormones. And the others can be ignored because they simply aren't important—who really cares how the dishes are loaded?

Today, step back from your watchful stare and listen to the words you speak. If your teens were to quantify the negative speech they hear from you, would it be 50%? 75%? Get intentional about the directions you give and the criticisms you make, and season them with much encouragement and levity.

## → Connection Point

*Father, please forgive me for the times I've set impossible standards for my teens. Help me to lighten up on the things that don't matter to the big picture and then give me the right words to say to effect lasting change on the things that do matter. Amen.*

## Are you there?
### Debi Lee

*There, in the presence of the Lord your God, you and your families shall eat and shall rejoice in everything you have put your hand to, because the Lord your God has blessed you. Deut. 12:7, NIV*

Have you noticed how childhood seems to be getting shorter and shorter lately? Even babies and young toddlers are sent off to be cared for by people their parents barely know, while Dad and Mom work 40 to 50 hours a week. Children are expected to read by age three, and they have schedules as packed as adults.

I'm privileged to be an at-home mom as my kids are growing up. A few years ago with three kids in high school, a seventh grader, and a kindergartener, I decided to take a class for eight weeks which would take me out of the house several hours a day. When my junior higher heard this she was not happy.

"Honey, I'll be home when you leave in the morning and home when you get out of school in the afternoon," I explained. "But I don't like knowing you're not there," was her response. She assumed that when I as not with her, I was at home waiting for her.

So, are we there? So often parents are guilty of being busy, busy, busy! Our kids need us to be there physically, mentally, and emotionally. Me time is important, but, quite frankly, it's not the priority. Our primary responsibility is to raise our kids to love Jesus. If they are out of our sight the majority of time, how can we do that?

For me, there is no greater reward than to see my children growing up to love God and to watch them develop an authentic relationship with Jesus Christ. And to do that, I must be there...

1. What changes can you make that will help you be there more for your family?

2. Are there adjustments in your schedule that could improve the spiritual climate in your home?

## → Connection Point

*Father, help me to really be there in all ways, so that my teenagers learn to depend on me as a steady in their lives. Let me always be able to answer their needs and to use life's good times and bad times as vehicles to point them to you. Amen.*

Powerline365

## Leapfrog Parenting
*Nicole O'Dell*

*My friends, I don't feel that I have already arrived. But I forget what is behind, and I struggle for what is ahead. Phil. 3:13, CEV*

Do you ever feel like you're taking two steps forward and three steps back as you parent your teens? When my oldest daughter was about 13, she and I had a bit of a challenging year. We would have a great day, and I would drop into bed feeling pleased about our interaction for the day and about my parenting. But just as I'd start to fall asleep, she'd come in and tell me about something I'd done horribly wrong or something I said that hurt her. It was deflating to me. I felt like all the good that had happened was erased by the negative.

It only lasted for a couple of months, and I think she was trying to find her way and figure out her place as she matured. I don't really believe that all of a sudden I became a horrible mom for a few months and then snapped out of it just as quickly. Can we all say "hormones?"

But there are many things that have that draining affect on our confidence. Finances, outside pressures, self-imposed expectations… we do fine for a bit and then something happens to set things up and we feel like we're back at the beginning.

First, use even your negative experiences as opportunities. Mentally place your hands squarely in the mistake you made and leapfrog right over it by learning from your mistake so you do it better next time and by sharing it with others so they can learn from it, too.

Second, let me encourage you with the truth that God doesn't forget the good every time you make a mistake. He knows how hard you've been working. He sees your efforts. Your errors or missteps don't erase all the good you've done. Don't let mistakes set you back, rather, let them propel you forward as you leapfrog the bad in pursuit of God's best for yourself and for your teens.

## → Connection Point

*Father, I know I'm not perfect and I make mistakes, but please help me to put my mistakes in the past and move forward with my eyes set on the future. Help me trust your forgiveness well enough that I can forgive myself, and please show my teenagers that I mean well even when I mess up. Amen.*

## High-Low
*Nicole O'Dell*

*Count it all joy, my brothers, when you meet trials of various kinds, for you know that the testing of your faith produces steadfastness.*
*James 1:2, ESV*

My family loves playing the High-Low game at dinner. Well, we call it a game, but it's really just a conversation starter. The rule is that each person has to share the high point of their day and the low point. And no one can say the same thing twice in one week. It's the best way I've found to get my teenagers talking about their experiences.

I've learned so much about them by listening to what torments them and to what they treasure. I love when I hear that the low point of a particular day had to do with someone else's pain. That shows they are growing in compassion. Or if their high point isn't materialistic or popularity-driven I know we're growing in that way, too.

A secondary benefit to this activity is my teenagers get to learn from me about what I value and what hurts my heart. The more they hear me open up about what truly does pain me and the more they discover what excites me, the more they'll explore those areas in their own lives.

Lectures and heavy-handed parental lessons don't always do the trick, but trying simple and fun tactics like this one will get everyone talking. The end result is that as we learn about our teenagers, they learn about us. And no one feels put on the spot or judged.

This kind of open communication, the celebration of hurts and triumphs, is not limited to the high-low game. We need to be intentional about finding ways to have ongoing, open dialogue with our teens. It's up to us, parents.

How can you release inhibitions and increase communication in your home this week?

## → Connection Point

*Dear Jesus, thank you for my amazing teenagers. I want to know them so much better. Please help them lower their guard and resist the enemy who wants them at odds with me. Give me wisdom as I push through the defenses and look for ways to get personal. Amen.*

## Innie or Outtie?
*Nicole O'Dell*

*Before I formed you in the womb I knew you, and before you were born I consecrated you; I appointed you a prophet to the nations.*
*Jer. 1:5, ESV*

Does your teen like to be surrounded by people and busyness or t alone in a quiet house? Being an introvert or an extrovert doesn't necessarily indicate how your teenager feels about others or reveal personal insecurity. Rather, it's about energy and peace.

Innies require less interaction because they find their energy and inner peace from their own imagination and quiet thoughts. Outies gain those things from others. They are buoyed by action and activity, and their imagination is sparked by companionship.

Neither social style is wrong, but the way we respond to our teens as we parent them will either support their comfort level and self-confidence, or it will make them question why they are the way they are. It's easy to understand what makes our teens tick when they're just like us. If you're outgoing, you'll naturally relate best to a teenage extrovert. If you're a homebody who doesn't like crowds, you'll understand when your teen prefers solitude.

Do you respond with shock or disdain when your teenager says she'd prefer to stay home on a Friday night? Do you force your son to go to the prom because you couldn't imagine he'd actually be okay with missing that experience?

You're raising someone who is different than you; aren't you glad? But it does make it harder to dig through the nuances to find the needs, and we might jump to conclusions and react to things that aren't actually problems. So, take some time to pray that God would show you when you need to respond to issues like this. If it's just a matter of style, let your teen develop into the social person God molded before time began. He has a reason for creating your child the way He did. How exciting it will be to see that unfold.

## → Connection Point

*Dear God, my teens and I are so very different. That's a good thing, but it's also confusing to me. Please help me to know when I need to step in and correct something and when I need to keep my hands off of things that aren't problems. Amen.*

## The Best Laid Plans
### Sherri Wilson Johnson

*My days have passed, my plans are shattered. Yet the desires of my heart turn night into day; in the face of the darkness light is near.*
Job 17:11-12, NIV

In the classic *Of Mice and Men*, George and Lennie, two migrant farm workers, dream of buying a farm and living off the fat of the land. George doesn't want to take orders from anyone ever again. Lennie's big dream is to own rabbits. A large and clumsy man, he doesn't know his own strength and causes great trouble for them. In the end, George's plan for their future doesn't turn out like he'd hoped. Lennie's life ends, and he doesn't get to be a part of their big dream.

Often, our parenting years don't go as we've planned and they mimic the line from *To a Mouse* by Robert Burns (the origin of the book's title), which states: "The best laid schemes o' mice an' men gang aft agley." (The best laid schemes of mice and men often go awry).

Why do plans go awry? Usually because we get distracted by things beyond our control or things that we simply allow to take precedence in our lives.

Sometimes we've planned incorrectly or over-optimistically. It's important to make a plan and try to stick with it, but it's equally as important to be flexible. If things aren't going according to what you wanted for or with your teen, it might be time to change your ideals. Scrap what isn't working. Dig deep and try to figure out where things went wrong. Admit where you've failed your child and help him own up to where he's failed you. And pray!

You aren't a failure as a parent, nor is your teen a failure. Resist the urge to compare yourself to other moms and dads and your teen to other teens. Step away from your disappointments, and reassess. Pray over your ideas. I bet you'll be amazed at how you can adjust things and keep your plans from going awry.

## → Connection Point

*Lord, help me follow your plan for my teen. Help me encourage even when I feel doubt or disappointment. Let my teenager see me as a trustworthy lighthouse in the storm. Please walk in step with me, and let me lean on you as I do this parenting thing. Amen.*

## Qualified?
### Nicole O'Dell

*Therefore I do not run like someone running aimlessly; I do not fight like a boxer beating the air. No, I strike a blow to my body and make it my slave so that after I have preached to others, I myself will not be disqualified for the prize. I Cor. 9:26-27, NIV*

How can we ask our teens, who are far less prepared to deal with temptations than we are, to make good decisions if we're not modeling the right choices? How can we expect them to overlook our shortcomings and choose better for themselves if we take the easy way out, look out for ourselves, and give in to sin? When things get tough, they'll use our failures as an excuse to justify their own.

In the verse above, Paul warns against preaching the truth to others but living in such a way that you miss it yourself. To offer the best life to your teen, you need to be living it yourself. This doesn't mean you have to be perfect, thank goodness. But you do need to be honest about your struggles and temptations. Let your teens know that living for Christ, defending truth, and standing up against sin aren't simple tasks for you either. And be open about the cost of doing the right thing so they'll know they're on the right path even when it hurts.

Imagine if, when you were a teen, your parent had said, "You know what? I struggle with that too. It's not easy for me to make the best choice when it comes to that either. And, to be perfectly honest, sometimes I don't. But I try. I try because I know it's God's best for me, and that's what I want." How would that have made you feel? Would you have respected that honesty and maybe made a different choice?

It helps teens to see their parents as human beings with weaknesses, failures, and struggles. They don't feel so alone in the battle when they see we all need God's grace and the power of the Holy Spirit. Empower your teens with that truth. It's not about you…it's not about them. It's all about the power they have through Him.

## → Connection Point

*Lord, I wish I could always be the perfect example for my teens, but it's not going to happen. Please help me use my failures as proof of my human weakness and your amazing grace. Let them see that my efforts pale in comparison with your mercy. Amen.*

## Pure Joy
### Nicole O'Dell

*Consider it pure joy, my brothers and sisters, whenever you face trials of many kinds, because you know that the testing of your faith produces perseverance. Ja. 1:2-3, NIV*

If you're like me, it kind of annoys you when you're dealing with something really difficult and someone says, "Consider it pure joy to face this trial." Yeah, I get it. James taught that we should welcome hardships because they will make our faith stronger and, in that way, be a blessing to us in the end. But, come on, even Jesus didn't *want* to suffer the bad stuff if it could be avoided.

Jesus trumps James any day, right?

Our Lord had a cup of suffering from which He was to drink. He asked His Father to take it from Him if it were possible. That prayer was answered with a "No, Son." No matter what, Jesus would do the will of His Father, but He didn't desire the pain that He was to endure. His Father's will was carried out and then, ultimately, the cup of suffering was removed when Jesus had victory over the grave. Did Jesus skip to the cross? Did he laugh in the midst of his trial? No, of course not. So what is James talking about with the pure joy comment?

Jesus didn't delight in His present sufferings, but He delighted in doing the will of His Father so much that He willingly endured the cross. And now that is His joy.

Parents, you will face all sorts of trials, temptations, and tests as you parent your teens. You will experience heartbreak. You will feel like a success one day and a failure the next. Follow Jesus' example of praying for God's will in all things. Be willing to endure whatever He asks of you in order that His will be done in the lives of your teenagers. When that happens, you will consider all of the pain pure joy because you'll see how they worked together for good in the lives of your children.

### → Connection Point

*Blessed be your name. I trust you. I surrender my family, my children, my parenting...my life...to you. Please show me your will and then help me joyfully walk in it, no matter what. Amen.*

Powerline365

## Do as I Do
### Nicole O'Dell

*These people honor me with their lips, but their hearts are far from me. Matt. 15:8, NLT*

"Because I'm the parent, that's why!" Parents expect kids to obey as a first-line response to a direct order. But, speaking from personal experience, there's a filtering thought process that happens before the obedience comes.

When you tell your teenager not to do something like lie to their teacher about a missing homework assignment, for example, they cycle through thoughts like these first:

- What is the cost to me if I obey?
- What will happen if I do it anyway?
- Would the outcome be worse if I lied or missed the assignment?
- Has Mom or Dad done it?

And the last question is probably the one that seals the deal. Maybe they are unsure of what will happen if they lie to the teacher. And maybe their consciences do feel a little uneasy about being untruthful. But if they can examine that last question and remember they heard you make up a story to get out of a commitment the day before, you can be pretty sure they'll go for it.

The surest way to erode the values you're teaching is to expect one thing from your teens but do another yourself. They trust you. Out of the womb they have an innate expectation that they can take you at face value. And it's actually because of that deep faith that they take your behaviors (more than your words) as a model for their lives.

As parents we must live above reproach before we can begin to expect godly behavior and good choices from our teens. This doesn't mean being perfect, but it might mean being honest about our imperfections and their consequences. Let your words and actions always be ones which you would be proud to see repeated by your teens...because they will be!

## → Connection Point

*Father, please open my eyes to the ways I hold my teens to a higher standard than I hold myself. Help me to be honest with them and with you so I can be an example they can follow. Amen.*

## Awake with Your Teen
*Laura Kurk*

*Therefore, as God's chosen people, holy and dearly loved, clothe yourselves with compassion, kindness, humility, gentleness and patience. Col. 3:12, NIV*

I've often wondered if a natural law dictated that the closer to midnight it is, the higher the probability that our teenagers will need to vent. The midnight kind of venting is never simple, either. It usually starts slow, and, as a parent, you recognize that tongue-tied look on your teenager's face. She wants to talk—she *needs* to talk—but getting the words to flow may take a while. Eventually, though, a key turns, a lock opens, and a heart melts.

Sometimes we hear a confession from our child. Sometimes it's an anxiety that has taken root or a new soul-deep understanding that needs validation. And this is a beautiful moment between you and this child you have seen through life's storms. So what's the problem?

The problem is you are tired. You are officially at loose ends and your reactions have slowed to glazed stares and long blinks that could be misinterpreted. A teenager in the throes of affliction demands a lot from you, but deep down you know that this is where parenting gets good. And even these late nights will be gone too soon.

Simone Weil wrote that "the capacity to give one's attention to a sufferer is a very rare and difficult thing; it is almost a miracle; it *is* a miracle." Do you feel the miracle stirring in your weary bones when your teen needs your attention? We must empty ourselves completely and practice the art of attentive listening and be awake to see our teens in all their messy truth, just as they are, just as they are becoming. If we don't seize the opportunity to hear them out, the world will.

When was the last time you reached your teen by asking, "What are you going through?" Sometimes your recognition that their suffering is important to you is all it takes to create a strong bond.

## → Connection Point

*Jesus, please help me tune in when it's time to be alert and on duty. Help me prioritize my teenager's needs no matter what time of day or night it is. Then, please, renew my tired mind and body so I can be ready the next time. Amen.*

## Bible 101
### Nicole O'Dell

*And these words which I command you today shall be in your heart. You shall teach them diligently to your children, and shall talk of them when you sit in your house, when you walk by the way, when you lie down, and when you rise up. Deut. 6:6-7, NKJV*

I don't know about you, but it's pretty busy in my home. That verse says we're to focus on God's Word when we sit down, when we walk, when we lie down, and when we rise up? How is that even possible?

Years ago my daughter would jump out of the car and run next door to share her Sunday School lesson with our elderly neighbor each week. He listened as she told him stories about Jesus calming the seas and feeding the five thousand. He chuckled as she mispronounced Zaccheus and put Moses on the ark and Noah on Mt. Sinai. But he loved that time because the spiritual intimacy they shared built a bridge that spanned generations.

How many moments do we waste each day on empty activities like watching television, tinkering in the garage, or reading magazines? I'm not suggesting all television is bad or all magazines should be banned. But a little introspection could reveal the value of the time we spend.

- Is what I'm doing necessary for my well-being?
- Is this activity beneficial to my family's spiritual growth?
- Would I be doing this if Jesus were here?

That last one gets me every time. It's not that I would be ashamed at what I'm doing as though it's wrong. But I almost always realize that I wouldn't be doing it because I'd want to sit with Him. Talk. Learn. Soak up His glory. We can help our teens sit with Jesus. Talk with Him. Learn from Him. Soak up every good and perfect gift He has prepared for them. That...or reality TV. That...or Monday night football. It's time we make the sacrificial choice and spend more of our time and theirs on things that have lasting value.

## → Connection Point

*Lord, please give me the wisdom and energy I need to be the best teacher of your Word that I can be. Help me push past the eye-rolls and sighs of boredom and build a passion within them that craves more and more of you. Amen.*

## Your Real Goal
### Nicole O'Dell

*Our fathers disciplined us for a little while as they thought best; but God disciplines us for our good, that we may share in his holiness. No discipline seems pleasant at the time, but painful. Later on, however, it produces a harvest of righteousness and peace for those who have been trained by it.* Heb. 12:10-11, NIV

What is your main goal in raising your kids? Most Christian parents would answer with something like, "My only wish is that they'd be happy and healthy and follow God throughout all of their lives." That's a great answer, but is that really what we want most of all?

The "follow God" part is valid, for sure. I know I want my kids to seek Him and know Him. I want them to pursue His will for their lives and to surrender their plans and desires to Him. You want that, too, right? Honestly, I don't think you'd be reading this book if those things weren't top of your list for your teens.

But what if God's best for them doesn't include the happy and healthy part? What if they have to learn about Him through hardship and heartache? What if illness, injury, or great loss enters their lives and it's through those circumstances they surrender to God?

That's a bit more difficult, isn't it? I think logically we can say that we're okay with whatever God uses to draw our teens to Him. But in practice, when we see them suffer or can't see the end of the tunnel they're in, we want to rescue them. We want to fix it.

The next time your teenager faces something tough and you feel the urge to swoop in to save them from pain, consider that pain may be just what they need. Ask God to show you how their painful experiences will help them know Jesus better and point others to Him.

Then let go.

## → Connection Point

*Dear Jesus, please show me when and where you're at work in my teens' lives. Help me know when I need to step back so you can have your way. Please give me the patience to wait it out when I need to, and help me stay surrendered so you can draw them to yourself. Amen.*

## Sleep on It
### *Nicole O'Dell*

*It is of the LORD's mercies that we are not consumed, because his compassions fail not. They are new every morning: great is thy faithfulness. Lam. 3:22-23, KJV*

Waking up for your day is like turning on your computer. It's like we reboot overnight and then every new issue that occurs throughout the day is like an open window that takes up space in our heads. Eventually, the computer bogs down and maybe even crashes.

That's how I feel at the end of a hard day. Sluggish. Unclear. Ready for a reboot. And when my teenagers come at me with needs, questions, or bad attitudes, I'm too spent to parent well. I still believe it's important to do our best in those moments—to take the moments they're willing to dole out, but we also need to know our limits and give our spirits the rest we need.

And it's not just me. Scientists believe that sleep helps people sort through facts and memories in order to see things more clearly. The brain does an automatic overnight info dump. Sleep also separates reality from emotions like fear and worry, which can cloud the thinking and get in the way of making a rational decision. Scientifically speaking, sleep is good medicine.

Even more important than the great biological effects of sleep are the spiritual ones. It's through the renewed mercy and compassion of God that His faithfulness is revealed afresh each morning so we can handle the concerns of yesterday with clarity and confidence.

When worry or anger begin to creep into your parenting brain, when you feel confused or frozen at a decision you have to make, power off. Pray that the Holy Spirit would speak truth into your situation while you sleep, and then face a new day refreshed.

## → Connection Point

*Heavenly Father, thank you for renewing your mercy and compassion each day so my concerns don't pile up and consume me. Help me know when I need to shut down and then please make it possible that I do so. I treasure my rest in you, and I lay my parenting burdens at your feet as I lay down to sleep. Amen.*

## Pioneer Parents
### Mary DeMuth

*That means we will not compare ourselves with each other as if one of us were better and another worse. We have far more interesting things to do with our lives. Each of us is an original. Gal. 5:26, MSG*

Some of us grew up in stable, Christ-loving homes. Others did not. What happens when people from difficult upbringings want to raise their kids in a Christian home? How do we pioneer a new path?

Pioneer Parents are parents who don't want to duplicate the homes they were raised in. They share many common traits, the most common being fear. Will the hurtful words my parents said to me fly out of my mouth in a moment of anger? Will I repeat my parents' mistakes? How will I parent if I've had no godly example? Why, when I read Christian parenting books, do I feel like the author can't relate to me? How do I protect my kids from my parent's negative influence without harming their relationship?

**Find a mentor.** Of all the ways I've tried to improve my parenting, finding a mentor was the most effective. It's so important to engage parents who are raising stable, well-adjusted kids.

**Forgive your parents.** Choosing to forgive causes the chain to fall away, setting you free to parent your children differently.

**Stop the comparison game.** Few acts are more destructive than comparison. God asks us to concentrate on ourselves and what He has given us to do or to be.

**Find like-minded support.** My parenting skills increased when I found other pioneer parents. With them I'm able to laugh at my mistakes and continue down the pioneer-parenting path.

Being a Pioneer Parent is no easy task. In granting ourselves grace, seeking mentors, saying I'm sorry, seeking inside-out healing, forgiving our parents, eliminating comparison, and finding friends who bear our burdens, our families will be blessed by God's grace.

## → Connection Point

*Thank You, Jesus, for drawing me to you, despite my upbringing. Help me to pioneer generation after generation of Christ-followers that start right here with my teenagers. Please help me battle my insecurities and parent with confidence. Amen.*

## Righteous Pray-er
*Nicole O'Dell*

Jesus walked on a little way. Then he knelt down on the ground and prayed, "Father, if it is possible, don't let this happen to me! Father, you can do anything. Don't make me suffer by having me drink from this cup. But do what you want, and not what I want."
Mark 14:35-36, CEV

*If I'm good enough, my prayers for my teens will be answered.*
*If my teens mess up, I'm sure I did something wrong.*
*If I sacrifice...if I pray enough...if I give enough...if I do enough...*
Have you fallen into the trap of believing that the answers to your parenting prayers are dependent on your righteousness?

There was once a great man who prayed with deep conviction but didn't receive the answer He most desired. Jesus asked His Father to take the burden of suffering from Him if it were possible. No matter what, He would do the will of His Father, no doubt about it. But He clearly could have done without dying if His Father said it was okay.

We all know how His prayer for release was answered. Jesus received a "No." There is none more righteous than Him. He had God's favor. He was sinless. He was cherished and loved by His Father way more than we are able to love our own children. Yet His prayer was not answered in the way He would have preferred. His daddy said no.

If Jesus couldn't earn His way to changing God's mind, then why do we think that our missteps have anything to do with God's will? Decide now that you will no longer judge your righteousness or God's favor for you by the choices your teenagers make, by the success they have in school, or by any other worldly metric that says nothing of God's heart

Seek first the Kingdom of God and His righteous...then all the rest will be added unto you and your teens. In His time. In His way.

## → Connection Point

Father, I'm an open book to you. You know my sins and my successes. you know the secret longings of my heart and the struggles I face each day. Yet you hear and answer my prayers. Thank you for looking beyond my weakness and loving me still. Please help me to trust in your will as I parent my teens. Amen.

## Take Inventory
*Nicole O'Dell*

*Examine yourselves to see if your faith is genuine. Test yourselves. Surely you know that Jesus Christ is among you; if not, you have failed the test of genuine faith. 2 Cor. 13:5, NLT*

I worked in retail management for many years. Every year, at least twice, we went through the process of taking inventory. It was a dreaded task because the work was tedious, unending, and often scary. We had to count, label, and record every single item in the store, and then a third-party company would match those records to our sales records to identify any problems like employee or consumer theft, too many careless damages, or shipping and receiving discrepancies.

Taking inventory was vital. After all, how could we plan a budget for the coming year, staff correctly, train more effectively, etc, if we didn't know where the problems were? It's from the inventory process we identified that a certain brand of jeans was getting stolen like crazy. That information led us to move them to the back of the store and put security tags on them.

The same is true in your spiritual walk and your parenting. How can you know where you're headed if can't see where you've been or identify the effects of your journey and what worked and what didn't?

Instead of mindlessly moving ahead, putting foot in front of the other toward some unseen end, be intentional about your goals and plans by learning from the past and being honest about the results.

Fight against the urge to do what comes natural to you. Instead, stretch yourself beyond the way you've always done it, and ask God to fill you with renewed energy and creativity. See change as an opportunity and fear as a challenge.

If your inventory reveals a communication problem, a trust issue, or even a spiritual weakness, it's time revitalize your system. Pray for guidance and be ready to act.

## → Connection Point

*Lord, help me see the weak spots in my parent-teen relationships and not let another year pass without making changes so I can be effective in the spiritual training of my kids. Show me new plans and practices that will help me raise my teens to know you more. Amen.*

## Sticks and Stones
### Nicole O'Dell

*For if you forgive men when they sin against you, your heavenly Father will also forgive you. But if you do not forgive men their sins, your Father will not forgive your sins. Matt. 6:14-15, NIV*

One time, in a fit of teenage desperation, I told my mom she wasn't doing her job as a parent. I won't share my exact words because, well, I'm ashamed to even remember them. I was so angry at life and at myself...even at God...and I wanted her to hurt like I did. There was no logic to it at the time, but looking back I can see that I was subconsciously trying to unload some of my pain, not knowing how to express myself. And I didn't trust that anyone would care if I was truly honest about what was going on inside of me. So I lashed out to the person closest to me. The safest target.

Fact is, sometimes teenagers are mean. They feel powerless and angry. They don't understand why they can't make sense of anything. They feel like we're against them. They don't like anyone—including themselves and especially us.

In the throes of this hormone-induced fog, they often say things they regret. Whether that regret comes immediately or many years later depends on the Holy Spirit and your teenager's level of surrender. For me, it took a little time for me to seek and believe in God's forgiveness and much, much longer for me to trust that my mom could forgive me. Sometimes still the feelings of inadequacy and regret creep in, and I cringe at the memory of the bratty teenager I was.

Trust me, when your teens lash out at you, they cringe inwardly. They wish they didn't feel the way they do, and they want you to push past it so badly. The best thing you can do is to be a constant. Smile. Say *I love you*. Hug the unhuggable. Love on the unlovable.

Jesus did.

## → Connection Point

*Father, please help me to forgive my teenagers as you have forgiven me. Help me to overlook their carelessly spoken words and to see past their mistakes and into their hearts. Please give me the grace to show my love for them no matter what they say. Amen.*

## Modeling Obedience
*Tricia Goyer*

> *Look, today I have set before you life and death, depending on whether you obey or disobey. I have commanded you today to love the LORD your God and to follow his paths and to keep his laws, so that you will live and become a great nation, and so that the LORD your God will bless you. Deut. 30:15-16, TLB*

When I was a teenager I wandered away from God, and I couldn't have cared less what the Bible said. I thought the Bible had too many rules. I stopped worrying about being good. I was tired of being a church girl. I started drinking, cussing, and sleeping around.

Later, I realized I didn't like these consequences, so I thought I'd shape up. When I found myself pregnant, I sought God. I told Him I'd messed up—big time—and I asked if He could do anything with my life. I wanted to obey Him and His Word because I saw that going the other direction led to no good.

I now have many little children. What is their reason for obeying me? Since my kids are still immature, the fear of consequences is their number-one goal. Thankfully, I've matured past my children, and my focus isn't just on fear of consequences. Yet to teach this to my children, I need to model obedience for them, and I need to teach that obedience brings GOOD things to their lives.

God knows obedience is the only way we can be truly happy. Everything He asks us to do is for our own good. He wants us to follow Him, not to make our lives miserable, but so He can give us more than we could ever dream. And that's what we need to model for our teenagers so they will obey God out of a desire for the very best He has.

Is there more to obedience than just rules? Yes! Jesus says, "If you love me, obey me," (John 14:15, TLB). We shouldn't obey because we are afraid of God or because we don't want to be punished. The real reason we obey is because we love God and want to please Him. Jesus loves us more than we can imagine!

## → Connection Point

*Jesus, thank you for loving my family and me. Help me to be a perfect model of obedience—seeking your will and walking it in all ways—so that my teenagers will pursue your will for their own choices. Amen.*

Powerline365

# Breakfast in Bed
*Nicole O'Dell*

> *Some people have gotten out of the habit of meeting for worship, but we must not do that. We should keep on encouraging each other, especially since you know that the day of the Lord's coming is getting closer. Heb. 10:25, CEV*

It's been a long week! Your Monday was like any Monday. Tuesday was stormy, and you got stuck in traffic everywhere you went. Wednesday you were home with a sick kid, which meant a late night of playing catch-up before the big meeting on Thursday, which was followed by a parent-teacher conference that didn't go so well. Friday, the furnace went out, which meant waiting around all day Saturday for the repairman to show up. Caring for an elderly parent. Shopping for groceries. Paying bills. Acting as chauffeur. Helping with homework...

Phew. I'm tired just typing that all out! Tomorrow morning is Sunday. What would it hurt to give yourself a break and sleep in? Would the family really mind if you all took a Sunday off of church? Maybe they even need the break like you do. Surely God would understand if you sat out just this once. Oh, how tempting it can be to nourish the flesh rather than the spirit!

Hebrews 10 warns us not to let that happen. We need fellowship in order to nourish our souls and prepare us for another week of duties. It's one way the Holy Spirit helps us to regroup and refresh for a new week. What if you decided to skip church and then had another week just like the one I described? Church isn't the only way to connect with God and get recharged, but corporate worship is a gift to body.

We also need to be aware of what we are teaching our teenagers about priorities. If we send a message that staying home from church is any sort of a break, we can be sure they will follow a similar pattern. Instead teach them by example that some of the best sources of renewal are through community worship, Bible teaching, and prayer.

## → Connection Point

*Jesus, please forgive me for isolating myself at times. Help me make fellowship a priority for myself and in my parenting. Convict my heart when it seems like the easy way is to sit out. And help me to raise teenagers who love and serve their church body. Amen.*

## It's Addicting
### Nicole O'Dell

*Be sober-minded; be watchful. Your adversary the devil prowls around like a roaring lion, seeking someone to devour. I Pet. 5:8, ESV*

Where is that sweet little girl who used to climb onto your lap for a story each night? Where did that adorable boy with the skinned up knees and grubby little fingers go? What about the ten-year-old who said she wanted to be a missionary and help people?

Those are the questions Christian parents ask themselves when their teens turn to drugs or alcohol. They remember happy, well-adjusted, energetic little kids with dreams and goals and big smiles across their faces. But now they see eyes shrouded in darkness, grim or vacant expressions, and sad or angry hearts.

Teenage addiction? When did it start, and why didn't I see the signs? Countless parents ask themselves those questions every day. Sometimes the cause of an addiction stems from choices made following a life-changing event like a death or divorce. Other times it's some other sort of trauma like abuse, rape, bullying, a tough break up—or even nothing tangible at all.

What was the tipping point? Where did that one last temptation come from, and why did it have the effect it did? Only you know the details about your family. I will say this, however, if you're dealing with teenage addiction, now is not the time for guilt. It's the time for action.

*Preventing is far better than curing.* Addiction is definitely one issue that is much easier to tackle *before* it takes root. Once it's a problem in your teen's life, it's much more difficult to stop the progression and break the stronghold. Ensuring that drugs and alcohol are not accessible to your teens is the first step in prevention. That requires you to take the time and steps necessary to make sure that's the case wherever your kids go.

### → Connection Point

Lord, please give me eyes to see what's really going on in my teenager's lives, ears to hear their needs, and the guts to take the steps necessary to really make a difference in their lives. Please protect my children from any kind of addiction as well as the temptations that lead to experimentation. Amen.

## Dashed Dreams
*Nicole O'Dell*

*"For I know the plans I have for you," declares the LORD, "plans to prosper you and not to harm you, plans to give you hope and a future." Jer. 29:11, NIV*

The hopelessness the disciples must have felt as they watched Jesus die and be buried in the tomb is unimaginable. He'd promised them so much, but then they heard the word, "It is finished." But...wait! Wait! It couldn't be finished. Sure, He promised His return, but it's difficult to believe in life when death has already happened.

Do you ever feel that way with your teenager? A school suspension. Legal troubles. A failing grade. Hateful words. Broken relationships. Lost virginity.

Each of those things can seem fateful and permanent in their own right. They hit hard. In the moment the mountain before you can seem insurmountable.

When I told my parents that I was pregnant as a teenager, I watched their world crumble around them. I expected them to react hard, but seeing it happen because of something I did was difficult. I'd wanted nothing more than to make then proud, and there I sat, a complete disappointment. Eventually they came around, of course, but I've long struggled with the impact those moments had on me.

As a parent myself, I've consciously prepared myself so that when something my teenagers do rocks my world they will first feel love and acceptance from me, long before they suffer regret or see the angst they might have caused. I know one of the things I love most about my God is that His love surpasses all my mistakes. When he looks at me, it's through eyes that approve of ME even when they disapprove of my sin. I want to look at my teens with those eyes. Don't you?

## → Connection Point

*Dear God, please let my teenagers see nothing but acceptance in my eyes. Let them know that disappointment or dashed dreams have nothing to do with the love I have for them. Let me be a living example of the way you feel about them. Amen.*

## Hold On Tight!
*Wendy Fitzgerald*

*But when I am afraid, I will put my trust in you. Psalm 56:3, NLT*

Our youngest daughter is eight and, until last week, she had only ever crawled into bed with us one time. Last week, however, this child who has never needed this kind of fortification, crawled into our bed, wrapped her arms and legs around mine, and shivered in fear as she sobbed in my arms. I have never felt her grip so tightly needing mine.

It is important that you know that our youngest daughter is adopted. From an early age, she learned to rely on her own strength and abilities. Often her natural reaction is to push away our help and conquer obstacles on her own, but on that night in the midst of her terror, she knew that she could cling to me for protection.

As adults, we too often attempt to handle problems on our own, but our heavenly Father longs to protect and help us through our trials. As our children grow through their teen years, it is easy to forget to run to God's arms with the problems we face. Sometimes we try to jump the hurdles on our own, but God longs to help guide us through these scary and tumultuous years.

Before you are afraid, after you are afraid...whenever you are afraid, trust in Him. He will carry you through. Like my arms around my daughter's, God longs to hold you through your fears.

## → Connection Point

*Father, I want to rely on you in all circumstances. Help me to run to you when I am overwhelmed and afraid. Guide me through my parenting fears to your arms of refuge. Amen.*

## Free Stuff
### Nicole O'Dell

*You know the commandments: 'Do not commit adultery,' 'Do not murder,' 'Do not steal,' 'Do not bear false witness,' 'Do not defraud,' 'Honor your father and your mother.' Mark 10:1,9 NKLV*

How much do you know about file sharing and movie, music, book, and graphic copyrights? Probably about as much as I did when I got my first lesson. It has become a conquest for teenagers (and adults) to score (steal) downloaded or shared copies of all sorts of media.

I knew a student whose school issued each student a MacBook on which they did homework, read textbooks, and turned in assignments. It was also the means by which much of the student body and some teachers passed around music and movies in a massive file-sharing explosion. Public theft was being done in school, on school computers, involving students, and perpetuated by the teachers!

Another example involves a church worship director I follow on Facebook. For weeks I watched as he posted of the movies he obtained for free. I was just about to confront him when the postings stopped. Someone must have beaten me to it. Did he not know what he was doing, or did he not care? Has our society gone so far to the extreme that we can't even depend on our teachers and pastors to lead our youth to a moral high ground?

How would you react if you found your teen with a hundred CDs stolen from Target? Most parents would be horrified at such a finding, but many think nothing of their kid downloading hundreds of songs without paying a cent. It's the same thing.

It's time to ask your teenagers if they understanding what is legal and what isn't when it comes to sharing digital files. Offer to help rid your home of any stolen product. Join a website like Pandora that allows free streaming of music legally. And, best choice, help your teens earn money to purchase songs and movies.

## → Connection Point

*Dear Jesus, please forgive me for turning a blind eye and letting sin creep into our home in this way. Please help me make swift and right changes and speak to my teenager's heart as we focus on doing things the right way. Amen.*

## Joy in the Journey
### Nicole O'Dell

*So that by God's will I may come to you with joy and be refreshed in your company. Rom. 15:32, ESV*

You're well into this devotional, and I commend you for remaining committed to your connection with your teens and their connection with God. It's not easy, is it? The toddler and elementary school years seem like a breeze compared to the teen years, don't they?

I just want to encourage you to take a deep breath. Now exhale.

Clear your mind of the fear, the anxiety, the angst. Don't think about the last argument you had with your teenager or the worry you're facing. Let. It. Go. If only for a moment.

Now, with a clear head, quickly list three things you most enjoy about your teenager. Go!

Are you smiling?

Capitalize on *that* emotion. Let your teenager see that you take pleasure in his sense of humor or in her kind acts of service. Talk to them about the good they do and the ways they bring joy to your heart. And don't, whatever you do, follow your words with a "but."

What can you do together this week to feed some pleasure into your relationship? Think of a way to reinvigorate the joy you've lost in recent weeks or months.

- Go to dinner. Go for a walk. Make a batch of cookies.
- Color a picture--seriously, no one is too old for a brand-new box of crayons.
- Paint a room—help your teenager pick a new color and bring new life to a dated teenage bedroom.

Whatever you find to do, do it with a smile. A little levity goes a long way toward building a lasting relationship.

## → Connection Point

*Jesus, have I lost sight of the awesomeness within my teenagers? Please forgive me for overlooking some of the things that make my teens unique. Help me to restore the joy I once knew as a parent and just give myself a break. Thank you for your grace. Amen.*

## All Teens Drink
### Nicole O'Dell

*Therefore let us not pass judgment on one another any longer, but rather decide never to put a stumbling block or hindrance in the way of a brother. Rom. 14:13, ESV*

"Every teen will experiment with alcohol; it's really no big deal."
"Oh, come on. I don't condone it. I just look the other way."
"It's better if they drink at home than at a party."

Those are actual statements parents have said to me. Some parents even provide alcohol to their teenagers and their friends. I'm sure that's not you, or you probably wouldn't have picked up this book. You're looking for ways to connect with your teens and to connect them with God. But just in case, let me take a moment to caution you against permissiveness in this area.

As teens get a bit older, many parents are so eager to be friends with their kids they allow things they never thought they would. But do they really believe substance abuse (and it is abuse whenever a teenager drinks any amount of alcohol) stops at home? Or is it just a teaser for what's coming later at the party?

There are many things that can go wrong with any amount of teenage alcohol consumption. Lapses in judgment, drunk driving accidents, alcohol poisoning, promiscuity, and a host of other problems, including legal ones. Also, vital areas of the brain need the teen years to finish developing. They are more sensitive to the toxic effects of substances than an adult brain. The maturation of those key areas of the brain can be permanently impeded by alcohol. Permanent is much longer than a party.

And the younger a person is when the drinking starts, the more likely it is to become a problem. In other words, partying as a teen makes a person more susceptible to alcoholism later in life. That's a gamble I don't want to take.

## → Connection Point

*Father, please help me recognize and reject the lies of the enemy who wants me to give in to the pressures and temptations of this world. Help me to never, ever be a stumbling block to my teens, but to uphold your righteous standards in all things. Amen.*

## Those Joneses
### Valerie Comer

*Keep your lives free from the love of money, and be content with what you have because He has said, "I will never leave you; I will always be by your side." Heb. 13:5 The Voice*

"But, Mom, I'll just die if I can't..." Fill in the blank.

I'm sure you've heard it all. Your teens need that new pair of jeans, or that new smart phone, or that new video game to be as cool as their friends. Don't they know you're not made out of money? Don't they know that a new fad will hit next week/month/year and this precious object will be replaced by some other desperate need?

From where do they get this sense of entitlement? Could it be from their parents?

Are you demonstrating an attitude of gratitude for what God has given to you, or are you, like your teen, always comparing yourself with others? The in-laws bought a brand new car. The guy at the office just got back from six weeks in the Mediterranean. Your neighbors are doing a top-to-bottom remodel on their three-year-old house because it's not good enough anymore.

Do you wish it were you?

It's tough to keep the green-eyed monster at bay sometimes, but focusing on what God has provided is key. Rather than be depressed about our lack of wealth, let's focus on the beauty God has created in our lives. He doesn't love the rich more than the poor. He didn't set us here to fight each for the earth's limited resources, but to turn our hearts toward Him.

Step one in turning your teen's sense of entitlement to a deep gratitude is to help them stop for a moment to look back in thankfulness, rather than always peering ahead in desire.

## → Connection Point

*Dear Lord, please forgive me for teaching my kids to crave more stuff. Help me lead the way in caring more for your presence than for the abundance of possessions.*

Powerline365

## Straight Talk about Pornography
### Nicole O'Dell

*I will set nothing wicked before my eyes. Psalm 101:3, NKJV*

Pornography is an uncomfortable topic, but your teens need to hear about it from you now before it sneaks into their lives another way. You can have every sort of safety feature and filter in place, but evil will always find a way into your teens' lives unless they have their guard up. So don't wait until your daughter's naked images are splayed as wallpaper on an ex-boyfriend's laptop or posted on some website. Don't wait until you find out she knows how to use a webcam for all the wrong reasons. And please don't wait until you find out your son has been objectifying women and then treating his own girlfriend badly. Act now.

In talking about pornography, avoid just making rules about what they can and can't do—you want your teen to be your ally in the battle against porn. Instead, focus the conversation on their thoughts about it, and use words that will make an impact like rape, objectifying, degrading, immoral, sin, sexual acts, pedophiles, drugged, victims, illegal, etc.

Then counteract those words with words of life. Beauty, purity, marriage, love, tenderness, cherish, adore, etc. When your teenager feels the difference between the two worlds of good and evil sexuality, we pray they will choose the path of wholeness.

I know the battle can seem futile at times. With scary statistics and a world that wants nothing more than to pull your teenagers down, it's hard to have faith they'll come out of the teen years with a solid grounding in God's will for their lives. But, trust me, Mom and Dad, the battle you fight for your kids' safety, purity, and well-being is one worth fighting. The battle against pornography starts in your conversations. It starts now.

## → Connection Point

*Please, Lord, guard my teenagers' hearts from evil desire, guard their eyes from visuals of sin, and guard their minds from lustful thoughts. Help me to be on guard and aware of the dangers that come in contact with my teens, and help me to arm them with truth and inspire them to run from evil. Amen.*

## Big Mistake
### *Nicole O'Dell*

*So let's keep focused on that goal, those of us who want everything God has for us. If any of you have something else in mind, something less than total commitment, God will clear your blurred vision—you'll see it yet! Now that we're on the right track, let's stay on it.*
*Phil. 3:15-16, MSG*

House flipping. I would rank that up there as a big mistake I made in my life. But don't tell my husband I feel that way! We bought a turn-of-the-century Victorian home that needed a lot of work. Okay, in reality, it needed a complete overhaul. New plumbing. New electrical. An actual shower. And so, so much more. We had a goal of fixing it up and then selling it for a lot more money. But then I got pregnant with the triplets. And the bottom fell out of the housing market. And we really learned about how much things cost. So now instead of flipping a real incredible Victorian home, we live in a half-remodeled home where we will probably retire.

Don't get me wrong, I'm grateful. I'm grateful that we have this home and this yard for the kids to play. I'm grateful that I'm married to a guy who can fix most things. I'm grateful our mortgage payment is low. But I do regret the decision.

Does regret always mean we didn't hear from God in the first place? And which part is wrong, the initial decision or the feelings that follow?

What mistakes do you dotting the landscape as you look back on your parenting journey? We all have a bucketful of answers to that question. But what we really need to be asking ourselves is what we learned through those mistakes. Is it God's will that we mess up? Of course not. But it is His will that we use those mistakes or lapses in judgment as building blocks to a solid foundation and strong relationship with Him.

### → Connection Point

Lord, you and I both know I've messed up. And sometimes my mistakes have hurt my teenagers. Would you help me to repair any damage I've done and learn from my missteps? Please help me to live without regret as I focus on learning from you. Amen.

## Masterminds
### Nicole O'Dell

*Where there is no guidance, a people falls, but in an abundance of counselors there is safety. Prov. 11:14, ESV*

Who are your masterminds? I'm part of a mastermind marketing group made up a handful of brilliant brains...and me. People I respect. People whose advice I follow almost unquestioningly because they have proven they get it right. They are smarter than I. They're more successful than I. They're funnier than I am. And I love them.

But who are my parenting masterminds? I'm intentional about surrounding myself with genius in the professional realm, but what about in a much more important arena, my parenting life? Whose advice do I seek? Who do I want to emulate? What traits do those parents have? There are certain traits we should look for in the people we call mentors. Masterminds.

- They love the Lord and live in a way that testifies to that.
- They hold (or held) their teenagers to certain standards.
- They aren't afraid to set boundaries and execute discipline when necessary.
- They have or had open and honest relationships with their teenagers.
- They enjoy their lives and their kids.
- When they offer advice, it's rooted in Scripture.

Parents who are ahead of you on the journey and who meet those qualifications are people you can emulate as you parent your teens. Having the perfect mentor doesn't mean you won't make mistakes. Trust me, your mentors made mistakes, too. But it's valuable and right to learn from those who have gone before. Who has God given as a parenting mastermind for you?

## → Connection Point

*Heavenly Father, thank you for sending people to guide me on this parenting journey. Thank you for establishing the natural order of counsel and guidance in the church. Help me to trust the advisors You've placed in my life. Amen.*

## Letting them Learn
*Brenda Yoder, MA*

*All things are lawful, but not all things are profitable. All things are lawful, but not all things edify. I Cor. 10:23, NASB*

"You let us figure things out on our own. You didn't baby us." My nineteen year-old responded when I asked him what things his dad and I did right in parenting him and his siblings. My husband and I were teaching a parenting class, and I wanted input from our kids on what they thought we did right – or wrong.

I smiled when I read his response. I remember hovering over our older two who are now college-age. But apparently, from their point of view, once we told them what was expected, we let them figure it out.

Taking your hands off your children during the teen and young-adult years is a leap of faith. We don't want our kids to make bad choices. We don't want them to embarrass us or the family name. We want them to walk in God's ways.

But God gives *us* choice to figure things out on our own, so we need to do the same with our kids. Cheering them on from the sidelines. Praying. Guiding. But I'm thankful God understands the pain of taking your hands off your child to let them learn about life and faith on their own. I'm thankful I can trust God when I'm not sure the path my child is taking.

Where do you need to let your children go so they can find their way, trusting Jesus with the results?

## → Connection Point

*Father, help us to entrust our children to you in all areas. Help us not to baby them or restrict their ability to learn from their mistakes. Thank you for loving them more than we do. Amen.*

## Looking Ahead
### *Nicole O'Dell*

*But Jesus told him, "Anyone who puts a hand to the plow and then looks back is not fit for the Kingdom of God." Luke 9:62, NLT*

That sounds harsh, but can you blame Him? He's talking about second-guessing our work for the Kingdom. The saying refers to stepping forward in God's call and then looking back as though the abandoned still has appeal. A person looking backward while plowing leaves a crooked line in his wake. Jesus is saying, "Look, if that's you, then you might as well stay back. If you've tasted this much — enough to step forward in faith — and still want to look back, then maybe it's not for you."

The Lord doesn't want us dwelling on what once was — not in our walk with Him, not in our marriages, and not in our parenting. Our enemy does. He wants us to feel discouraged and helpless over what we face today. He wants us to drown in regret over mistakes we made or in self-pity about the better days. But God wants us to look ahead to the future. The future is where He is. He promises to give us hope if we face forward.

Has parenting teens left you discouraged? Do you look at your kids and wonder how anything is going to come from the mess of choices and bad attitudes? Do you see parenting mistakes and wonder why you should bother putting one more foot in front of the other? Let me encourage you to look to the future. That's where He is. That's where His promise waits. It's not in the past. It's nowhere to be found by looking back. Look ahead. Look beyond what you can see.

When you do, when you press toward the promise in the future, you're automatically freed from the bondage of the past. And so is your teenager.

## → Connection Point

*Jesus, please help me to lay aside my parenting regrets and the longings I've had for the things I thought would be. Let me find contentment in reality and hope for the future — my teenager's and mine. Let me walk in your will, boldly into the future, leaving the past behind. Amen.*

## Root of Addiction
### Nicole O'Dell

*So if the Son sets you free, you will be free indeed. John 8:36, ESV*

Every addiction begins with a single kernel of desire for something. For a teenager that desire can be born from things like the deprivation of relationship, a desire for popularity, or desperation for escape.

When that desire is fed, the teenager feels fuller, richer, and rewarded. Then, when the feeling passes, the teen feels empty, lonely ... longing to feel full again. That desire grows again until it's uncontrollable and the teen is compelled to reach out and meet that need again. Thus begins the vicious circle, the cycle that leads to addiction.

Most teens who drink, smoke, or use drugs do *not* become addicts. But genetics play a big part in predisposing a person toward addiction. You won't know if your teens are at risk for addiction until they test it out. That's not a game worth playing.

Different brains deal with pleasure and need in different ways. So the point where drug or alcohol use becomes an addiction is different for each person, and no one can truly know where his or her own tipping point is until it's too late. Teenagers have a harder time controlling their impulses to drink or use drugs than adults do because they don't have as strong a grasp on consequences and lifelong effects, and their desire for experiences and testing boundaries often outweighs any perceived risk.

The true problem, though, is when teens look to any earthly thing or substance to meet their spiritual and emotional needs. As parents we need to keep our eyes and hearts open and sensitive to the Holy Spirit. We need to be a conduit of the God's love in order to meet the true needs within our teens.

## → Connection Point

*Dear God, please show me the dangers within my teens. Reveal to me the truth about any drug or alcohol use, and please help me deal with the real reasons for the problem. Help me meet the needs within my teenagers by sharing your love with them. Amen.*

## Escape Route
### Nicole O'Dell

*If you are tired from carrying heavy burdens, come to me and I will give you rest. Matt. 11:28, CEV*

"Calgon, take me away!" What was it about that commercial that resonated with every overworked and exhausted woman or tired father? What was it about that phrase that has stood the test of time and speaks to us still today? If I sigh and speak those words, you know what kind of day I had, and that I'm in search of an escape.

That's the keyword right there: *escape*. "Calgon, take me away!" is symbolic of the need to get away from exhaustion, schedules, kids, etc. The image of that bubble bath and a locked door is a picture of getting away from all of the trials of the day.

We often say things like that as a way to communicate how hard we worked that day. It's like a parenting badge of honor sometimes. But I've been convicted to avoid that phrase and others like it in my home. No matter how tired I am, I don't want my kids to think I need to escape from them. Because we all know they aren't the problem. It's all the stuff going on around them.

If you are constantly feeling the need for escape at the end of the day, maybe something needs to change. You might need to free your schedule or say no to a new obligation. Maybe you need to work escape into your schedule so it's proactive rather than a desperate reach when it's almost too late.

And instead of saying something like "Get me out of here!" the next time you need escape, try a phrase like, "Jesus, refresh my soul." That's really what your flesh is crying out for, after all. Spiritual nourishment and godly refreshment are far more fulfilling than any bubble bath.

## → Connection Point

*Jesus, please refresh my soul. Help me to order my schedule in such a way that escape is not necessary. And when I am over-burdened, help me remember to look to you for my refreshment. Amen.*

## Transparency Parenting
### Bethany Jett

*If we say we have no sin, we deceive ourselves, and the truth is not in us. If we say we have not sinned, we make him a liar, and his word is not in us. 1 John 1:8, 10, ESV*

If there is one thing teens are great at spotting, it's a phony. This is great, really, until your child asks you about an embarrassing topic, such as your sexual past, or your drug and alcohol history. Awkward.

When I was in eighth grade, the topic of smoking was brought up and my mom said, "I've never smoked. Never taken even a puff." I had never been offered a cigarette at that point but four months later, the girls at my bus stop passed around a box of cigarettes, and my mom's words echoed in my head. I determined to be able to tell my own kids, "I've never smoked, not even a puff." Had she not shared that story, I don't know what decision I would have made that day. It may not have carried the same importance as it did once I knew my mom's history.

What happens if our teen wants to know about something we *have* done? The verses in 1 John can give us a glimpse into how we should react when our teens ask us about our past. Honesty is important, but it doesn't mean your teen should know everything. Discretion is key, and the age and maturity level of your child should play the biggest role in how much information to share. Full disclosure isn't necessary or inevitable—you control the boundaries of what you share.

While it can be uncomfortable, for many situations, a simple: "I made a mistake in this area, but God forgave me, and this is how He restored me..." is sufficient. This not only shows your teen that you're human, but demonstrates a great example of looking to God for forgiveness.

No matter what situation or topic your teen wants to discuss, rejoice that your child is coming to you for answers. Not only is that rare, but it's a special time for you to provide teachable moments and perhaps prevent your child from walking down the same road.

### → Connection Point

*Jesus, please guide me in this. Help me to know what to say and when so my teens will learn from both my good and bad choices. Amen.*

## Attention Seeker
### Nicole O'Dell

*The Lord is close to the brokenhearted and saves those who are crushed in spirit. Psalm 34:18, NIV*

When you were raising toddlers and school-age children, they would get hurt and cry and run to you for comfort. You held them and nursed their boo-boos, and while you cuddled them their cry would change a little bit. You knew they were past the injury and need for physical relief but craved more snuggles anyway. They faked their tears for a while so you would keep holding them and stroking their heads and rubbing their backs. They crave the attention so they prolonged the expression of pain.

Your teenagers are really no different. They crave your attention and the attention of others, so they will do whatever it takes to get it. How are they shouting, "SEE ME!"? Acting out, disobeying, breaking curfew, inflicting pain on themselves…How are they crying out to you?

In order to find out what's going on in the minds of your teenagers, the best thing to do is ask them.

Do you feel like you get enough attention and affection from me?

It's really that simple. And it doesn't matter how much attention you think you show her how much affection you think you give, if they are feeling slighted or needy, something needs to change. You either need to ramp up the time you spend, the encouragement and praise you give, or the physical affection you offer, or you might need to bring in someone who can get to the bottom of the issue.

Ultimately the most important thing is that you don't minimize or sweep away the concerns your teenagers have. They need you. Don't take it as a personal attack, take it as a cry for help.

When we are needy, our Father begs us to come to Him, to sit at His feet, to drink from His fountain. Let us be the same haven of comfort and rest for our teenagers.

## → Connection Point

*Thank You, Father, for filling me with every good thing I need. Thank you for the gift of Your Son and the blessing of your presence in my life. Help me to be that kind of nourishment to my teenagers. And please use me to meet their spiritual and emotional needs. Amen.*

## Judgment in the Carpool Lane
### Nicole O'Dell

*Who are you to pass judgment on the servant of another? It is before his own master that he stands or falls. And he will be upheld, for the Lord is able to make him stand. Rom. 14:4, ESV*

Dear haggard lady who looked like you'd been up all night and used curse words in every other sentence as you spoke to your teenager this morning, I'm not judging you. Dear business-suit-wearing man whose son is always waiting for you long after everyone is gone, I'm not judging you. Dear teenager who just put your cigarettes away before your parent showed up, I'm not judging you.

Judgment is always driven by assumption and is not what we are called to do as followers of Christ. I could assume that the worn-down woman was out late partying or up all night surfing the Internet. I could assume that businessman was too busy worried about making more money than picking his kid up on time. I could assume that teenager is acting out against his parents because they're not spending enough time with him.

But what if that lady is a single mom undergoing cancer treatments and is in a lot of pain? What if that businessman is about to lose his job and his home, and is doing his very best to balance it all... and is about to take his son home to play ball in the yard? What if that teenager is suffering his parent's divorce and is crying out for help?

Every one of us could be judged for our parenting actions on a moment-by-moment basis. But the judgment of others doesn't hurt us, it hurts them. Jesus calls us to love and encourage each other, not criticize and undermine. When we operate with a critical spirit, it eats away at our joy and leaves us empty. Instead, love others with the love you have been shown.

### → Connection Point

*Dear God, please help me not to jump to conclusions about other parents and teens based on what I see on the outside. Let me bring my concerns to you in prayer, out of love, not criticism. And please help others do the same for me. Amen.*

## Wait Watchers
*Nicole O'Dell*

*In all toil there is profit, but mere talk tends only to poverty.*
*Proverbs 14:23, ESV*

If you're like me, a diet starts on a Monday morning. Okay maybe Tuesday. Oh, okay, Wednesday is soon enough. Well since it's already Wednesday, might as well wait until Monday. Sound familiar? That's how it goes for most people when starting a new habit like an exercise program, a financial plan, a housecleaning system, a daily devotion schedule. But why do we do that? Once we've identified a positive step for our lives, why do we wait? What is it about the bad behavior or inefficient habits that we cling to? Our human nature thrives on the path of least resistance, but our spiritual self strains for righteousness and growth.

Consider your parenting and ask yourself and God what aspects might need attention. Where do you need to make some changes? Have you been rebelling against immediacy in favor of procrastination?

How about now? What's wrong with starting now? Have that family dinner today. Do your family devotions today. Go out for a walk with your teenagers today. Whatever has been nagging at you as something that you should instill in your family routine, don't wait till Monday. Tuesday. Wednesday...or beyond. Choose today.

## → Connection Point

*Dear Lord, please help me to recognize the next best step for me to take as a parent and then help me do it right now. Help me to reject the spirit of complacency and procrastination that makes me put off the hard work in favor of what comes more easily. Give me the energy I need to make the changes you've called me to make right now. Amen.*

## Pro-Life with Exceptions?
### Claire Culwell

*"For you created my inmost being; you knit me together in my mother's womb. I praise you because I am fearfully and wonderfully made; your works are wonderful, I know that full well. My frame was not hidden from you when I was made in the secret place, when I was woven together in the depths of the earth. Your eyes saw my unformed body; all the days ordained for me were written in your book before one of them came to be." Psalm 139:13-16, KJV*

Are you pro-life with exceptions? Is there such a thing? Many people believe that abortion in the case of rape is okay. Statistics show that abortion only intensifies the pain of rape. And we must ask ourselves, is one baby less valuable or less of a person because of how they were conceived? While rape is vile and unfair, a baby is not.

What about when pregnancy or birth poses a threat to the baby or the mother? What if that mother-to-be was your daughter or your son's girlfriend? As a mother myself, I know that if asked to choose between my life or the life of my child, I would never choose to save my own life. I don't know any mother or father who would. God is the only giver and taker of life. Who are we to say that our plan is better than His? His track record shows that His plan is always better.

You are either pro life or you're not. This extends from the choices you'd make yourself, to the counsel you offer friends and acquaintances, and to what you'd tell your teenager if the situation presented itself. Exceptions are nothing more than excuses made in hopes of avoiding the tough situations in life. Imagine if Jesus made excuses so he could ignore His Father's wishes and avoid the tough things He had to face.

Be pro-life without exception, and be prepared to talk with your teenagers about the sanctity of human life. And use these truths as a way to support abstinence.

## → Connection Point

*Heavenly Father, thank you for the gift of life. Please help me to uphold it at all costs. Give me the words to say when people don't understand my stance, and help me lead my teens to a firm commitment to life with no exceptions. Amen.*

Powerline365

## Chocolate Temptations
*Nicole O'Dell*

*No temptation has overtaken you that is not common to man. God is faithful, and he will not let you be tempted beyond your ability, but with the temptation he will also provide the way of escape, that you may be able to endure it. I Cor. 10:13, ESV*

What if, when you were a child, your parents told you chocolate was bad for you before you ever tasted it? What if they told you it was bitter and would make you fat and ruin your life? What if they even told you that God didn't want you to eat it? You'd easily promise never to eat it.

But one day, years later, the smell coming from the fudge shop at the mall stops you in your tracks. You peek inside. The customers are smiling and none of them are even fat. Had your parents been wrong in their warnings? That's it. You have to know for yourself. You take a nibble. Then a bite. It melts on your tongue, and you must have more.

Sex is very much like that chocolate. It's easy to elicit a promise of purity from a child who plays wedding Barbie. A preteen who hasn't been on a date will promise to wait for her knight in shining armor. But what about the teenager with a boyfriend or girlfriend? What happens when their bodies first respond in a physical way? Like the smell from that chocolate shop, that feeling is intoxicating. They'll assume Mom and Dad never felt that way, and they'll wish they'd never made such a foolish promise, if they remember the promise at all.

We have to be honest with our teenagers. We have to assure them that we know what they're facing and feeling. We have to come right out and tell them that purity is very, very difficult because the body wants what the body wants. Don't shame them about their sexual responses. Don't pretend that physical desire doesn't exist. Instead, talk about it. Be open about what they will feel. Then tell them that God asks for purity anyway. Tell them God's plan is for them to sacrifice, withhold, and withstand for this stage of life so they can have the very best one day.

## → Connection Point

*Lord, help me be real with my teenagers. Help me have the guts to tell it like it is and then give me the words I need to inspire them to push past their physical desires and chase your best plan for them. Amen.*

# 160

## Inconceivable
### Nicole O'Dell

*All you need to say is simply "Yes" or "No"; anything beyond this comes from the evil one. Matt. 5:37, NIV*

In the movie *The Princess Bride* Vizzini says, "Inconceivable!" over and over. I love when Inigo Montoya says, "You keep saying that word, but I do not think it means what you think it means."

Sometimes I think our teenagers use the word no, or plan to, but don't really know what it means. They make promises to us and agree to our boundaries easily enough. But they soon realize that sin is easy and fun, and the lines become fuzzy.

The first time they face real peer pressure or temptation, they say, "No!" and mean it. They make it through that difficult moment and get to the other side with their commitment in tact. But they soon see how difficult it is to stand up against peer pressure. They learn how it feels to let their friends go on ahead while they stay back with their resolve. Their friends are even having fun, and it doesn't look so bad.

The next time temptation rears its head, the "No" is followed by a question mark. It means, "No...unless you do a really good job of convincing me." Maybe they can even make it through that time. But there's always the next time and the next time and the next time.

So, how do we empower our teens to uphold their standards? We need to talk openly about the things we expect from our teenagers. What do we want them to say no to and why? And how do we expect them to do it? We also need to make it easy for them to make good choices within the boundaries we set. If you make a rule but then have loose boundaries, you're setting your teenager up for failure. But if you make a rule or set a standard for behavior and then construct good restrictions and safeguards to make it difficult to give in, then your teens have a much better chance. Both your communication and your support mean everything when it comes to the word NO.

### → Connection Point

*Father, please help me to be an example of what it means to say no and mean it. Help me empower my teens to uphold your standards, and please show me how to establish the boundaries. Amen.*

## The Last Laugh
*Nicole O'Dell*

*A joyful heart is good medicine, but a crushed spirit dries up the bones. Prov. 17:22, ESV*

Looking back at my week, I'm not very proud of the amount of time I carved out for relaxing and laughing with my teens. There was some, sure. But not enough. The school day chewed up a lot of time. On top of that there were commitments related to student council, marching band, National Honor's Society, church, community, ministry...oh, and a few doctors appointments, and more. There was a sick pet and some sick Kindergartners. Everything was rushed, and there was a lot of heavy sighing on my part.

My daughter Natalie loves to run to the store with me because she knows those moments will be uninterrupted, and we will soon be laughing about something silly as we grab list-minute dinner items. I love moments like those when my teenagers and I really connect over something that tickles us in way others can't understand. Laughter is like music to the household and it knits us together in relationship like nothing else can. Inside jokes are like glue.

What fun things have you done with your teenagers this week? Or did the week get away from you, and schedules, activities, and commitments of all kinds pressed in and squeezed out all the fun like they did for me?

I always regret these crowded weeks when I look back on them. I don't remember with any great fondness even one moment of unnecessary busyness we endured. It's in the joy and laughter where the true memories are made. We must plan ahead to fill our homes with rest, peace, and joy. Waging war on our schedules must be intentional, and we can't do it alone. How can you turn your sighing into laughing in this coming week and beyond?

## → Connection Point

*Jesus, I give my schedule to you. I let go of all the have-to's so I can grab hold of the levity you provide through the gift of laughter. Help me to enjoy my teenagers through the true joy of humor and please give us some inside jokes to bind us together. Amen.*

## Age Doesn't Matter
*Jill Hart*

*Trust in him at all times, you people; pour out your hearts to him, for God is our refuge. Ps. 62:8, NIV*

Do you ever wonder if your teen wants to spend time with you? As our sweet children turn into tweens and then teens they often begin to pull away, spending less time with us and more time in their rooms. They are often less willing to talk with us, less willing to share what's going on in their lives.

Or is this true? Could it be that they are more self-conscious about seeking us out? More reserved as they work to figure out what this next stage of life will look like for them.

Over the last several years as my daughter has opted for more time to herself and less time with me, I have ended up with hurt feelings on several occasions. I took her standoffishness personally and assumed that she didn't want to be around me.

As I prayed about this, I felt the Holy Spirit impressing on me that I should reach out to her. I'll admit I was scared. I was already feeling rejected and really wasn't up for more hurt feelings.

However, as I made my way down the hall and knocked on her room, hope filled me. I went in and sat on her bed and we chatted a little. I tried to let her talk, to see where the conversation would go. Surprisingly, she shared many things with me that had been happening in her life. She seemed eager to talk with me and pleased that I had made the effort to seek her out.

As I left her room, I realized that it wasn't that my daughter didn't want to talk with me or didn't want to be around me. The truth is that she needs me more than ever, but that times have changes and I'm going to be the one who needs to make the effort, at least for now.

Have you noticed your teen becoming more withdrawn from family life? How can you reach out to them today?

## → Connection Point

*Dear God, please help me to be aware of what my child needs. Help me not to take their changing personally, but help me to seek them out and build a strong relationship that will weather the coming years. Amen.*

## On the Lookout
### Nicole O'Dell

*Therefore, preparing your minds for action, and being sober-minded, set your hope fully on the grace that will be brought to you at the revelation of Jesus Christ. I Peter 1:13, ESV*

Teenagers often have blinders on when it comes to risk. They just don't have a firm grasp on the dangers of their choices or even on the likelihood they'll get caught doing wrong.

My mom used to pray that no matter what I did as a teen, I'd get caught. As a parent myself, I completely understand that she wanted me to have to face my mistakes, deal with their consequences, and then realize my need for forgiveness. But teens don't always get caught with their hand in the cookie jar. Sometimes they begin to change, and we just can't put our finger on the source of the problem.

Take drug and alcohol use, for example. There are certain emotional, behavioral, and physical changes that may occur when teens begin using these kinds of substances. Be on the lookout for emotional signs like irritability, aggressiveness, mood swings, depression, excitability, and restlessness.

Behavioral and physical changes might include things like lack of care for personal hygiene, a big change in personal style, weight loss or gain, drowsiness or sluggishness, bloodshot or glazed eyes, drop in grades, lack of focus...etc.

Now, it's true that each of these symptoms can be explained by other things as well, but they should encourage you to dig a little deeper and watch a little closer. And no symptom you observe will ever come close to matching the power of your parental instinct. If you're in prayer and asking the Lord to reveal any trouble spots in your teens' lives, then that gut feeling is most likely the Holy Spirit answering your prayer.

## → Connection Point

*Holy Spirit, please guide me to the truth. Help me see whatever I need to know about in my teenager's life. Sharpen my instinct and guide my actions as I parent my teens. Amen.*

## Subtle Erosion
*Nicole O'Dell*

*Submit yourselves therefore to God. Resist the devil, and he will flee from you. James 4:7 ESV*

Can you feel the waves of change relentlessly battering the shores of your peace? It's subtle, and can become familiar as the tide. You won't recognize the change until your shoreline is moved.

Did you approach the teen years with solid ideals and expectations? Did you have a plan for holding your teen to certain standards and limitations? Were you sure you'd be a hands-on parent – not at all like your own?

How have lines in the sand shifted by the changing tide? Why did those changes occur? In other words, where have ideals and expectations relaxed as pressure from your teens or from the outside pelted you? Can you identify why you may have given in? Did you realize it was happening?

- It happened before you realized.
- It happened because you weren't prepared for the fight.
- It happened because of conviction you didn't want to face.
- It happened because the enemy fought to erode commitment.

There is hope. Take charge and right the wrongs. Restore the order and the rules originally intended to define your home. It'll take some work and be met with resistance. You can do it!

**Step one:** Identify where things went wrong.

**Step two:** Call a family meeting. Place no blame on anyone. In fact, apologize for the erosion, and share your vision for correction.

**Step three:** Enlist your family's help so they take ownership of changes too.

**Step four:** Be consistent in follow-through and unwavering in your resolve.

You've got this!

## → Connection Point

Dear God, please forgive me for the ways I've strayed from my convictions. Restore my commitment and give me the strength I need to make the necessary changes in my home. Please prepare my family to receive my renewal with open hearts and minds. Amen.

## Really Bad News
### Nicole O'Dell

*You are my hiding place; you will protect me from trouble and surround me with songs of deliverance. Psalm 32:7-8, NIV*

One day, when my daughter Natalie was about three, she came to me with a very sad, resigned look on her face. She stood at my side and said, "I have really bad news." She scrunched up her face like she was about to deliver a deep, emotional blow that was sure to scar me for life. Then she held up one chubby little finger that had a scratch on it.

I looked at that scratched finger wondering what on earth the bad news was. She looked at me wondering when I was going to grieve her injury, confident that it would hurt me more than it had her. I quickly scooped her up and covered her with kisses until her boo-boo was better.

Our teens still want to see that their "really bad news" hurts us more than it hurts them. They want to know we're walking with them and carrying their burdens. Even when it seems they don't want us to be involved, they really do.

I am kind of a toughie and have a high pain tolerance. So to me, a scratched finger is pretty mundane. It took me a minute to remember than my little one saw it as bodily damage that needed to be mourned. Consider that your teenager may not respond to things the same way you do. It's important to learn which love language speaks to your teenager's heart, and reach out in that way.

So, this week, when your teenager walks in the house and hesitantly lets you in on some hurt or worry they're enduring, maybe you won't smother them with kisses, but you can shed a tear. You can take the time to work on a solution. Offer a hug. Say a prayer. Show them that their problems are more important than your own, and be a lighthouse in their storm.

## → Connection Point

*Dear Jesus, please help me to show the right amount of concern for my teenager's needs. Help me to show love in the way my teenager will best respond. Let me be a vessel for deliverance in my teenager's life. Amen.*

# Eye on the Prize
## Lyn Parker

*I press toward the goal for the prize of the upward call of God in Christ Jesus. Phil. 3:14 NKJV*

There is nothing like the feeling of attending your favorite sporting event and cheering on your team to victory. Our hometown team went to the Super Bowl this year. Until that game, many of us took ownership in their success and celebrated as though we'd coached them to victory ourselves. But we didn't have anything to do with the way the team members played. They had to make up their minds and find their own motivation to win the game and push on to the final prize — the Super Bowl win!

Are you a soccer mom or a football dad? It's invigorating to sit in the stands and cheer your kids on to victory. And doesn't it feel so much better from those seats even than it did when your role was on the field? Living vicariously through our kids gives off an electric charge like nothing else can.

But as much as we would like to help our teens accomplish their dreams, ultimately, they have to find the motivation, passion, and desire to go for that end goal. What we can do is to pray for them, position them with opportunities that lead to their goals in even small ways, and help them through the disappointments. Finally, we can help them stay focused on the end result — victory!

## → Connection Point

*Father God, thank you for the dreams and passions you've given me. Help me stay focused on the prize of the call you have placed on my life. Thank you for the people you have strategically placed in my life to accomplish your purpose in me. Amen.*

## Back to Basics
### Nicole O'Dell

*But in your hearts honor Christ the Lord as holy, always being prepared to make a defense to anyone who asks you for a reason for the hope that is in you; yet do it with gentleness and respect.*
*I Peter 3:15, ESV*

How are you on your knowledge of the basics of your salvation? If your teenager asked about why you believe in God, would you have an answer? Would you know how to defend your faith if challenged?

Satan knows the Word of God. He knows it so well that he can twist is just enough to make the truth a lie that still looks a lot like truth. We have to know God's Word so well that we can shield our teen from his schemes.

If you can name the Bible verses where you would turn to begin a defense of your faith, if you can name some outside resources that support your belief, if you can talk openly and freely about the gift of salvation and the reason that the shed blood of Christ was required, then you're well prepared.

If you cannot, please take some time to do some studying and ingrain those truths on your heart and your mind so you can answer the questions your teenager will have. In fact there are really great programs at most churches that take you back to the basics of faith and give you good foundational grounding in facts and truth. If you haven't taken one of those, or if it's been a while and you aren't feeling confident, sign up for one and dig in. Even better, bring your teenager with you so God can heap more solid truth on the foundation that's already there.

## → Connection Point

*Lord, would you teach me more about yourself? Please show me the truth of your Word, and help me to understand it fully so I can share with others about you while I also teach my teenagers to be defenders of truth. Amen.*

## Teenage Wrath
*Nicole O'Dell*

*Fathers, do not provoke your children to anger, but bring them up in the discipline and instruction of the Lord. Eph. 6:4, ESV*

I remember stomping down the hall and slamming the door to my room where I buried my face in the pillow so I could let out my frustrations. For me, anger exploded when I didn't feel heard. If I knew there was more to a story, and my parents weren't hearing me out, it was maddening. I was powerless, yet I felt like I had information they needed and should want. Why didn't they want the full truth? Why wouldn't they hear me out? I felt like simple human respect would dictate that they would at least let me finish what I needed to say.

For the record: they would say that they did hear me out over and over. That I didn't feel heard unless they agreed.

Regardless, sometimes the conversation needed to end, and it was my job to respect them first and foremost. However, knowing what made me tick and that I was a talker, I do contend that they should've let me finish what I needed to say. *Ahem.* For that reason, I try to examine the intricacies of each child's personality and decide what I need to do to get through to them.

Some other things that can provoke a teenager to wrath are when parents:
- are over-critical
- can't let go even a little bit
- falsely accuse
- take sides with others
- make painful comparisons

Consider whether you struggle with any of those things and how they might affect your teenagers. In what ways do you provoke your teenagers to wrath by not meeting their individual needs and showing them basic human respect?

## → Connection Point

*Heavenly Father, please help me be wise in how I deal with conflict with my teenager. Help me to know when I'm provoking negative reactions that are damaging to my teen and to our relationship. Give us a calming spirit in our home. Thank you, Jesus. Amen.*

## Fix my Eyes
### Nicole O'Dell

*Let us also lay aside every encumbrance and the sin which so easily entangles us, and let us run with endurance the race that is set before us, fixing our eyes on Jesus, the author and perfecter of faith. Heb. 12:1b-2a, NIV*

Fix our eyes on Jesus. What I love about this verse, this idea, is that we're to look up from all the stuff, all the chaos and sin that entangles us if we let it. We're to fix our eyes on Him and let the rescue happen according to His will.

It gives the picture of stalwart, resolute, unwavering attention placed on our provider and protector, the one who offers security and help at the time of our need. The war could be raging all around us, trouble with our teenagers could be knee-deep or deeper. Yet our eyes are fixed on Him because we know He's the one that will perfect us through our trials.

Now the second thing in this verse I want to point out is that we are to fix our eyes on Jesus even when the answer, the help, is not visible yet. It's not about the rescue; it's about faith in the rescuer.

I like to think of what it feels like when you're driving uphill at sunset. You keep your eyes on the horizon as you head up the hill. You can't see the other side at all, but you press ahead in faith. You keep your eyes locked on your destination, and you're confident that when you crest the hill the other side will be there. The road will continue on, and you'll be safe.

This week let's parent our teens with that same amount of faith, trusting in the rescuer more than we depend on the rescue. Keep your eyes fixed ahead on the horizon, on Jesus, and be confident that He is at work no matter how chaotic life gets. He has a plan. Keep your eyes on Him, the author and perfecter of your faith.

## → Connection Point

Lord, please forgive me for the times when my faith has been weak. Those times when I have tried to find the answers and worked to create my own rescue. Help me keep my eyes fixed on you and your promises. Help me trust in your word as I parent my teens. Amen.

## Who am I?
*Cara Putman*

*Take delight in the* LORD, *and he will give you the desires of your heart. Psalm 37:4, NIV*

The teen years are filled with so many questions. Who am I? Who am I supposed to be? Why am I here? Do I matter? Can God use me?

I well remember those years. Years of offering myself to God again and again, because I knew that ultimately nothing else mattered. But how was I supposed to find my way through the maze of options to the place He had for me? The place He could use me?

Then I settled on this verse. "Delight yourself in the Lord, and He will give you the desires of your heart." I've meditated on it for years. Claimed it as my life verse. Wondered exactly how it works. Is there a magic formula embedded in the verse? A promise that if I do this, it's God's promise to give me everything I want?

No. Over time, God has shown me that as I delight in him I am changed. My heart changes. What I desire changes. In the delighting, my heart becomes entwined with Him. And there. In the mixing of Him with me, I am forever altered. The things that appealed to me before, aren't nearly as important. Instead, what is left behind are the desires, gifts, drive that He embedded in me.

Now with a teenager of my own and more growing to that stage, I'm focused on transmitting that desire to them. My heart is that they would understand when their focus is on God first; He clears the way for their desires to change and come to life.

Have you seen this principle in your life? How have you been changed by delighting in God and His presence?

## → Connection Point

*Heavenly Father, please help me figure this out for myself, so I can pass it on to my teens. Help me to first order my desires so they are always in line with Yours. Help me to stay Kingdom focused in the things I do and say, and also in how I parent my teens. And please give my teenagers passion to pursue Your perfect will. Amen.*

Powerline365

## Such a Chore
*Nicole O'Dell*

*Laziness brings on deep sleep, and the shiftless go hungry.*
*Prov. 19:15, NIV*

More and more I'm seeing families where parents are afraid to give their teenagers chores. What's up with that? What kind of culture are we creating with their teenagers if we can't ask them to pitch in around the house? What are we afraid of as a society? As parents?

Why do we think that we can raise a generation of spoiled, lazy, entitled human beings who will one day turn into self-reliant in independent and hard-working about? It's illogical.

I believe that teenagers need to contribute to the household. They need to learn what it takes to keep a home clean and to prepare for their own independence. They also have a lot to be thankful for and can show some of that gratitude by helping out.

My teenage girls are responsible for all of the dishes, for example. We set that rule long ago and soon discovered that they prefer to be on one week and off the next. They worked out that rotation and it works fine for all of us. Now, though, my older daughter is working two part time jobs, going to school, and working to keep her grades high enough to earn help with college. Honestly, I would feel petty if I held the dishes over so she could do them when she finished all that other stuff. She's not being lazy, she's striving for good things. I can do her dishes now and then.

But I do have to realize—we all do—that our teenagers will be busy their entire lives. We must instill a sound work ethic, organizational skills, and a good set of living standards in our teens. This will carry over into their future career, marriage, parenting, and all of life's demands. Help them now so they don't suffer for it later.

## → Connection Point

*Lord, please show me what's appropriate. I want to help my kids, but I don't want to help them right into dysfunction. Help me know what's right so I can be the parent they need me to be, preparing them for a rock-solid future. Amen.*

## Attention Seeker
### Nicole O'Dell

*Making your ear attentive to wisdom and inclining your heart to understanding... Prov. 2:2 ESV*

I have young children and teenagers in my house right now. The little ones get hurt and cry for my attention. They crawl on my lap and let me rub the owie away. At some point, while I'm comforting them, I notice their cry changes. They have gotten over the injury but still crave more snuggles. I sure don't mind the cuddles, so I let them whimper until they're bored and run off to play.

Teenagers are no different. We complain about drama—how they make everything so serious and earth shattering. We wish they wouldn't turn everything into a gripe session or cry every time their feelings get hurt.

But they are just like those small children. Their problems are different, but their needs are the same. They want our attention.

What are your teenagers doing that is crying out for your attention? Are they acting out, disobeying, breaking curfew, inflicting pain on themselves... How are they crying out to you?

In order to find out what's going on in the minds of your teenagers, the best thing to do is ask them.

Do you feel like you get enough attention and affection from me?

It's really that simple. And it doesn't matter how much attention you think you show or how much affection you think you give, if they are feeling slighted or like there's something lacking, something needs to change so they know for sure how important they are to you and to Jesus.

Ultimately the most important thing is that you don't minimize or sweep away the concerns your teenagers have. They need you. Don't take it as a personal attack; take it as a cry for help.

### → Connection Point

Father, I don't claim to speak teenager. I just need to know what my teens need from me. Please help me understand and meet their emotional needs, and let them see how much I love them. Amen.

Powerline365

# 173

## What's after Kissing?
*Nicole O'Dell*

*Therefore put on the full armor of God, so that when the day of evil comes, you may be able to stand your ground, and after you have done everything, to stand. Eph. 6:13 NIV*

*Adapted from Hot Button Sexuality Edition*

"So, what's next after kissing?" Have you ever asked your teenager that question? Seriously, just come right out and ask it that way. Most teens would be adamant. "Nothing! That's where it stops for me!"

Wonderful. And hopefully that's true. But what would your teenager say if you pursued that question even deeper? Does your teen know where the progression of physical activity would lead from there? Often, they don't think it through to that level until they're in the situation and feeling the tingly urges. One thing leads to another...

Sometimes, in the heat of the moment, someone snaps out of it and calls a halt. But in a family where there's no ongoing dialogue about sexuality, the experience often gets filed under, "Hmm ... interesting." And isn't revisited again until the next heated moment.

Next time it goes a little longer and a little farther. Same thing the next time. Until one day ... the rest is history.

When I was a 13, a friend asked me if I would have sex before I turned 16. I admitted that I hoped I wouldn't but expected I probably would. Even then, I believed I was powerless to stop the inevitable, unable to stand up against the pressure to fit in, wanting to be loved. Circumstances didn't go quite as I expected, but ultimately, I was right.

We must parent proactively with an eye on the possibilities and the promises of God, not resigned to the inevitable. Speak life into good choices and hope into the issue of peer pressure. When your teens act like circumstances are spiraling out of their control, remind them that they shouldn't be in control. They should be surrendered. Power is found in surrender.

## → Connection Point

*Father, please help me to always remember that you're the one who holds the power of life and death in your hands. Help me point my teens to that power as they strive to overcome temptation, peer pressure, and sin. Guide them in your truth to good choices. Amen.*

## Unfriended
*Debi Lee*

*How can a young person stay pure? By obeying your word. I have tried hard to find you—don't let me wander from your commands. I have hidden your word in my heart, that I might not sin against you.*
*Psalm 119:9-11 NLT*

Last night I did the unthinkable. And I would do it again. I had come across a picture my 13-year old's friend posted of a half-naked girl with some inappropriate caption, so I went into my son's Facebook account and unfriended the boy. This boy's been in our home many times. We like him. But I can't ignore that behavior or expose my son to it.

So, I wrote my letter. "Dear xxx, this is Caden's mom. I want you to know that I am unfriending you because I don't want Caden seeing the pictures you post. I think they're inappropriate and disrespectful. I want you to know, though, that you are still his friend in real life."

Within a minute his friend responded, "Oh. I'm sorry about that thank u for letting me know I appreciate it have a nice night." That was a great first step. And the next morning I had a sweet message waiting for me when I read my mail, "I'm sorry that I posted that stuff I should have known better to post that kind of stuff."

He got it!

If we are so naïve to think we should never snoop, never question, and just trust our young teens and their friends are okay on their own, we are in for a rude awakening. I love my son so much that I invest time in him---not just cooking his meals, washing his clothes, providing for his needs, but also keeping both ears and eyes open at all times. I must teach him what God's Word says and how he can guard his mind from harmful things. Someday he will thank me! And, in this case, even his friend appreciated the instruction and the boundaries.

What if I had said nothing? Neither boy would have been called to a higher standard and it would only go downhill from there. Parents, let's do the hard work to teach our kids these valuable lessons.

## → Connection Point

*Father, please forgive me for taking the easy out and overlooking some red flags. Please help me know exactly how to handle the issues I need to address with my kids and their friends. Amen.*

Powerline365

## Better to Give
*Nicole O'Dell*

*For the love of money is a root of all kinds of evils. It is through this craving that some have wandered away from the faith and pierced themselves with many pangs. I Tim. 6:10 ESV*

Teenagers come with all sorts of expenses. There are school dances, picture day, team sports fees, extracurricular activities, class rings, graduation, youth group activities, and more, more, more. And none of those are things you have to do as a parent like providing food, clothing, and shelter. It can be more than overwhelming. And if you're like I am, you have to multiply all of that a few times.

Have you ever sat down and shown your teenager exactly what kind of expenses go out of the house for things that aren't considered necessities? Things you provide because you think you're supposed to, or because you want to, but that are not necessary? I think it's important that they see the sacrifices we make just to keep them up-to-date on all as much of that as we can, because it can really be draining. And it often causes us to make choices we wouldn't necessarily think are best for the family. Are we taking on extra work, agreeing to overtime, building up debt, or scrimping in other ways because we've spoiled our kids to the point where we can't say no without looking like a bad parent?

It's time to redefine the expectations.

Let your kids earn some money. Let them pay for their own formal dress or class ring. Plan ahead for the next time a band instrument will need to be serviced and let them earn the money to pay for it. In the end it will mean more to them to have earned the money and it will teach them the value of hard work even if they don't realize it now. You're not a bad parent if you empower your kids to put in some effort. Teach your teenagers a bit of independence and a strong work ethic. They'll thank you for it later.

## → Connection Point

*Lord, please help me know the difference between spoiling and providing for my teenagers. Help me teach them good lessons about finances. And please show me when it's right to say no. Amen.*

## 176

## The Gong Show
### Nicole O'Dell

*If I speak in the tongues of men and of angels, but have not love, I am only a resounding gong or a clanging cymbal. I Cor. 13:1, NIV*

Sometimes, when I've been nagging a lot, I feel like the words coming out of my mouth have about as much impact as a bell. Do your homework. Clean your room. Load the dishwasher correctly. Don't use that tone. Send a thank you note. Call your grandma. Did you memorize your verse... do your devotions... read your Bible. Put down your phone...

Gong. Gong. Gong.

It's at times like those that I really detest even the sound of my own voice —how much more must my teenagers want to just shut it off? Do you ever feel that way?

Nagging is often borne out of fear — fear that things won't get done, fear someone will see the messy house, fear the garbage won't make it to the curb in time, etc. But, teenagers report that when they feel nagged, they stop listening. They subconsciously decide that there's nothing they can do to make us happy, so it's pointless to try. They tune us out and do their own thing.

1 Corinthians 13 tells us that unloving speech is about as effective as the ringing of a bell, it means nothing. It becomes an incessant, annoying noise that falls on deaf ears. Speech filled with love and grace communicates God's love and is edifying to all. We need to stop dictating life to our teens and, instead, embrace them as we walk the journey together. If you adopt that mindset, I can promise you that your speech will automatically reflect that heart. Accomplish things God's way, and reap the rewards of His blessings in your communication with your teens.

## → Connection Point

*Father, please help me control my tongue and realize my relationship with my teens isn't about being the boss. Give me words of grace and love to speak to them, and help me to be an example of your love through the things I say. Amen.*

Powerline365

# Book of Wisdom
## Nicole O'Dell

*Brothers and sisters, I do not consider myself yet to have taken hold of it. But one thing I do: Forgetting what is behind and straining toward what is ahead. Phil. 3:13 NIV*

About eight years ago, my husband and I decided to take on a rehab project and bought an old Victorian home. We prayed about it a little bit and looked a the logic behind the decision...then we jumped in. Let me tell you, this flipping house project ranks right up there with a few other big mistakes I've made in my life.

Yes, we got it for a great price. And, yes, we've been slowly able to make the necessary changes to make it safe and increasingly pleasant. But it has taken almost a decade to be able to say that. But we'd prayed about it, right?

Does regret always mean we didn't hear from God? That's something I ask myself about this house. And there are other mistakes like that one that pepper the landscape of my past, and yours too if you're human. Just because we regret a choice, does that mean we were wrong all along and just didn't see it?

This question magnifies in our parenting as our choices affect our teenagers. We want to do right, but mistakes from the past shake our confidence. Or mine anyway.

God is showing me that every choice, every mistake, every regret is part of the book of lessons He's been writing in my life. It's where I get the wisdom to pass on to my kids, to my friends, and even to you. You have your own book of wisdom that you've been working on since your early days. Consider that your regrets aren't just a list of things that shouldn't have happened, but they have shaped you into the person you are and are now part of your own parenting resources.

## → Connection Point

*Jesus, thank you for redeeming my mistakes and not just letting them rot on a heap of regret. Help me harness the value in my missteps so others can learn from them. Please make my teenagers open to learn from my regrets and avoid them. Amen.*

## Happy Memories
*Tricia Goyer*

> But Mary treasured up all these things, pondering them in her heart.
> Luke *2:19, ESB*

What is your favorite memory of your teen years? How many of them involve your parents? So much of life is stressful, I believe it's very important to be intentional about creating happy memories with your teens. So how do we go about doing that?

To get an idea of what things will mean the most to your children, think about some of your own favorite memories. To take the exercise one step farther, discuss these with your teens. Your teens will learn more about you, and you might be surprised at what you remember when you talk these through.

- What was your favorite pastime as a child?
- Think about one special memory about each of your siblings.
- What was your favorite meal?
- What were some of the most memorable books you read?
- Think of one particularly memorable event.
- What scent or sound immediately takes you back to childhood?
- What meaningful advice did you receive from an adult?
- Think about someone who influenced your life profoundly.
- Think about your proudest moment.
- What made you laugh the most?

Next make a list of fun things you can do with your teen. As you do these things, talk about the details and then revisit those memories in conversations over the years so you can make sure the good ones stick. You are the one who will give your teen wonderful memories. It's up to you, so let's get started!

## → Connection Point

*Jesus, thank you so much for all the good memories I have. Please help me create awesome memories with my teens that overshadow some of the dark times we've had. Help me be creative about ways to excite my teenager and invigorate our relationship with great memories. Amen.*

## Dash of Salt
*Nicole O'Dell*

*Let your conversation be always full of grace, seasoned with salt, so that you may know how to answer everyone. Col. 4:6, NIV*

Ever use 1/8th of a tablespoon of cayenne pepper when the recipe calls for 1/8th of a teaspoon? Trust me, and don't test that one out. There's a reason recipes are so specific, down to even the tiniest 1/8th of a teaspoon. Someone else already tested it. They came back with the best combination they could create. If it only calls for a tiny amount, like 1/8th of a teaspoon, there's a very good reason. And when even that measurement is too large, some recipes say to add a pinch or dash. How could such a small amount have any impact at all?

When it comes to our speech, God gives us the perfect recipe. This applies to how we speak to our co-workers, our friends, and even our teenagers. We are to be rich in grace — that means we're always ready to show love and mercy to others. But, our words should also to be slightly seasoned with salt. Salt is both flavor and a leavening agent. Salt in conversation is how we affect change in those around us. But notice grace comes first, like asking someone to pass the shaker, please. We have to master the courtesies before we earn the right of using the saltshaker. Salt without the grace element will ruin the recipe.

As parents, we need to be a living example of God's unending grace and always be willing to season our speech with enough salt to convey the truth of God's expectations to them. In the right measurement, this is the perfect recipe of truth.

## → Connection Point

*Lord, please help me to balance my speech with the proper amount of grace mixed with the right amount of salt. Let both my words and my guidance be pleasing and effective in the lives of my children and others around me. Amen.*

## End the Legacy
### Nicole O'Dell

*So they are no longer two, but one. Therefore what God has joined together, let man not separate. Matt. 19:6, NIV*

It is sad to realize there is virtually no family that remains completely untouched by divorce. Almost everyone has felt the pain that comes as a family is torn apart or has dealt with the after effects, or even the side effects. Whether it's you and you are raising your teens alone, or whether it's your parents, siblings... or anyone else you look up to, divorce is painful. It cannot be denied that it usually leads to more divorce. It's contagious because once it's made a viable option, then other family members see it as seemingly reasonable way out of a tough situation.

Remember that my parents are divorced, and so am I. My kids have been raised as a product of divorce from all angles. So trust me when I say that I speak in love and from experience on this issue.

If your teens have been touched by divorce, please tell them every chance you get that no matter how brave everyone seemed, it was horribly difficult to break up a marriage. It is not an easy way out, and it's not God's way out. Please don't shield your teens from that truth either as a way to protect them or yourself.

Face the truth that God has a better plan than divorce, and it starts long before marriage. It starts by choosing the right mate. Then, a godly marriage requires unwavering commitment. And finally, keeping a marriage together requires faith in God's sovereignty and His might. God's desire is that marriage be a lasting covenant between two people He joins together. Help your teenagers to purpose in their hearts now that marriage is permanent. Pray with them for the right mate and also that God would prepare them to be someone else's godly choice in a partner.

### → Connection Point

*Jesus, please prepare my teenagers for marriage. Help them break the legacy of divorce by surrendering to You in marriage and in all of life. Amen.*

# It's Private!
## Nicole O'Dell

*So we fix our eyes not on what is seen, but on what is unseen, since what is seen is temporary, but what is unseen is eternal.*
2 Cor. 4:18, NIV

There comes a point in every young person's life when they crave privacy more and more. It starts in small ways. Young girls love diaries with keys, but they often leave those keys hanging right from the lock, unconcerned with who might look inside. They like the idea of locking them, but they really have nothing to hide nor any reason to think they should. Young boys have treasure boxes they stash under their bed or up in a tree. As they get older, they hide those boxes better and better.

As the teen years approach and technology increases, parents have passwords and email addresses and Internet content to contend with. Privacy takes on a whole new meaning. There is so much privacy available to our teens that some of the programs even delete cyber content within seconds of being viewed.

Society is working against disclosure when it comes to our young people, so it's up to us to keep our eyes open and our fingers on the pulse of what our teens are being exposed to. From the very earliest age we need to be involved. They need to understand that privacy has to do with bodily functions, not worldly exposure. They need to view complete privacy as something we can't allow because we love them. Because God loves them.

## → Connection Point

*Lord, please make me wise. Help me be gentle in my exploration but wise in my pursuits as I protect my kids from their own desire for privacy. Amen.*

## Every Day is a Gift
### Tara Fairfield, Ed.D.

Shortly after my teenage years, my best friend died in a small plane crash. This devastated me. She wasn't supposed to die. We had our whole lives planned out. We were going to raise our children together! Anger and disbelief warred within me as I struggled to grasp the new reality of a life without my dearest friend. I felt robbed. My world tilted off it axis and grief immobilized me... until I attended her funeral.

Raised in a Christian home, her family exemplified what it meant to trust in Christ. My friend's funeral was a celebration of her life and of her love for Jesus. Stories were shared of how she impacted the lives of so many in such a short time. Even in death she witnessed to me what it meant to live a life of hope. God does not want us to waste a moment outside of his plan for us.

Every day with our teenagers is a gift, and we each must choose how our moments will be spent. We often take time for granted and waste days or years on guilt, hard feelings, unforgiveness, or anger.

Don't let the enemy rob you of the life God has planned for you or what He wants your teens to learn through your example. I could have chosen to wallow in my grief but to do so would have tarnished the memory of everything my friend stood for and stolen the life God called me to live. Everyone experiences pain, suffering and grief but do not let those emotions become the legacy of who you are, let it be an opportunity to witness the overcoming love of Jesus Christ. I have no doubt I will see my friend again and can only hope I leave a fraction of the impact on others that she had on me.

## → Connection Point

*A Psalm of David. The Lord is my shepherd; I shall not want. He makes me to lie down in green pastures. He leads me beside still waters. He restores my soul. He leads me in paths of righteousness for his name's sake. Even though I walk through the valley of the shadow of death, I will fear no evil for you are with me; your rod and your staff, they comfort me. You prepare a table before me in the presence of my enemies; you anoint my head with oil; my cup overflows. Surely goodness and mercy shall follow me all the days of my life, and I will dwell in the house of the Lord forever. Ps. 23, ESV*

# Parent of the Year
## Nicole O'Dell

*For am I now seeking the approval of man, or of God? Or am I trying to please man? If I were still trying to please man, I would not be a servant of Christ. Gal. 1:10 ESV*

I'm going to an award banquet this weekend where I'm a finalist for one of those "of-the-year" awards. For the sake of this writing, it doesn't even matter which one. The fact is, I doubt I'll win, but it truly is an honor just to be nominated.

I often joke that a particular parenting flub like forgetting birthday treats, not sending the field trip permission slips, forgetting to send invitations on time, etc. Those things won't earn me the Parent of the Year award, that's for sure. In fact, one time I went to the school and waited 20 minutes to pick up my daughter. I got annoyed that she was keeping me waiting so long and was about to go into the school to find her when I remembered that she had been home sick all day. With me. Yeah, not winning any awards for that.

So, who is the Parent of the Year? In my book it's the one who wakes up each day renewed. Who lays the mistakes and trials of the day before aside, surrenders the day to the Lord in prayer, and commits to raising their children in the grace and truth of Jesus Christ. And at the end of the day that parent has kept the faith and is ready to lay mistakes aside and start over. 365 times. That is the parent of the year.

The Parent of the Year award goes to you. You who reads this devotional book. You who shows up and puts your hand to the plow day after day and asks for a do-over when things don't go well. You who works for eternal rewards not momentary pleasures. You.

Congratulations to you, Parent of the Year.

## → Connection Point

*Lord, it's my turn to pray for these parents. Please give them wisdom for the journey they face and power to withstand the tasks on the road ahead. Show them what you have called them to do as parents, and protect their teenagers along the way. Shield them and keep them only to yourself. Amen.*

# 184

## Bozo Buckets
*Nicole O'Dell*

*Look carefully then how you walk, not as unwise but as wise, making the best use of the time, because the days are evil. Eph. 5:13 ESV*

Do you remember Bozo the clown and his sidekick Cookie? He was the star of Bozo's Circus, based out of Chicago, which is where I grew up. In order to visit Bozo's Circus and be a member of the studio audience you had to request free tickets years in advance. One of the teachers at my elementary school had the foresight to request them every year so each class would reap the benefits of the claim she made years before.

I remember sitting in those seats wishing they would call my name to play Bozo's Buckets. They called a boy's name and then it came time for a girl. I waited and waited, and there it was. My name. I jumped up and skipped down the steps to stand on the huge concrete floor with my toes right on the line. I tossed my ping-pong balls just as carefully as I could and tried to make it into as many buckets as possible. If I remember correctly, I got three buckets. Not a bad showing, but certainly not worthy of any major prize. But I'd had my chance! Not many kids could say the same thing...especially not at my school.

It's important that you prepare your teens to face the Bozo buckets of life with confidence. They're entering years where each action or inaction feeds into the next one. Our encouragement, our preparation, and even our example will greatly affect the way they stand at that red line and throw their ping-pong balls.

Have you made the most of the opportunities you've been presented? Have you learned from the times you haven't? Have conversations with your teens about this. Share an example of a time when you had a great opportunity and faced it with confidence and then reaped the rewards with gusto. And then share an example of a time when you did just the opposite. Talk about ways you can learn together from those experiences and prepare for the next God-given opportunity that waits right around the corner.

## → Connection Point

*Father, help my teens embrace life with confidence. Let me be a great example of endurance and eagerness to try new things. Amen.*

## Ruby Slippers
### Nicole O'Dell

*Jesus replied, "Anyone who loves me will obey my teaching. My Father will love them, and we will come to them and make our home with them." John 14:23, NIV*

There's no place like home.

I got to play Dorothy in a fourth grade rendition of the Wizard of Oz. As I learned my lines, my mom made my blue-and-white gingham dress with its classic white apron. I remember pacing backstage, nervous, but ready to utter those all-important words. *There's no place like home.*

Poor Dorothy wanted nothing more than to go home. But look at what she had to go through to get to arrive at that feeling. She ran away from her troubles and found herself in all sorts of messes before she could truly discover the blessings she'd had all along at home.

The same is true for the biblical prodigal son who ran away from his family and squandered his inheritance. After he hit rock bottom, he realized how great he once had it with the people who loved him.

Your teenager might be walking that road of disillusionment, preparing to walk or run down that road of escape. But sometimes it's necessary to run in order to figure out what's really best. Letting them experience some of the hardships and realities of life will only serve to remind your teens of the wonderful blessings they've been given. It's not easy to see them suffer, and of course we would wish another way for them, but gratitude and sacrifice don't come easily. If you do have to walk that journey and watch your teenager pull away from you, hold tightly to the truth that one day they'll remember that there's no place like home.

## → Connection Point

*Lord, would you give me patience to trust that you're at work? Help me remember your promise that when I train up these teenagers according to your Word and your will we will all reap the rewards. Hold my teens close to your heart and continually drawing them to you. Amen.*

## Rebellion: Not just for Teens
### Wil O'Dell

> He said in a loud voice, "Fear God and give Him glory, because the hour of His judgment has come. Worship Him who made the heavens, the earth, the sea and the springs of water."
> Rev. 14:7, NIV

"Worship Him" is not a suggestion. It's a directive from God. We are to give God glory (Rev 15:4) and worship Him with gladness (Ps. 100:2).

"It's not my thing."

"I worship in my own way."

"I'm not a showy person."

God has shown us how to offer worship and praise to Him. If we hold back, it really is an act of rebellion. And if we do that in front of our teenagers, they will surely wonder about their own worship. They will hesitate and wonder if demonstrative worship is weird. They might be reserved and afraid to enter into corporate praise.

Yes, we are all different. And God does see through our actions to our hearts, but why wouldn't we want to model complete surrender to God before our teens? Why not display adoration and praise rather than stoic and rigid behavior?

We should come to church prepared to worship in the way God has called us as individuals. In our personal time with God we should spend time in the Word asking for divine help to worship Him freely. Our teens look to us for their first cues about relationship with God. If we send a message that worshiping with abandon is something to be ashamed of, they will be ashamed, too.

Do you have sin in your life? Doubts? Fears? Insecurities? Leave them at the door. Don't let Satan turn you from the obedience that God desires and deserves. In the name of Jesus, claim power over all that entangles you. The Holy Spirit will do the rest. Do not give the devil even one victory over you as you approach God with your worship.

## → Connection Point

*Gracious Father, please receive my sacrifice of praise and let my worship be an example to my teens. Help me be unrestrained in my offering and teach my teens that true worship is a vital part of a thriving relationship with you. Amen.*

## People First
### Nicole O'Dell

*Do nothing out of selfish ambition or vain conceit. Rather, in humility value others above yourselves. Phil. 2:3, NIV*

I've often said that my Papaw was the one human being who really helped me understand what Jesus was like. In my eyes, he was a complete extension of Christ's love in my life. He had so many Christ-like qualities, but mainly, he was sacrificial. He put people first. His kids, grandkids, great grandkids, friends, and others. The man loved to serve. He put people far above things.

I can't claim to have mastered that ability yet. Many times I've had to refocus after allowing material possessions, professional ambition, personal goals, and a host of other things, take priority as my relationships took a backseat to all that other junk. It wasn't until my grandfather's example flashed in my mind that I was able to reorder my priorities and make the needs of others the priority.

People first.

Ultimately, stuff fades away, but love is eternal. The things you have or don't have in this life will be nothing when you stand before Jesus one day. And your teenagers, though they might want the most trendy clothes or the newest smartphone, as they get older, they will appreciate that you prioritized spending time with them over working overtime to buy the latest gadget. Teach them the value of relationships and sacrifice. Be present.

People first.

## → Connection Point

*God, please help me have good priorities. Help me see what's important and what is worth the sacrifice of my time and energy. Help me to see the needs around me in and out of my home, and then give me the mercy and strength to meet those needs whenever I can. Amen.*

## Building Blocks
### Nicole O'Dell

*Built on the foundation of the apostles and prophets, Christ Jesus himself being the cornerstone. Eph. 2:20, ESV*

The most important thing in any construction project is a solid foundation. Those first blocks that are laid—or the first layer of concrete floor—strengthens or destroys the structural integrity of the building. Similarly there are tried and tested building blocks that go into raising teenagers who love Jesus and to make Him known.

Those two things, loving Jesus and making Him known to others, don't come naturally. You won't wake up one morning and find that your teenagers have adopted an evangelistic style at school and are passionate about their personal pursuit of Christ. It has to come from somewhere. Are you laying the blocks to that kind of solid foundation?

Those foundational building blocks include a solid prayer life, regular study of God's word, fellowship with believers, and a lifestyle that backs up faith. All of those things start with your example and then follow through with your teaching. What can you do this week to gird up the foundation you're laying in your teenager's life? Here are a few simple steps:

- Pray with them before school.
- Incentivize them to memorize scripture.
- Attend a social church function.
- Turn off a questionable TV show and talk about that choice.

Be open about your desires to draw closer to your teenagers while drawing closer to God. Let them see it in you first, and persist, layer upon layer, until you have a break through.

## → Connection Point

*Lord, make me a light in my home. Help me to lay solid foundation in my teenagers' lives so they can build upon them and draw closer to you all of their lives. Amen.*

## Carousel
### Nicole O'Dell

*"You don't really understand human nature unless you know why a child on a merry-go-round will wave at his parents every time around - and why his parents will always wave back."*
William Tammeus

Enjoying the ride. It's exciting to ride that brightly painted white steed up and down, around and around, completely independent for a moment. But then, at just the right second, Mom and Dad come back into view. They grin and wave until they disappear from sight again. The little one rides off grinning, but as the carousel makes its rotation, the child frantically leans forward to catch that first view of Mom and Dad right where they're supposed to be, waving.

Is your teenager on life's merry-go-round? Enjoying the ride, experiencing new things, and taking off alone? Often they think they're ready to be independent, and they set out in search of new ways to break away, but at this age, they always circle back to what is familiar and encouraging. They're not yet ready to disconnect and ride off into the chalky sunset like Mary Poppins and her charges did at the County Fair. They need that connection. That stability. They need to know that every time they return to their home base, you'll be there encouraging and supporting them.

At this stage as the transition is beginning, make a conscious effort to keep some of the comforts of home in place. Let them enjoy the peace-giving familiarity that only you can provide.

## → Connection Point

*Lord, please help me stay connected to my teens as they explore their own interests and excitement. Help me be that steady rock in their lives always encouraging and supportive, but gracious as they ride away. Protect them and go with them on their ride. Amen.*

## When Check-ups go Wrong
### Vicki Tiede

*My grace is sufficient for you, for my power is made perfect in weakness. 2 Cor. 12:9, NIV*

Great. You did what you're supposed to be doing. You checked up on your teenager's Internet history and social media activity... but what you found is less than encouraging. Porn. Now what?

Punishment and correction are not your goal. Restoring your child and helping them recalibrate to God's design for sexuality needs to be your priority.

That said, do you remember how Jesus approached the adulterous woman in John 8? He was compassionate and kind, but He didn't mince words. Now would be a good time to put to use your best Jesus impersonation.

It's vital that you act swiftly to ensure your child isn't on the path to addiction. Here are some important next steps to take to change the atmosphere in your home and set tighter boundaries:

- Allow no coarse jokes or hints of immorality.
- Be sensitive to sexually charged media or resources in your home.
- Establish rules about media use.
- Ensure that any device that connects to the Internet has proper filters in place.
- Seek the help of a professional, Christian counselor who can uncover deeper issues, facilitate tough talks, and reinforce your findings.

Finally, you cannot be porn cops for the rest of your child's life. This really comes down to training your child in the power of the Gospel of Jesus Christ and helping him/her steward their sexuality in a way that honors Him.

This is a battle that we parents cannot afford to lose.

## → Connection Point

*Father, please open my eyes where they need to be opened, and help me do the hard work to raise my kids to honor you in all their choices. Protect their hearts and minds against the schemes of the enemy who wants to destroy the beauty of marriage and the family. Amen.*

Powerline365

## Turn up the Heat
*Nicole O'Dell*

*The God we serve is able to deliver us from it, and he will deliver us from Your Majesty's hand. But even if he does not, we want you to know, Your Majesty, that we will not serve your gods.*
*Dan. 3:17-18, NIV*

King Nebuchadnezzar was about to throw Daniel and his three comrades, Shadrach, Meshach, and Abednego, into the fiery furnace for refusing to worship false idols. Check out Daniel's response. Basically he said, "I'm not going to do it no matter what." He didn't say that he knew for sure his God would save them. But he did know his God was ABLE to save them. He was surrendered fully to God's will, and knowing what He was capable of was more than enough for Daniel.

Do you know what God is capable of in your life and in the lives of your teenagers? The truth is we don't know what He has in store for us. We don't know the fires He's going to let us walk through as He refines our faith and molds us into a finished work. We don't know what He will save us from; in fact we have no idea of all He has already protected us from. But as long as we know what He is able to do, we can be at peace.

Peace is different than acceptance. We don't have to be excited to endure hard things or be tested, tempted, or tried. Suffering or watching our teenagers suffer is not easy. The apostle Paul knew that very well. But peace is different. It passes all understanding. It doesn't make sense. Peace fills our soul with faith in God and in His place plans for our lives. When we are at peace as individuals, our spirit is at rest and united with the plans of God. That enables us to parent from that place of surrender, not knowing exactly what God is going to do, but knowing what He is capable of doing.

## → Connection Point

*Dear God, help me to trust you today with peace I cannot understand. Help me trust you and your plans, letting your peace crowd out my anxiety. I trust in you. Amen.*

## Target Practice
### Nicole O'Dell

*Do not be deceived: "Bad company ruins good morals."*
*I Cor. 15:33, ESV*

How in tune are you with your teenagers' relationships? Do you really know friends and acquaintances...and their families? How much time do you spend with them as they interact with their friends? It's a good idea to take inventory now so you can help your teens focus on connections that will make a difference.

This activity is a great way to understand your teens' relationships and discover how they identify them.

Draw a small circle and then three larger circles around it. Point to the center circle and say do you teenager, "This is your bull's-eye. Who are your bull's-eye friends? Who are the few people that hit right on target?" Don't explain what that means, your goal is to do some discovery here. Next point to the circle slightly outside the center. Who are your next-tier friends? Not quite right on target but closer than others. And continue to move outside the circle until you get to those people outside the circle. Now ask your teenagers to describe the characteristics of each level of relationship.

Follow it up with one question:

*How can these friendships most impact you for or against your relationship with Jesus Christ?*

Then just see what they say. The goal here is to get them thinking. What are they looking for in a friend? What draws them to people? What qualities really make them feel comfortable with others? And what does God think of it all? It's time for them to be intentional about who they spend time with and to focus on those relationships that are most edifying.

## → Connection Point

*Dear God, please help my teenagers surrender their friendships and relationships to you. Help them see that you're at work in every relationship they have, both good and bad. Let them draw near to those who will encourage and uphold their faith journey. Amen.*

Powerline365

# 193

## Hidden Words
### Nicole O'Dell

*I have hidden your word in my heart that I might not sin against you.*
*Psalm 119:11, NIV*

I know a woman who was abducted and brutally assaulted when she was in middle school. While the attack was happening, she recited scripture, out loud, one after the other. It sustained her. It gave her faith. It probably saved her life.

That kind of preparation was within her because her parents led her to the Word. They helped her store countless treasures in her heart so that when she needed to call for strength, she was already equipped. I encourage my teens to memorize God's Word and hide it in the hearts so when hard times come, it's there as a comfort. When they face temptations, it's there as a reminder. When they face tough decisions, it's there as counsel.

If you're ready to introduce scripture memorization and need a place to start, these are some of our favorites:

**Jeremiah 29:11** -- For I know the plans I have for you," declares the Lord, "plans to prosper you and not to harm you, plans to give you hope and a future.

**Romans 6:23** -- For the wages of sin is death, but the gift of God is eternal life in Christ Jesus our Lord.

**Romans 8:28** -- And we know that in all things God works for the good of those who love him, who have been called according to his purpose.

**Romans 12:2** -- Do not conform to the pattern of this world, but be transformed by the renewing of your mind. Then you will be able to test and approve what God's will is—his good, pleasing and perfect will.

**Galatians 2:20** -- I have been crucified with Christ and I no longer live, but Christ lives in me. The life I now live in the body, I live by faith in the Son of God, who loved me and gave himself for me.

Ephesians 2:8, I John 1:9, I John 3:16, I Timothy 4:12

## → Connection Point

*Lord, please fill my teenagers with Your Word. Give them a desire to study and learn scripture until they know it backward and forward. Help them understand your truth and hide it in their hearts. Amen.*

## Missing the Mark
### Brenda Yoder, MA

*And Jesus increased in wisdom and stature, and in favor with God and man. Luke 2:52, KJV*

There have been times I've sat in the bleachers wondering where I went wrong. Though all four of my kids have been and are active in sports, none of them have been the top player, the MVP, the one who makes the crowd go wild.

They haven't been in the Homecoming Court, and the oldest two finished third and fourth respectively in their graduating classes, just missing the mark.

Do you ever feel jealousy over other children's accomplishments or popularity? When I feel the I-didn't-do-it-quite-right feeling, God reminds me I'm raising kids for a lifetime, not just high school. He reminds me being popular among peers often means making choices that aren't pleasing to Him. He reminds me that having integrity and a good attitude while sitting the bench speaks louder to others than making the winning shot.

I'm thankful that Jesus is our model for raising kids, not high school popularity. When we raise our kids to please God, favor with others goes hand in hand. God's favor with others may not make the headlines, but it's the kind that others see when no one else notices. That's the winning prize in the bigger game of life.

Do you struggle with wanting your kids to excel or be popular? Allow God to show you His favor for your child today.

## → Connection Point

*Dear Lord, help me to see the value you see in my child. Help me see their successes in your eyes, not the eyes of the world. Equip me to raise them for your favor, then bless them to receive honor in the sight of others, too. And if you can use me as a vessel to work out your perfect will for them, I'm ready. Amen.*

## Tick-Tock
### Nicole O'Dell

*Remember not the former things, nor consider the things of old. Behold, I am doing a new thing; now it springs forth, do you not perceive it? I will make a way in the wilderness and rivers in the desert. Is. 43: 18-19, ESV*

The clock is ticking. 40 is the new 30. The parenting finish line.

Concepts like that drive me crazy. Your effectiveness is not based on your age nor on the amount of time you have left as either a parent or as a follower of God. In fact, your perceived success in any capacity of the work He has called you to is only because of Him. Whether you have three years with your teenagers in your home or three days, God is on the throne, and He is able to work miracles in your teen's life and in your relationship.

God owns the outcome of your efforts, and He will use your bright moments and your dark failures as opportunities to teach you and others. So don't fall for the lies that tell you you're running out of time, or you wasted too much time to be effective now, or if only you had... No! Today is the day of renewal and change. Today is the day of miracles. No matter how damaged your relationship is or how futile it seems, put your faith in Jesus Christ then leave the rest up to him.

Surrender the past and embrace the future. He's not asking for your yesterdays; He's asking for your today and your tomorrows. If you need to renew your commitment to walking solidly with Jesus as you parent your teens, pray this with me:

## → Connection Point

*Heavenly Father, please forgive me for the times I've dropped the ball. My intentions are good. You know my heart, but I'm weak. Help me get back on course right now. I give you this day and every day forward to work in my teen's life through me. Please show me what you have called me to do. Amen.*

## Jesus vs. Santa
### Nicole O'Dell

*Ask and it will be given to you. Luke 11:9, NIV*

One of my young triplets asked me, "Mommy, why do we pray to Jesus if Santa brings the presents?" Ouch! Now we're not a big Santa family. We don't get militant about it, but we're not really active in promoting the whole chimney, reindeer, North Pole thing. But a six-year old picks up on things, no question.

Many take the above verse to be somewhat of a Christmas wish list. Like little children who line up to sit on Santa's knee, naming off the toys they hope to see under the tree on Christmas morning. They make their requests, fully confident they will receive exactly what they ask for.

The problem with that verse, though, or rather with the usage of that verse, is that it's so often taken out of its full context. It is not a promise that God will give you whatever you ask for.

That verse is part of a lesson in which Jesus has described what matters most—being His disciple. He teaches His followers how to pray, and models a prayer that focuses on His Kingdom. It's then that he says, "Ask and it will be given to you." If you seek His Kingdom and His promises, you will receive that which you seek. It's that simple.

As you parent your teens, seek God's will, desire His Kingdom in their lives, pray for their salvation. Those prayers will not go unanswered. They are His will.

## → Connection Point

*Father, thank you for being the giver of all that is good. Please help me to trust you when you say no to the things that seem right to me. Thank you for walking with us and drawing us to you in everything you do. Amen.*

## Home-Based Business
### Nicole O'Dell

*If any of you lacks wisdom, let him ask of God, who gives to all liberally and without reproach, and it will be given to him.*
*James 1:5, NKJV*

In launching Choose NOW Ministries, I had to research what it took to be successful with a home-based business. I've read many business manuals and took seminars on how to thrive. When we decided to become a nonprofit organization, it took more research and lots of paperwork. In my experience, the top five steps to be successful in any home-based business are to plan ahead, put money aside, organize your time, organize your space, and stay focused.

As Christian parents, we are in the throes of our own home-based businesses. Our business is Jesus. In order to be good business managers in our homes and successful with our teens we need to plan ahead to set aside time for study, prayer, and teaching. We also need to be good stewards of our finances so we can be called upon to serve God with those resources as needs arise.

With proper time organization, we will be available to serve the body outside the home and the family inside the home. Our homes should also be organized and inviting so that our teenagers feel at peace and visitors feel welcomed. And we need to stay focused on the reason (Jesus) and the goal (leading our teenagers and others to Him).

Even though parenting our teens and serving God are much more important than any actual business, looking at our parenting steps in such an objective way can push the motions aside and help us do the right thing even when it's difficult. Setting boundaries, learning from the past, and preparing for the future are habits of successful business owners and effective parents.

## → Connection Point

*Dear God, help me to be objective when I consider the needs in my home-based business. Help me make changes swiftly when necessary and to do all things to bring glory to your name. Amen.*

## Make a Joyful NOISE!
### Wendy Fitzgerald

*God has given each of you a gift from his great variety of spiritual gifts. Use them well to serve one another. 1 Peter 4:10, NLT*

As the mother of five children, quiet is a luxury. When my eleven-year-old son started playing the piano that sits in our front room, I lamented the extra noise his curiosity imposed. However, within a few months, I realized that his intrigue for creating music didn't subside, but rather increased. After careful consideration, we decided that we would invest in piano lessons, and the noise became more methodical and pleasing.

Fast forward three years and he now owns six guitars, two keyboards, and a drum set, and he teaches music lessons. His love for music is a gift that I could never understand. He grasps things about music that will always be like Greek to me, even though as a child, I took piano lessons for years. But the most exciting thing about his love for music is that almost every weekend, he is playing one instrument or another as part of the worship team at our church. God gave him a gift that he is now giving back to God. In leading worship, his spirit is exuberant!

As parents, we need to help our children discover what special gifts God has given them and how they can use those gifts to honor God. And we have to step back while they explore and learn, even when it's noisy. When our teenagers use the gifts they have been given to serve others for God, they will be filled with joy...and so will we.

## → Connection Point

*Father, please help me to see and understand the unique gifts that you have placed in each of my children. Give me wisdom to know how to help them develop their gifts so that you are honored, the world is served, and their spirits rejoice. Amen.*

## Don't Relate
*Nicole O'Dell*

*Don't copy the behavior and customs of this world, but let God transform you into a new person by changing the way you think. Then you will learn to know God's will for you, which is good and pleasing and perfect. Rom. 12:2, NLT*

No matter how hard you try, you're Mom or Dad—you'll never be hip in the eyes of your teenagers. Especially if you didn't blink at the use of the word hip. But, trust me, this is a good thing. And you may have moments when your teens think you're the greatest, but isn't that usually because they've gotten their way about something?

Instead of trying to relate to your teen as a contemporary, instead of turning a blind eye during a champagne toast at a wedding or allowing them to watch a questionable movie just to keep the peace, prove your consistency with them by standing firm. Even if they're frustrated or angry with you because "everyone else's parents are so much cooler," deep down they're relieved that you care enough to stand firm.

Your teens don't want you to be a drinking buddy; they want you to guide them toward safety. They certainly don't want you to look the other way while they embark on dangerous behaviors—they want you to set boundaries and teach them the way to walk. If they can't count on you to want the best for their health and happiness, not to mention their Christian walk, whom can they count on?

You can't parent well if your focus is on looking cool to your teenagers and their friends. And they don't want you to fill the role of BFF; they want you to be the *parent*. Your kids get to choose from millions of potential friends in the world, but they only have access to a couple of parents. Be the parent God has called you to be by standing on the Word of God for strength and wisdom.

## → Connection Point

*Jesus, please keep me focused on my calling. Help me to remember that it's never about being my teenager's friend or about keeping the peace. Give me the strength to do the uncool things that will call my kids to a higher place. Amen.*

## Praying Scripture (Part 1)
*Nicole O'Dell*

When we're knee-deep in the parenting mire, it can be difficult to even know how to pray for our teens. I've learned over the years that quoting and paraphrasing scripture as I pray for my teens is one of the most powerful ways to refocus myself on God's will, surrender my own desires, and lift my teens to Him daily.

I've seen it over and over and now fully believe that when we're afraid or weary, or when we're feeling alone on the journey, it's impossible to pray in the Word and not be changed.

Here are some of my favorite scriptures that I pray for my teenagers on a regular basis. Go ahead; give it a try:

- Create in (name) a clean heart, O God, and renew a right spirit within him/her. (Psalm 51:10).

- May (name) walk after you, God, and fear you and keep your commandments and obey you. May she/he serve you and hold fast to you no matter what may come (Deuteronomy 13:4).

- Please help (name) be strong and courageous in the face of peer pressure and not fear or be in dread of life's trials, for it is you, Lord, our God, who goes with him/her. You will never leave him/her or forsake your promises (Deuteronomy 31:6).

- May (name) walk before You, God, as King David walked, with integrity of heart and uprightness, doing right thing according to what you have called. Help him/her stand up against all sorts of evil and temptation and hold tightly to your truth. (1 Kings 9:4).

## → Connection Point

*Thank you, Lord, for providing your Word as a tool to keep my focus on you as I parent my teens. Amen.*

## Praying Scripture (Part 2)
### Nicole O'Dell

How did you like yesterday's list of scriptures to pray for your teens? Powerful, right? Well, those few weren't nearly enough for me, so I'm going to give you a few more of my favorites.

- Like Timothy, may (name) be an example to believers in speech, in conduct, in love, in faith, and in purity (1 Timothy 4:12). Let others see you when they look at (name).

- Thank you, Lord, for working all things out for the good of (name), because (name) loves you and is called according to your purpose. Please reveal that purpose to him/her. (Romans 8:28)

- Please bring about Godly repentance and sorrow in the heart of (name) and help keep him/her pure according to Your word. Convict of sin and then restore by your grace; write your laws upon (name) heart. (Psalm 119:9)

- You are for (name), so no one can be against him/her. Show the fullness of your protection and surround (name) with your favor as with a shield. (Romans 8:31)

- Thank you for making a way out of temptation for (name) and for helping him/her to be faithful to stand strong and resist it. Please strengthen (name) against peer pressure. (1 Cor. 10:13)

→ **Connection Point**

Your Word is alive and I am so grateful for the power it holds. Please use your Word to build my faith as it draws my teens closer and closer to you. Amen.

## Go In the Strength You Have
### Amy Joob

*The Lord turned to him and said, "Go in the strength you have and save Israel out of Midian's hand. Am I not sending you?... " The Lord answered, "I will be with you..." Judges 6:14,16a, NIV*

During a time of great difficulty for the Israelites, God called Gideon to lead the troops and defeat their enemy, the Midianites, who were oppressing them. Gideon was not a *qualified* individual. In fact he felt incapable, weak, afraid. Perhaps you feel that way too. Or maybe you are in a hard season or going through a difficult trial and you don't feel qualified to handle what you're facing. Well, you are in the same place that Gideon found himself when the Lord put him to work. He was at the end of his strength and his resources, and he had no choice but to look to God and to trust in His power and strength to carry out the mandate God called him too. Basically, if God didn't show up, the Israelites would be defeated by the Midianites whose army numbered into the thousands. Guess what? God did show up. And with only 300 men, Gideon and the Israelite army won.

Perhaps your family is facing a challenging circumstance today. A challenging diagnosis. A teen pregnancy. A teen who is pulling away from you...or from God. Maybe it looks impossible in human terms. Maybe you or your loved one is ready to concede defeat. Can I encourage you to get up again and go in the strength you have today?

Even in the midst of this difficulty, keep moving forward. One step at a time, one day at a time. God has given you strength for this moment, for this day. Trust Him. He will not leave you alone. His power and His plan will meet your obedience and your faith and then you will see the Big Picture. You have the strength and the wisdom to come through this battle. This too shall pass!

## → Connection Point

*Father, please fill me with your strength and courage today. Give me faith to believe your word even when everything seems dark and impossible. Give me your grace to take one step at a time. Thank you for giving me insight to see the Big Picture for my family. I commit these circumstances and this day into your capable hands. Amen.*

Powerline365

# Universalism
*Nicole O'Dell*

*Turn away from godless chatter. 1 Tim. 6:20, NIV*

Universalism is a social philosophy that says nothing is right or wrong. In fact, it claims that any belief system that teaches black and white values is wrong. Wait! That means something *can be* wrong? See the flaw in that teaching? Anyway, that's not the point. The Universalist is convinced that God, or anything resembling absolute values, simply doesn't exist.

Abortion is a great example of the abandonment of pure morality. God says mankind was created in His image, which makes us bigger than a mistake. He says He knew each of us before he created the world, which means life begins before conception. He knows even the number of hairs on our head, which means He cares about what happens to us. But our society waves all of that away in favor of personal rights and the freedom from morality.

This is all part of Satan's plan because, if your teenagers believe that they are the result of an accident, it undermines their passion to follow Jesus. It also leads them down the path of doubting God's existence. If we're nothing but an accident...then...? Dangerous road.

The apostle Paul urged Timothy to "turn away from godless chatter and the opposing ideas of what is falsely called knowledge" (1 Timothy 6:20). We must follow that advice, too. It's vital that we teach our teens right and wrong are defined, not by the culture in which we live, but by God.

## → Connection Point

*Almighty God, you and you alone define truth. Please protect my teenagers' hearts and minds from the lies of the enemy. Shield them from worldly viewpoints and distractions that strive to pull them from your path. Give me wisdom as I lead them ever closer to you. Amen.*

## It's on You
### Nicole O'Dell

*Discipline your son, and he will give you rest; he will give delight to your heart. Prov. 29:17, ESV*

My teenager won't let me... I'm not allowed to... That's off-limits...

I had a conversation earlier today with someone who should know better than that. This person said about her teenager, "Oh, I'm not allowed to talk to her about that." And then later in the conversation she said, "Anything in my daughter's bedroom is totally off-limits to me." Um, who's running the show here?

I stood there with my mouth open as I listened, and then I couldn't hold it back anymore. I had to confront the imbalance in that parent/teen relationship.

Who is the parent in your home? Not only are you *allowed* access, *allowed* to talk about the things you want to talk about with your teenager, and *allowed* to ask the questions you feel you need to ask... but it is your responsibility to do so.

I feel a sense of urgency to empower you. What is on your heart right now? What concerns do you have about your teens? What is niggling at your conscience, just hinting that something might be wrong? Mom, Dad, that's the Holy Spirit. You must sit up and take notice of those little feelings you get and the questions you have. You must.

This is on you. It's not on them. The mistakes they make at this age, if you ignored the signs and let them happen — it's on you. If you don't set good boundaries and stick to them, it's on you. If you don't ask the questions and hold your teenager accountable for truthfulness, it's on you. Don't let another day go by without doing the digging you need to do and confirming what you need to know. And then dig deeper. Be your teenagers' best line of defense against temptation, sin, and wrong choices. Take the heat; it's on you.

## → Connection Point

*Lord, forgive me for turning a blind eye and being weak in some areas. Help me boldly confront the issues that need to be confronted. Open my eyes to anything I have not seen, and give me clarity and wisdom to attack them head on in your name. Amen.*

Powerline365

## A Day in the Life
### Nicole O'Dell

*But above all, my brothers, do not swear, either by heaven or by earth or by any other oath, but let your "yes" be yes and your "no" be no, so that you may not fall under condemnation. Ja. 5:12, ESV*

Every once in a while I have to fill out one of those "A day in the life of..." explorations into my daily existence. Bloggers or media folks want to know what it's like to walk in the shoes of a writer or a publisher or mom of multiples or... You get the point.

But if I'm being honest with you and with myself, I have to wonder how truly transparent I'm being with them. Sure, I may have made a French toast breakfast for the kids and reported it on my interview. But did I do it only because I wanted to be able to write it down? Sure, I might have cleaned my bathroom and swept the floor before nine in the morning. But was it only because of that interview? Is that list of perfect order with a hint of non-essential and funny mishaps an accurate picture of my home life?

And if not? Why am I, why are any of us, compelled to tell our stories that way? Honestly I don't have anything major to hide; it's not that. It's more of a desire to rise above the mundane burden of normal human existence. But why?

I want to challenge you, and myself obviously, to be authentic with your teens. Let them see your struggles. Talk to them about what scares you, about your pressures, and about the mistakes you've made. Let them hear you. Let them help you. There's no better way for them to learn to live authentically than to see it modeled for them. And there's no better way for them to be okay with who they really are than if they see you loving yourself just the way God made you.

Tomorrow, post the uncropped picture of your cute kid even with the pile of dirty laundry in the background. And share your struggles with someone. Maybe even your teenager.

## → Connection Point

*Jesus, may my teenagers learn to love themselves because you do. Help me live authentically, embracing my failures and my joys so they will learn to do the same. May love and grace abound in our home. Amen.*

## Helping your Teen Cope
### *Laura Kurk*

*For I am the Lord, your God, who takes hold of your right hand and says to you, "Do not fear; I will help you." Is. 41:13, NLT*

Teens who struggle with anxiety or depression feel isolated and parents fear focusing on the struggles will lead to further ostracism.

First, if you're trying to help a child who struggles, know that you are not alone. In 2013, the CDC released a report estimating that 13% - 20% of U.S. children are affected by a mental disorder in a given year. The good news is that because of new attention on mental disorders affecting children, we have solid data that will help kids.

Anxiety can be especially scary for you and your child. The physical signs—rapid breathing, light-headedness, palpitations, and paleness—make this difficult for children and their parents. You can model deep breathing and relaxation. You can create a quiet moment for your child in the middle of the storm she feels.

Memorize a few powerfully positive statements that your child can repeat, such as "God abides in me," "I've handled this before and I can handle it now," and "Once I'm in the situation, I'll feel better."

Teach your child that a rush of adrenaline causes the feeling of panic. Patiently breathing through that rush will help the adrenaline reabsorb faster. Above all, reassure your teen that what she is feeling is common and normal, and will not hurt her.

Remember, our children don't have to rely only on our inadequate ability to comfort. Even our best attempts cannot do for them what God's peace will do. When we have taken every step toward helping them through this storm, including seeking professional guidance, we can rest in the knowledge that He covers them with His hand.

Have you seen in your own life, or in the life of your child, how God is able to use anxiety for good? Through it, He draws us to Him and His sufficiency. He is the true anchor in the storm.

## → Connection Point

*Dear God, please be a calming force in my life and in my teenagers' lives. Help up all look beyond our fears and anxieties to the light you shine in the storms of life. And please give me the words to say whenever my teenager is dealing with emotional struggles. Amen.*

## Peace in our Time
### Nicole O'Dell

*Don't worry about anything, but pray about everything. With thankful hearts offer up your prayers and requests to God. Then, because you belong to Christ Jesus, God will bless you with peace that no one can completely understand. And this peace will control the way you think and feel. Phil. 4:6-7, CEV*

This world is in a complete state of unrest. Tensions are soaring, and violence, hatred, and poverty are at all-time highs. And sometimes it seems like our global conditions are mirrored in our homes. Siblings battle constantly. Parents and teens are at odds. Sin, hate, and temptation relentlessly knock at every door.

We pray for peace in the world and peace in our homes, but they both seem elusive. So we battle on with little hope of victory.

I know as well as anyone how chaotic life can be. The busyness and stress squeeze in from all sides until there's no time or energy left to pray. But, as we see in that scripture quoted above, the main ingredient in the recipe for peace is prayer.

You know those days when you want to throw in the towel? When your schedule is killing you, the kids are fighting, and you can't bear the sound of another negative word, you just don't have time *not* to pray. It's during those times when you need to draw close to Jesus most of all. He'll give you what you need to see it through. He'll help you control your temper. He'll remind you of His promises. And the very act of prayer is surrender. When you're surrendered, peace ushers in.

Honestly reflect on your prayer life this week. Is it a good picture of the level of peace in your home? If you're in need of more peace, make more personal and family prayer a priority.

## → Connection Point

*Father God, you're the only way that we can truly find peace in our home. Please calm the tensions that come from the explosion of a lot of busy lives. Help up find order and calm. Draw us near to you as a family. Amen.*

# ROI
### Nicole O'Dell

*He who guards his mouth and his tongue keeps himself from calamity. Prov. 21:23, NIV*

ROI is a business term that refers to return on investment. If you put money, time, or any resource into an effort, you should measure the result to see if it's a good expenditure. For example, businesses will look at the return on the investment of the marketing dollars they spend. If they put $1000 into an ad, they will watch to see if they gain more than $1000 in profit strictly related to the exposure that ad provided.

Another way you can look at return on investment is what you're paying for goods and services as a consumer. Look at how upset everyone is at the price of gas (myself included!) But let's say gas costs an average of $3.50 a gallon. Did you know that olive oil costs $47.63 a gallon? And orange juice comes in at $7.19. And folks, this one is going to hurt, but a Starbucks latte costs $32.00 a gallon!

What about our words? What's the ROI on the words we speak? Of all the thousands and thousands of words spoken each day in our homes, how many of them are fruitful and godly? As a parent, you will get the best return on investment from the encouraging, supportive, Christ-centered words you speak to your teenagers. Fill your time and use your words on things that edify and build them up. Call them to a higher place; don't criticize. Empower them to make good choices; don't judge. Model passionate pursuit of Jesus; don't preach. And most of all, tell them you love them every single day. Maximize the opportunities you have, and use your words as an investment into the Kingdom of God.

## → Connection Point

*Father, would you guide my words today? Would you close my mouth of the speech that tears down and destroys? Help me invest in the future of my teenagers by using my words to build and nurture and always point to you. Amen.*

## Ask for Directions
### Nicole O'Dell

*The wicked in his proud countenance does not seek God; God is in none of his thoughts. Psalm 10:4 NKJV*

Go to work. Bring home a paycheck. Do the laundry. Wash the dishes. Shop for groceries. Attend all team events and school activities. Be active in church. The list of duties every parent deals with is never ending. Entwined within those chores are the mental challenges of making wise decisions, dealing with relationships, raising the kids to have faith in God, and being an example of everything good we want our kids to embody.

Somewhere along the way we caught the idea it's wrong to ask others for help. We want to press on, deal with our challenges alone. We suck it up and make it happen. The problem is, God didn't design us to live that way, and we certainly can't function well like that. If we don't ask for help, and receive it gratefully, we don't stand a chance. The body of Christ is meant to support one another. When one is in need, the other is strong. The cycle continues until everyone's load is a bit lighter.

Some people would rather drive around lost for hours rather than to stop and ask for directions. But how often do you stop for a moment and ask the Father for directions? Jesus, knowing He needed guidance from His Father, constantly sought His Father's will by praying and asking for it. He depended on directions from God. How much more is that true for us?

Is it easy for you to ask for help from God? What about help from others?

## → Connection Point

*Jesus, forgive me for my pride and for not asking you for directions. Show me the way to go and lead me in it. Also, help me to feel comfortable in admitting my needs to others and asking for help when I need it. Amen.*

## Give Them a Presence
*Pastor Jason Lane*

*There is a lad here, which hath five barley loaves, and two small fishes: but what are they among so many? John 6:9, KJV*

Our culture is in such need of someone to step up and meet the needs of the hour. A large group of people had been listening to Christ teach all day. It was nearing the time for them to return to their homes, but Jesus didn't want them to leave hungry. The problem: no food. When Christ asked his disciples what they had for the people, they revealed they did not have enough to make a difference to the crowd. A young boy approached and offered a solution to the problem. He would give his lunch of five loaves and two small fish.

I love the first five words of that verse. "There is a lad here..." Because in a problem-filled situation a boy shows up on the scene to do what he can. Why did he trust his presence could make a difference? I believe it was a result of what he had seen.

Each day, as you parent your teen, know the importance of your presence on the scene. Having a presence not only in the home, but also in community, will show your teen how one person can make such a huge difference. Our culture needs the presence of God-fearing people to step up to the need of the hour, but they must first know how.

You can teach your teenagers a great lesson simply with the power of your presence. Show up. Be there. Stay there. Our son can learn to be a father who is there for his family when his dad is a constant presence in the home. Our daughters can learn to be virtuous women when mom exhibits all things godly as she lives and moves — as she's present. As you give presents to your teens make sure to give them your presence. They need that more than anything money can buy.

## → Connection Point

*Dear Heavenly Father, thank you for showing up as I needed you the most. I ask you to help me to be a presence in the life of my teens, revealing the need for them to step up as the need arises. Please use me to fill the empty places in my teen's heart and mind with my presence. Amen.*

## Deeply Rooted
*Nicole O'Dell*

*Let your roots grow down into him, and let your lives be built on him. Then your faith will grow strong in the truth you were taught, and you will overflow with thankfulness. Col. 2:7, NLT*

When you look at lush, mature trees, you can't see the root system below ground. In fact, if you're like me, you seldom even think about it. But in order for those trees to be tall and strong, they had to spend many, many years allowing the roots to dig deeply into the soil. And they had to soak up nourishment and bask in the sun so they could stay healthy.

In the same way, your teenager won't display the fruits of a mature tree until the root system is deeply embedded in the soil of God's word. Your teenager won't be consistent with good choices or strong in biblical knowledge until those roots have had time to dig in deep and grab hold. And your teenager must have time to bask in the Son.

Just like with any planting, you can fertilize the soil. You can prune back the dead branches and pick off the dying fruit. You can watch, water, and wait. But some things just can't be hurried. You must allow your teenager the time it takes to blossom.

Staring at a baby apple tree and willing it to produce will be fruitless, if you'll pardon the pun. God designed the process to be slow and steady. Let's embrace that process with patience, eagerly anticipating all that's to come.

## → Connection Point

*Father, please remind me that my teenager is growing. Let me be a fertilizer as you pour nourishment onto the process. Help me not to rush, push, or doubt your hand is at work as my teenager puts down roots. Amen.*

## The Envelope System
### Nicole O'Dell

*For which of you, desiring to build a tower, does not first sit down and count the cost, whether he has enough to complete it? Otherwise, when he has laid a foundation and is not able to finish, all who see it begin to mock him, saying, "This man began to build and was not able to finish." Luke 14: 28-30, ESV*

Score! My teenager has a job! She loves to work and has proven to have a great work ethic. But, I'm sad to say, saving does not come naturally to her. Sparkly, pretty things seem to capture her attention much more than a growing bank balance does. So, seeing bad habits and the potential for overspending unfolding in front of me, what am I to do about it?

I'm sure many of you are facing or will face similar situations as your teenagers embark upon income earning opportunities. It's important to help them plan for the future now. We need to help them develop good habits so when they have a family of their own or are responsible for much bigger things than they are now, the habits are already there.

I taught my daughter the envelope system. The point of this method of money management is to allocate funds appropriately the minute they come in. How much goes into the giving envelope? How much goes into savings? How much for car insurance, car repairs, and gas? Now how much is left for clothing and entertainment?

Most of all I wanted her to see the value of making good choices with her money. Notice the giving option came first. It's vital that we teach our kids to give first. If they begin at these young ages to instill bad habits of giving from the remains, eventually they will squeeze themselves out of giving at all.

### → Connection Point

*Heavenly Father, please forgive me for the ways I've not been a great example in my money management. Help me to instill better habits in my teenager than I had when I was young. Where I've done it right, let my teens learn. Where I've done it wrong, let them do it better. Thank you, Jesus for all the resources you have blessed us with. Amen.*

Powerline365

## Speaking my Language
*Nicole O'Dell*

*If the whole body were an eye, where would the sense of hearing be? If the whole body were an ear, where would the sense of smell be? But in fact God has placed the parts in the body, every one of them, just as he wanted them to be. I Cor. 12: 17-18, NIV*

You're arguing with your teenager until it escalates and someone storms away. You think back over the conversation and just can't quite figure out where things went wrong. Like last time, you're left feeling ineffective and your teenager feels like she's blown it again.

It's an all too familiar scenario for most families and it generally comes down to the question of what kind of language we're speaking. Dr. Gary Chapman wrote a series of books about the five love languages. They describe how important it is to understand how your spouse or your teenager feels most loved. It's different for everyone. And most commonly your teenager's love language is going to be different than yours. That makes it the most difficult. When you're showing your love in the way you best receive it yourself, your teenager may not see it that way at all. Your efforts can fall flat and both you and your teens are left feeling dissatisfied in the relationship. Hopeless.

Periodically over the next few weeks, we'll look specifically at the different types of love languages. We'll uncover what your teenager needs from you, how to speak that language, and then how to lay down your own expectations to be more effective in expressing your acceptance and approval in the most effective way. Intentionally parenting with the concept of love languages can be revolutionary to your parent/teen relationships.

## → Connection Point

*Lord, it's not about what seems natural to me or what I want. It's about what my teenager needs from me. Please open my eyes to the specific and unique needs my teenager has. Amen.*

## God's Grandchildren
*Valerie Comer*

*Just as you accepted Christ Jesus as your Lord, you must continue to follow him. Let your roots grow down into him, and let your lives be built on him. Then your faith will grow strong in the truth you were taught. Col. 2: 6-7 NLT*

Doesn't the title create a cozy picture? Visualize your children perched happily on a gray-headed God's knee, while you stand nearby, smiling indulgently. Yes, there's a biblical basis for part of this image. On several occasions Jesus took a small child on his lap and used the tot as an example of how we should all come to the Kingdom of Heaven.

But it's a fatal flaw to assume our teenagers are Christians simply because we are. Each person needs to make a decision on his or her own and become responsible for individual spiritual growth. As parents, we can't do this for our kids. We can guide them, teach them, and pray for them, but the decision has to come from their own hearts through the work of the Spirit in their lives.

Young King Joash acted like a follower of God as long as his Uncle Jehoiada was alive. He didn't internalize his faith but followed his mentor's example until it no longer existed. Then his shallow roots shriveled up and he fell away from Yahweh to the point of worshiping idols. Read this sad-but-true story in 2 Chronicles 22-24.

Joash didn't inherit his uncle's relationship with God. He couldn't. Salvation isn't received by a family connection. God doesn't have grandchildren, only adopted sons and daughters who come to Him and accept Jesus' sacrifice in faith.

## → Connection Point

*Father God, please help me to teach my tweens and teens to look to you for their salvation, so that they can become your own children, adopted into your family. Help them become rooted in their faith. In the name of Jesus, amen.*

## Training your Replacement
*Nicole O'Dell*

*Show yourself in all respects to be a model of good works, and in your teaching show integrity, dignity, and sound speech that cannot be condemned, so that an opponent may be put to shame, having nothing evil to say about us. Titus 2:6-8, ESV*

In the corporate world, in order to move up the ladder, you have to watch for talented individuals who might be capable of taking your place one day. And when you identify the potentials, you have to train them to step into a new role.

Your teenagers are the next generation of leaders, pastors, teachers, doctors... and parents. As they strain toward adulthood, how are you preparing them to meet the demands of their roles?

Feminism would shout that it's wrong to teach girls to cook and sew; rather you should teach them to change the oil in the car while you teach boys to do housework. Society is so busy fighting against people's natural inclinations that it's losing all sight of God's plan for the home. I say, teach your daughters and your sons to cook, clean, do simple car repairs, and anything else they want to learn. If they desire the knowledge, help them attain it.

My little boy (6) says he either wants to be a cake baker or a Jesus teacher. You can bet I'm nurturing both of those options along with anything else that comes along. The key is not to worry so much about what it is they are seeking and learning, but rather that you're on the journey toward growth and discovery together. That you're taking the time and being intentional about the budding adult that is rooted within your teenager.

## → Connection Point

*Father, please show me the path to take with my teenagers so I can help you mold them into the adults you've called them to be. Give me wisdom so I can encourage them and guide them to the right pursuits. Amen.*

## Identity Crisis
*Nicole O'Dell*

*See what great love the Father has lavished on us, that we should be called children of God! And that is what we are! I John 3:1, NIV*

Never too much. Always enough. Precious. Stunning. A beautiful creation, perfectly formed by God for a special purpose in this exact moment.

I believe those truths about myself now, but I didn't buy it when I was a teenager. To me, at that time, I was just wrong. I was too much. I was never enough. I was failing at life. Failing at being awesome. Failing at being loved. But no one would have dreamed I felt that way. My parents had no idea what I was going through or why. They didn't know that I felt like a walking black hole. Void of love or any sort of acceptance from anyone. And since they didn't know, they had no idea how to meet my needs.

I craved my parents' approval above all. But since I didn't love myself, I couldn't believe they would find value in me. So I pushed them away and launched a tug-of war that would last decades.

*Love and hate can't exist in the same place at the same time or in the same relationship.* If your teenager hates herself or himself, they can't receive your love with complete abandon. And when a parent's love seems out of grasp, how much harder would it be to believe in God's love?

Maybe your teenager has been pulling away from you, or lashing out in anger in efforts to push you away, or acting aloof about your relationship. Consider that those reactions may be nothing more than defense mechanisms put in place to shield from the fear of vulnerability.

It's time to confront the lies the enemy has been telling. Lay it all out on the table. Ask questions. Demand answers. Don't let the sun go down until you've fought hard to express your love, and then do it over and over and over until it sinks in. And then do it more.

## → Connection Point

*Jesus, please get through to my teenagers. Help them see themselves like I do and to believe in my love and your love. Help them feel worthy of your grace and approval. Amen.*

## Greenhouse
### Nicole O'Dell

*I am the true vine, and my Father is the gardener. He cuts off every branch in me that bears no fruit, while every branch that does bear fruit he prunes so that it will be even more fruitful. John 15:1, NIV*

I haven't spent much time in a greenhouse, but I do know temperature control, food supply, and precise pruning are all strategies used to grow robust plants. After the plants get big enough, and once the ground temperature is just right, most can be moved to a more permanent home outside of the protection of the conservatory.

Parents, aren't we like those sheltering greenhouses? We keep our kids safe, we nourish them, and we prune them with teaching, guidance, and discipline. We keep the environment as steady as possible while we're raising them. We want them to grow strong, not battered about by wind or rain. We want their roots to grow deep, not desperately seeking sustenance at surface level. We want them to reach tall to the Son, confident nothing will get in their way.

But, eventually, our job is done and our robust plants are released to a new environment. A new environment where they'll face challenges they never experienced under our shelter. But thanks to the time we gave them to grow strong, they can withstand all the world throws at them.

## → Connection Point

*Jesus, thank you for the greenhouse effect you provide for us. Thank you for the daily, spiritual nourishment and protection you offer. Thank you for your rich sustenance and even for your discipline in my life. Help me to be that same shelter and nourishment for my teenagers. Help me to know when it's time to plant them outside of my shelter. Amen.*

## Life-Long Learning
*Tricia Goyer*

*Do yourself a favor and learn all you can; then remember what you learn and you will prosper. Prov. 19:8, GNT*

When I became a mom at 17, I dropped out of high school and finished my credits at home. Soon after, I met and married my husband, started college, and moved to a new town. I learned how to take care of a house, how to clean, how to cook. I started a small business making hand-crafted teddy bears and learned how to be a business woman. I had another baby and learned how to care for multiple kids. I realized I was more interested in writing than making teddy bears, so I started doing that. I attended conferences and started learning about writing.

With each step came changes, and looking back I realize my greatest asset was my ability to roll up my sleeves and try something new. As a parent, you have the choice to take a step to follow a dream or to stay stagnant and continue on as things are. Your teenagers are watching your choices and will pursue learning as they see you do it.

**Learn who God created you to be.** When I first started pursing writing I KNEW I was made for it.

**Learn your learning style.** I learn best with books and papers piled around me. Figure out how you learn best and use your preferences to your advantage.

**Listen.** I've learned so much from listening to others. I build relationships with people who I respect and want to learn from. I read blogs written by people I respect. Pay attention to those around you.

**Teach**. The best way to incorporate your knowledge is to teach it. As a parent, you have a willing student in your teenager. They learn by watching, by doing, and by sharing. Involve them.

Learning can take you far—you just have to be brave and start! Once you start learning and growing, your life will never be the same. Your teenager's life will never be the same either as he or she learns to follow in your footsteps!

## → Connection Point

Jesus, help me know which opportunities are from you and how I can move forward in pursuit of them. Also help me to motivate my teens to get involved or at least learn about what I'm doing. Amen.

## Green-Eyed Monster
*Nicole O'Dell*

> But if you have bitter jealousy and selfish ambition in your hearts, do not boast and be false to the truth. This is not the wisdom that comes down from above, but is earthly, unspiritual, demonic.
> James 3:14-15, ESV

Jealousy is an insidious beast, and it can get its claws into anyone. I remember a time when I was so jealous of a particular friend I could hardly see straight. I thought she had it made. Like, really made. Perfect kids. Perfect husband. Perfect house. Perfect body. Perfect bank account. I knew in my head that nothing was ever exactly as it seemed, and I knew no one had the perfect life. But for some reason my head never explained that to my heart.

Jealousy is a powerful emotion since it's usually based on perceptions rather than on reality. I was jealous of what I thought I knew about my friend, so imagine my shock to learn that all those years she felt jealousy toward me. She was miserable in her marriage, struggled with horrible self-esteem issues, and ended up losing her home when the recession hit a few years back. She needed a friend, but I was too lost in my selfishness to see her pain.

As parents of teens we need to watch out for signs of jealousy in ourselves and in them so we can deal with them before they fester and cause damage. My feelings impeded the closeness of my relationship with my friend. They also kept me from being grateful for the blessings in my life and from fully appreciating my family because I was constantly comparing them to a nonexistent ideal.

Challenge: find out what seeds of jealousy might be sprouting in your teen or in yourself by asking the following questions.
- What do you think is most unfair about your life?
- Who do you think has the best life? How does that make you feel?
- If you could trade places with anyone, who would it be and why?

## → Connection Point

*Jesus, please shine a light on my jealous thoughts. Help me walk in gratitude and be an example to my teens. Give me wisdom to deal with any jealousy my teenagers might be feeling. Amen.*

## While the Sun Shines
### Nicole O'Dell

*In your anger do not sin: Do not let the sun go down while you are still angry, and do not give the devil a foothold. Eph. 4:26, 27 ESV*

I'm a parent of teenagers. I get angry. How about you? When was the last time you were angry? I'll tell you mine if you tell me yours...

It was just about a week ago, actually. It was a school holiday, but I still had to work. I came home several hours later to find the entire family home, where they'd been all day. *Lying around. Doing nothing. Assuming I'd come home and take care of everything like always.* So I jumped in and started my cleaning tornado, slamming drawers and huffing around the house to make sure everyone knew they'd blown it.

Now, let's break that down a bit.

Was I wrong for feeling like they should have seen what needed to be done and pitched in a little? Maybe not wrong for wanting help, but expecting teens to see the mess and take care of it without being asked might have been a bit much.

Was I wrong for feeling taken advantage of? No... if that *was* how they really felt, but maybe I jumped to conclusions about their motives. Was I wrong for being mad about having to rush around and take care of it myself? I certainly wasn't wrong for cleaning up, but in my fury, I didn't give them a chance to fix it.

The problems in the situation were too-high expectations, wrong assumptions, and passive-aggressive bitterness. Sin. My anger caused me to sin, so I had to fix it right away. Before the night ended. Before the sun went down.

How about you? In what areas of your parent/teen relationship has anger driven a wedge? That wedge is division, which is sinful if it's not repaired. Don't let another day go by without addressing it openly and praying for God's healing.

### → Connection Point

*Dear God, please forgive me for my anger. Help me see where my relationship with my teenager is fractured and then please give me the means to make it right. Help me never to let the sun go down on my anger again. Amen.*

Powerline365

# Christians and Therapy
### Nicole O'Dell

*For lack of guidance a nation falls, but victory is won through many advisers... Prov. 11:14, NIV*

Christian parents of troubled teens often wrestle with the question of whether or not it's wise or even okay to seek counseling or therapy for their teenagers. They struggle with misplaced guilt over needing to look outside their home and their faith to find the help they need. And their teens often rebel at the idea of talking to a stranger about whatever is going on with them.

But God gave us lots of resources to help us in our parenting. Scripture. Prayer. Fellowship. And the wise counsel of others. There are some times when there's no other option and it's the best, most loving parenting move you could make to enroll in a counseling or therapy situation. Signs that it might be time include:

- Sudden and serious changes in mood and/or behavior.
- A trauma or a major life-altering event.
- Sadness, depression, or anxiety that impedes normal function.
- Attitudes or behavior that have a damaging effect on the family.

Once you've identified the need for help, start with a medical doctor who can ensure there are no underlying physical problems. Hormonal changes and many other very real physical issues can cause emotional struggles. Treating these first might not eradicate the problem, but it can help get things started.

From that point, whether you do individual therapy, family therapy, group meetings, or a combination of those, be sure that your faith is the pivotal part of your treatment. You want to make sure that anyone who is advising your teen is doing so within the framework of Christ.

## → Connection Point

*Father, I'm worried about my kids. Please don't let me miss something important going on inside my teenagers. Open my eyes and reveal whatever I need to know, and then please help me seek the right resources in dealing with it. Amen.*

## Distractions
### Tim Hageland

*Yet a time is coming and has now come when the true worshipers will worship the Father in the Spirit and in truth, for they are the kind of worshipers the Father seeks. John 4:23, NIV*

Worship is not a form of entertainment on a Sunday morning. It is not the hype that many teens seek from their church experience. It is simply praise. It is the thankfulness that bubbles up from the depths of our souls that becomes a song on our lips. Music was created only to carry the presence of God, and it is worship that opens and softens our hearts to receive the Word of God.

Many times teens begin to close off to God. They withhold true worship by pulling back, getting busy with other things in the church, sitting in the seat whispering with their friends, or worse, messing with their cell phones.

If you have fallen for the deception that you just need to get them to church so God can move on their hearts to worship, I ask you to reconsider. Parents, as a worship leader, I can promise you that your teens are missing out. Set standards for conduct in a church service even if it means taking possession of the phone upon arrival. Encourage participation in all aspects—worship, teaching, giving. And be an example your teens can look to. They're watching.

It's much more than a song. It's the song of the heart. It's the connection to our heavenly Father. I pray that you will not only worship and bless the Lord on Sunday morning but that you will experience a deepening connection with your teenagers as you engage in worship together.

## → Connection Point

*Spirit of God, call my teens into your presence. Make them passionate for you with hearts that long to worship. Help me set expectations for conduct in church, but more than that, let them desire to draw near to you. Amen.*

Powerline365

# The Blame Game
## Nicole O'Dell

*For all have sinned and fall short of the glory of God. Rom. 3:23, NIV*

Many parents come to me in pain about the challenges their teenagers are forcing on the family. These parents often feel like it's a reflection on them or a sign of God's displeasure. Have you ever felt that way? Do you deal with parenting guilt?

Let me first say that your teens have free will, and most have no problem exercising it despite your very best parenting efforts. On top of that, they need to walk their own journey to discover God's will for their lives. Sometimes that means making mistakes. Big ones, even. Sure, we want to shield them from the consequences of their choices, but that's not always in their best interest. So, when they choose to go another way, there's no blame.

If you continue to worry that your teen's behavior is your fault, ask yourself these questions:
- Have I been a praying parent, surrendered to God's lead?
- Have I done the best I can, taking a new direction when necessary?
- Have I admitted my own failures and sought forgiveness?

If you are regularly (not perfectly) doing those three things, then you're securely on the right path and you should show yourself grace. Much grace. If, however, you can't answer yes, you might want to consider what needs to changes so you can.

But even if you manage to go all those things just right, that doesn't change the fact that your teenager has free will. Let the challenges you face as you parent your teens send you to your knees. Let them draw you closer to the Father.

## → Connection Point

*Dear Jesus, please forgive me for making it about me. Help me be an extension of you, reaching my teen in and among all the troubles of life, even the teen-inflicted ones. Amen.*

# 224

## Silver Lining
*Nicole O'Dell*

*And we know that in all things God works for the good of those who love him, who have been called according to his purpose.*
Rom. 8:28, NIV

Yesterday's devotion was about enduring the challenges our teenagers inflict on us and our families. Today I want to follow up with some thoughts about how those sorts of hard times are not only things we have to suffer through, but how they can also be a blessing.

The first thing I think of when I go through tough times (okay, maybe the second or third thing) is how it might bless or reach others in the future. Take, for example, a teen pregnancy. Your son comes home and tells you his girlfriend is pregnant. How do you react? Do you weep and wail or hide away in your bedroom for nine months? Do you gossip about the girl and her family? Do you take the blame upon yourself? Those reactions are all about you and your anger or disappointment. They do nothing to bless others or point them to Jesus.

What if you reacted differently? "Son, this is going to be tough, but it's nothing Jesus won't walk through with us. Let's pray together." That reaction will lead the way to more kind words and loving actions. When others see the grace with which you handled your challenge they will be able to identify the presence of Jesus throughout the hardship. When you've weathered a storm and remained submitted to God, He'll get the glory for seeing you through, and He'll be able to use you through it.

Surrendering to God makes it about Him, not about us or our teens. The more I'm able to live that truth in my life, the more the anger and defensiveness fades away and humbleness and gratefulness rise to the surface. It will do the same for you as, through the process of testing, you are refined.

## → Connection Point

Jesus, my heart wants to protect my family from hard things, but I also want to be submitted to you and your plans for us. Help me let go so you can move in our lives. And, please, prepare me now with the ability to react well when or if the tough times come. Amen.

## Tithing Teens
*Nicole O'Dell*

*I am the Lord All-Powerful, and I challenge you to put me to the test. Bring the entire ten percent into the storehouse, so there will be food in my house. Then I will open the windows of heaven and flood you with blessing after blessing. Mal. 3:10, CEV*

How early should you start teaching your teens to give to God? We've talked a bit about budgeting, but what about tithing? I must state the obvious here and say that if you're not a tither, you're going to have a very hard time convincing your teens to let go of the first 10% of their money. They will hold onto their cash as tightly as you cling to yours. It's what they know. So, before you embark on this life lesson with your teens, consider ordering your own financial priorities.

Why does God ask for a tithe when He can do anything He wants to anyway? It's for the same reason that you ask your teenagers to do their homework before they watch TV or finish their chores before they go out with friends. It's about priorities and obedience, and it's symbolic of surrender.

God owns it all. Everything that comes into our hands passes through His first. Handing back the first 10 percent is our way of showing gratefulness for His provision and faith in His continued blessings. If we are unable to let go of that money, it says a lot about our trust in God.

If your teenager is reluctant to start tithing, don't fret. Pray with your teen that God would soften hearts and open the floodgates of generosity. Let them hear you say those words. They will have an impact. I did that with my working sixteen-year old. It took one conversation and one prayer. The next week at church, she was to be in the nursery and not in the service. She handed me an envelope. "Will you put this in the offering for me?" I smiled and nodded as tears filled my eyes. A new generations of givers who will taste and see that the Lord is good.

## → Connection Point

*Father, thank you for your continued blessings in our lives. Would you give me the words to say to help spark a giving spirit in my teens? Let them commit to the priority of tithing and giving. Amen.*

## It's Addicting
### Laura L. Smith

*The wrong desires that come into your life aren't anything new and different...You can trust God to keep the temptation from becoming so strong that you can't stand up against it. 1 Cor. 10:13, NLT*

Do you check your email or your Bible first thing in the morning? Have you ever been late to a meeting or a game because you had to swing by Starbucks? Ever missed a family meal for work or a workout? Do you rearrange schedules to catch your favorite show? Ever splurged on a new sweater then marched right past the Salvation Army bell ringer outside the entrance of the mall?

Don't get me wrong. God invented coffee beans and made us creative. God gave humans intellect to design Smartphones. And we should absolutely take care of our bodies and be responsible at work. I love shopping as much as the next person. There's absolutely nothing wrong with enjoying life's pleasures.

In fact, those are great things. But when we put these pleasures ahead of God or family, we've crossed the line. When we catch ourselves, we need ask, "Am I putting my desires ahead of my relationship with my teens or ahead of Jesus?" If our actions indicate that we are, it's time to make some adjustments. Secondly, we need to ask, "What does this behavior speak to my teens?"

We worry about serious addictions like drugs, alcohol, sex, gambling. And those are all extremely dangerous and need attention. But Webster says addiction is an unusually great interest in something, or a need to do or have something. Are we paying enough attention to the subtle addictions that steer our teens and us further away from Christ and closer to worldly desires and standards?

If not, it's time for an alignment. Work with your teens to set healthy priorities and pray 1 Corinthians 10:13 as a reminder that God will never give them a temptation so strong they can't resist it.

## → Connection Point

*Dear Jesus, please help me keep you front and center despite all of the tempting distractions in this world. Thank you for the things I enjoy, but also help me prioritize them behind you and behind the needs of my family. Amen.*

## Bulletproof Vest
### Nicole O'Dell

*I have said these things to you, that in me you may have peace. In the world you will have tribulation. But take heart; I have overcome the world. John 16:33, ESV*

When a police officer wakes up in the morning and puts on a bulletproof vest before he goes to work it's because he realizes he faces some kind of danger. It's potential danger; it's not guaranteed. Yet he protects what's most important to him. His heart.

As Christians we're warned that our danger is a guarantee. Our enemy is out to get us, and we will face temptation and danger all of our lives as we serve Jesus. And even more so as we raise our teenagers to serve Him.

Knowing that you're stepping into battle everyday, what's keeping you from putting on that bulletproof vest before you face the challenges that are guaranteed to come? Studying the Word, prayer, worship, and communication. Those are some of the components of the strongest kind of protection. They are the means God has given us to know Him best and to fight the enemy. You can read more about the armor God has given us in Ephesians chapter six.

Think it through each morning and put on that bulletproof vest. Pray that armor of protection over yourself, your home, and your teenagers as they enter the world. Walk gingerly and guarded, but be confident knowing that the protection God is giving you is firmly in place and held tight by the Holy Spirit.

## → Connection Point

*Father, would you put your hands of protection on my entire family? Guard and protect us and give us the confidence to boldly go into the world and serve you. Let us not be unwise but assured. Amen.*

## Prayer Requests
### Nicole O'Dell

*Is anyone among you suffering? Let him pray. Is anyone cheerful? Let him sing praise. Is anyone among you sick? Let him call for the elders of the church, and let them pray over him, anointing him with oil in the name of the Lord. James 5:13-14, ESV*

This is a challenge. In fact, I'm taking it myself right this minute.

Okay, I'm back. Now it's your turn. If your teenager has a cell phone pick up your phone and send this text: How can I pray for you today?

You will accomplish so many things by asking that question by text. First of all, there's no pressure because you're not staring your teenager down. They aren't feeling self-conscious or nervous about answering because they feel protected by the privacy the phone offers. It's the same as when they talk to their friends, much more open and comfortable by text because of that sense of anonymity.

Secondly, you'll learn so much about what's going on with your teenagers by their answers. What do they ask you to pray about? Are they worried about school? Is there a problem in a relationship? Are they nervous about an upcoming audition or tryout of some kind? You'll get insight you might not get otherwise.

Finally, you'll be showing your teenagers you're thinking of them even when they're not around. You're concerned about their needs and are eager to bring them to the Lord in prayer. It's such an easy step to ask that simple question, but it accomplishes so much.

## → Connection Point

*Lord, be with my teenagers today, and help me see and understand the things that concern them. Fear, pain, regret... expose it so we can come to you in prayer to find healing and restoration. Amen.*

## Steal the Show
*Nicole O'Dell*

*But we have this treasure in earthen vessels, so that the surpassing greatness of the power will be of God and not from ourselves.*
*2 Cor. 4:7, NASB*

Are you a Toby Mac fan? I love his song that talks about putting on a performance. He's singing about the lights, the activity, the action, and even his talent, but he's saying, "Lord, it's all yours. Take over. Steal the show. Give the people what they want. Use me as a vessel."

What if we approached our parenting in the same way?

Rather than crumbling under our perceived failures or trudging through the day in defeat, what if we rose each morning with hands-in-the-air abandon to whatever God wants to do through us? We can purpose to continue putting one foot in front of the other as we follow His lead. But instead of feeling the pressure of self-judgment, we can simply move as vessels of the Lord.

Tomorrow, even before you get out of bed, pray: "I'm excited to see what you're going to do through me today. Steal the show from me; take the spotlight off of me. Anything can happen, and I can't wait to see what it is."

Can you see the shift in attitude? If we clothed ourselves with that kind of anticipation and release, the freedom we'd feel and the exhilaration that would take over our every move would be palpable. Our teenagers would notice a change. They'd feel less pressure, and we'd feel free.

Let go. Let go of the burdens you place on yourself and the expectations you have for yourself and your teenagers. Let Jesus steal the show and work through you on a moment-by-moment basis. Stand back and watch what He does.

## → Connection Point

*Lord, take over. Take the microphone from my hands, and fill my mouth with your words. Take the steps from my feet, and move me in your path. Take the work from my hands, and busy me with the work you would have me do. Steal my show. Amen.*

## Balancing Act
### Jill Hart

*Train up a child in the way he should go, and when he is old he will not depart from it. Prov. 22:6, KJV*

Because I run a website focusing on working from home, I often get asked how I balance work, marriage, and children. Trust me. It's not always easy. I've found that I need to be consistently re-assessing how I'm doing in different areas of my life.

Every few months I need to stop and take stock of what's changing in my life, what I need to change, and how I'm doing in the different areas that need to be re-focused. As my children grow and mature, their needs change. As my husband and I add years to our marriage, our needs as a couple grow and change as well.

So, I make it a point to take time regularly to ask myself questions like:

*What areas am I doing well in?*
*What areas am I weak in right now?*
*Where do I need to be more intentional?*

As I reflected on these questions not long ago, it struck me that my weakest area at the moment was in praying for my children. I determined to "beef up" this aspect of my parenting and shared this desire with a few friends. One sweet friend shared with me that she had purchased a Wide Margin Bible and was reading through it and praying passages for one of her children. She journals bits of Scripture and prayers throughout the Bible in the margins. At the end of the year she will purchase another Bible and do the same for her other child. What a great idea and an incredible way to impact your child's life.

Take a moment this week to reflect on how the balance in your life currently looks. Are there areas where you can improve? What steps will you take to keep a more even balance?

### → Connection Point

*Dear God, please open my eyes to the areas in my life where change is needed. Help me to be a more balanced and more intentional parent. Show me how I can find balance and if there are things that I need to do, or things that I need to let go of, in my life. Amen.*

# 231

Powerline365

## Parenting Partners
*Nicole O'Dell*

*Therefore a man shall leave his father and his mother and hold fast to his wife, and they shall become one flesh. Gen. 2:24, ESV*

We've already talked to single parents a bit, but today I want to address those of you who are parenting in a partnership. Whether you're a mom or dad, you are blessed to be parenting in joint effort with someone else who loves your teens. So, let's take a little inventory, and find out how your team is functioning.

- When is the last time you compared notes about how your teenagers are doing?
- When is the last time you considered new strategies for reaching your teenagers in a new and more powerful way together?
- When did you last sit with your teenager to talk about your relationship?
- When is the last time you prayed together for you teenager and for yourselves as parents?

Your answers to those questions will give you insight into how your partnership is functioning. This is a great time to remember that God joined you together, and He has a plan for you both on this parenting journey. His desire is that you work well together and serve Him as you parent your teenagers.

If your partner isn't on the same page as you spiritually, this may feel like a heavy burden. But God called you to behave in a certain manner in your marriage regardless of your spouse's actions. It's very important that you act in obedience to God as an example to your unbelieving or spiritually weaker partner. In fact, it's one of the best ways to draw them closer to Jesus.

## → Connection Point

*Dear God, I surrender my marriage to you. Please use us in a stronger way to parent our teenagers effectively. Bring us together spiritually and emotionally, and with united purpose. Amen.*

## Conflict Question
### Nicole O'Dell

*Let all bitterness and wrath and anger and clamor and slander be put away from you, along with all malice. Be kind to one another, tenderhearted, forgiving one another, as God in Christ forgave you.*
*Eph. 4:31-32, ESV*

Our teenagers will have enemies. There will be people who come against them at school and others who will wrong them as they walk through their whole lives. Enemies are inevitable, and false accusations are so hard to face. And it's difficult to know the right thing to do in the face of injustice and malice. So how do we teach our teenagers to respond to hurt inflicted by others?

Well, revenge is never the right answer. We need to model conflict-resolution skills that don't involve making the other person pay for their actions. Getting revenge doesn't satisfy the need we have for resolution. It might feel good for a moment, but that feeling will quickly fade and leave shame in its wake. Only God can right the wrongs in a fulfilling and permanent way. Plus, holding onto anger and resentment turns into bitterness, which fuels the rage in our hearts.

God has redeemed us. He's paid the price for all of the injustices that will be done against us, and by doing so, He allowed a huge injustice to be done to Himself. He stood in our place and paid the price for the wrongs we commit, so now we need not act as judge and jury, doling out punishments to everyone who wrongs us.

His kindness and grace were never intended to be gifts we hid away just for ourselves. They should be shared. Do you teach your teenagers to be an extension of God's love and grace even to those who hurt them? Ask your teens to name their enemies, and then challenge them to commit a good deed toward those people. It's an amazing experience that will draw you all closer to God's heart.

## → Connection Point

*Lord, this is a tough one. In order to teach my teenagers to love like this, I have to practice it myself. Help me be a forgiving person who shows grace and mercy to those who hurt me. And then help me guide my teenager to do the same. Amen.*

## Patience is a Virtue
### Nicole O'Dell

*But they that wait upon the LORD shall renew their strength; they shall mount up with wings as eagles; they shall run, and not be weary; and they shall walk, and not faint. Isaiah 40:31, KJV*

Waiting is hard. It's especially difficult when we're anxiously waiting for something that we believe is good. A change, an answer to prayer, or some need we believe God should want to meet. It's hard to trust that His timing is not always our timing when it seems like our best interests are so clear.

Why wouldn't a loving Father want to give us (and our teens) everything?

But the renewing of our strength comes as we wait in His presence. It's only when we're there that we fully surrender our needs to Him. Impatient waiting is actively withholding that surrender, but true patience is the act of letting go. It's absolute faith in God's provision and in His timing.

In what areas of your parenting do you need to practice more patience? Maybe you're worried your teenager isn't coming along in certain areas the way you would like, and things are moving slowly in the realms of education or spiritual growth. Maybe you feel your relationship has hit a rocky patch. Or maybe you're facing a tangible need with your teens like an illness or some other kind of hardship. If any of those things are weighing heavily on you and shaking your faith foundation, ask yourself if it's your timetable you're looking to or His? Are you open to being patient, even when it doesn't make sense to you?

## → Connection Point

*Father, help me be actively patient. I want to surrender my fears and expectations to you as I parent my teenagers. Please corral my energy and desires into something You can use for your glory. And please show me where I need to let go of my expectations and embrace your will. Amen.*

## Hyper-sexual Culture
### Mary DeMuth

*They have become callous and have given themselves up to sensuality, greedy to practice every kind of impurity. Eph. 4:19, ESV*

The truth: We live in an over-sexualized culture. It's difficult enough for adults to handle the way society is filled with sexuality at every turn. There is nothing sacred or private about sex or the human body. Our teenagers are assaulted with sexual images, ideas, and challenges on a daily basis. The battle for purity is one of the toughest ones we can fight as parents.

So, what's a parent of teens to do?

There are several things we need to focus on as we fight four our teenager's purity and a godly sense of sexuality. First of all, we need to praise the non-physical greatness in our kids. Focus on their unique qualities, talents, goodness...let physical traits and beauty be secondary to everything else.

We also need to watch movies and shows alongside our kids. When there are sexual references we need to talk about them. Pause the movie/show and ask, "What lesson does this teach us, and how does God feel about what we just saw or heard?"

And parents, please be affectionate with your spouse. The best defense of this sexualized culture is a marriage full of love and joy and harmony. Real love involves sacrifice and commitment, not sex appeal. It enjoys physical intimacy and isn't afraid to celebrate it.

Ultimately you are the first line of defense against the sex-focused attacks your teenagers will constantly face. The preparation you do with your teens, the open communication you have, and the time you spend on your knees will make all the difference.

## → Connection Point

*Dear God, help my teenagers draw the truth about themselves from what you say about them, not from any physical or sexual traits, and let them see others the way you do. Let their spirits cry out against the lies that drive a hyper-sexed view of this world. Keep them pure in word, thought, and deed. Amen.*

## Blind Spots
### Nicole O'Dell

> And Jesus answered and said unto him, "What wilt thou that I should do unto thee?" The blind man said unto him, "Lord, that I might receive my sight." And Jesus said unto him, "Go thy way; thy faith hath made thee whole." And immediately he received his sight, and followed Jesus in the way. Mark 10: 51-52, KJV

What you see is not always what you get. And it's seldom the full truth. In raising teenagers, I think we often parent with a huge blind spot... or many of them. That block can be in place because of something that happened to us in our past or a fear of something that hasn't happened yet. Regardless of why they're there, we need to identify those blind spots and see what truths we can uncover.

James 1:5 says that if we lack wisdom, all we have to do is ask God, and He'll give it to us. We don't have to try to navigate around our blind spots, we can ask the Holy Spirit to help us see through them. It's really a faith issue. Moving forward even when we can't see the whole picture is an act of trusting that God can see and that He'll guide us through.

What spots are blocking the full truth in your life and your parenting relationship with your teens right now? Consider asking your teenager what you're not seeing. Something like this, "What is going on with you or what issue are you dealing with that I'm missing?" Then, once those blind spots are out of the way, you can boldly parent your teens in complete acceptance. Which is what they so desperately want.

## → Connection Point

*Lord, that wisdom you promised, I'd like a huge dose of it, please? Help me see clearly the truth about my teenagers' inner thoughts and outward actions, and show me all I need to do to parent them effectively. Remove my blind spots and open my eyes. Amen.*

# 236

## Facebook Families
*Nicole O'Dell*

*We do not dare to classify or compare ourselves with some who commend themselves. When they measure themselves by themselves and compare themselves with themselves, they are not wise.*
*2 Cor. 10-12, NIV*

You probably know with this devotion is going to be about. You've heard it all before. But I have to take a moment to draw attention to the social media craze and how it affects our families. I'm a huge fan of social media. I'm the first one to run to Facebook or Twitter to share some news or post a pic of my kids or talk about what I make for dinner. In fact, I'm probably annoying. But one thing I try very hard to do is to keep my focus off of what other people look like, what they have, and what they're doing. I am on my own journey with my family and my kids and even with myself. When I get in the comparison game, no good comes of it.

Don't worry about where your friends went on vacation last year. Don't worry about the bathing suit photos your neighbor just posted. Don't measure your kids' success against the college scholarships your friend's teenager just received. Live your best for yourself, for God, and for your teenagers. Make wise decisions and good health choices for yourself because it's what God is called you to do, not because you want to fit in some stereotype your friends post on Facebook. Celebrate your teens' successes—academic and personal—for who they are and the effort they put in.

Furthermore, none of it is real. It may be a zoomed-in pixel of reality, but it's not the full picture. Be authentic and realistic, and keep your eyes on your own paper, so to speak.

## → Connection Point

*Jesus, would you give me insight into the truth and remind me that people only share the best of themselves on social media? Help me to stay out of the comparison trap, and free me and my children from the expectations it creates. Amen.*

## Clothed in Holiness
### Nicole O'Dell

*Put on your new nature, created to be like God--truly righteous and holy. Eph. 4:24, NLT*

Imagine if you set an infant in the middle of the room and didn't touch it, feed it, move it, change it. What would happen? It would grow for a very little while until it ran out of physical resources. And then it would die. Completely dependent, that infant needs to be nurtured and cared for so it can thrive.

That's how we are when it comes to our spiritual growth. We are dependent beings, and we need to be nurtured by the Holy Spirit. We need to be fed by the Word of God, bathed in truth, and encouraged through mentorship. All of those things work together to make us fit for our long journey as Christians and as parents.

Real growth and spiritual maturity comes about when we turn over our ways to the Lord. That means surrendering the way we react in a tough situation. The way we hand out discipline to our kids. The way we set boundaries and enforce them. All of those things, cloaked in holiness, will bring about far better results than actions motivated by fear or self-righteousness.

Your spiritual growth can't happen on its own. You can't raise yourself and neither can your teens. So consider your own needs when it comes to your spiritual growth. Make them a daily priority so you can be strengthened for the journey and have the reserves you need to pour into the lives of your teenagers.

## → Connection Point

*Father, in what ways am I expecting my spiritual growth to happen automatically? Please guide me and raise me up to a place of maturity where I can parent my teenagers effectively in your name. Thank you, Jesus. Amen.*

## Love and Shepherd's Pie
*Sara Goff*

*I pray that God, the source of hope, will fill you completely with joy and peace because you trust in him. Rom. 15:13, NLT*

Have you seen that commercial where a middle-aged man is up late at night baking a shepherd's pie? Then it cuts to a park the same night where a pretty teenage girl argues with her boyfriend. He throws up his hands and steps away from her. The message is clear: their relationship is over.

The girl waits at a deserted bus stop. She's sobbing. Back in the kitchen, the middle-aged man takes his shepherd's pie out of the oven. The girl bursts through the front door, sees her father holding the hot pie, and smiles through her tears. He looks burdened with worry and full of questions, but says nothing as he lovingly watches her eat.

Is this realistic? Another teen might channel all her pain into a pointed glare that says you've got to be kidding! I can't eat now! before charging into her bedroom to collect the pieces of her broken heart. But that's okay, too.

The commercial is long over, but the father's quiet outpouring of love for his daughter stays with me. Perhaps his instincts are right. He offers love and shepherd's pie, and then stands back, much like God's unobtrusive presence in our lives. He gives us the space to love and learn, and the courage to love again.

### → Connection Point

*God, show me how to be an example of your love. As I rush from one responsibility to the next, help me not lose sight of the details: a home-cooked meal, a loving gaze, the understanding that comes with silence. I know I can't safeguard my teens from heartache, but with your guidance I can give them time to learn from their mistakes and provide a safe place to heal. Thank you for your shepherd's pie. Amen.*

Powerline365

# Overwhelmed or Under-Prayed?
### Nicole O'Dell

*Try your best to live quietly, to mind your own business, and to work hard, just as we taught you to do. Then you will be respected by people who are not followers of the Lord, and you won't have to depend on anyone. I Thess. 4:11 CEV*

How does that scripture read to you? I wonder if you see what I see. "Live in peace, worry about your own stuff, have a strong work ethic – serve on the prom committee, chair the parent organization, run the band fundraiser, teach a Sunday School class, write a book..." Wait a second. All that's not in there?

Now before you start quitting everything, I'm not saying any of those commitments are bad. Some are quite worthy. However with a life like that, there's little time for your relationship with God.

It's easy to feel overwhelmed and pressured. Sit before Jesus, let Him order your steps, adjust your priorities, and pat you on the back. When you blow through life like a tornado, the wake of destruction isn't good for anyone – not your teens or yourself.

Mom or Dad, if your mantra is, "I'm overwhelmed," followed by a familiar litany of duties and deadlines, perhaps you haven't fully sought the will of God regarding your schedule. His desire isn't to overwhelm you. He recommends you do your very best to lead a quiet, simple life, while working hard at the things you need to do. Find peace releasing yourself from self-imposed requirements, surrendering to God's will.

The lives we lead before our teens are likely the lives they will construct for themselves. If success looks like a rat race while they're teens, they'll jump right into it later. Strive to live as an example of peace and order, not chaos.

How can you make changes that will bring calm to your home?

## → Connection Point

*Heavenly Father, please help me to order my life in a way that I bring peace to those around me and gain the respect of those who don't know you. Show me where you would have me place my energy and urgency, then help me to teach my teenagers why it's so important. Amen.*

## Truth and Consequences
### Nicole O'Dell

*Then David confessed to Nathan, "I have sinned against the Lord." Nathan replied, "Yes, but the Lord has forgiven you, and you won't die for this sin. Nevertheless, because you have shown utter contempt for the word of the Lord by doing this, your child will die." 2 Sam. 12:13-14 NLT*

Teenagers often have a disproportionate view of their own guilt. They confess when they're caught, apologize when there's no way out of it, and take the blame when there's no one else to point to. But regardless of the circuitous route that leads to repentance, we need to be ready with forgiveness just like God readily offers it to us.

However, in parenting those teens, we need to differentiate forgiveness from consequences. As in the scripture above, David confessed and repented of his horrific sin, and God forgave him. But that forgiveness didn't mean God took away all consequences. In fact, David's son died as a result of his sin.

It's not easy for us to allow consequences that we know will cause our teenagers pain or hardship, but just as God knew what David needed to learn, we must be open to those kinds of hard lessons in our teens' lives.

Disobedience requires repentance, which leads to forgiveness, but it doesn't always erase consequences. Be prepared to teach your teenagers that there are natural results to their sin, and avoid the temptation to swoop in with the rescue. Letting them learn from their mistakes is sometimes the most loving thing you can do.

## → Connection Point

*Jesus, give me eyes to see when you're at work amidst the hard times in my teenagers' lives. Let them face the consequences of their actions and learn their lessons well. Help me be strong enough to keep my hands off until you've done your work in them. Amen.*

## In the Bubble
### Nicole O'Dell

*Since he himself has gone through suffering and testing, he is able to help us when we are being tested. Heb. 2:18, ESV*

Sometimes I think Christian families can live in a somewhat of a bubble. We get very nervous about little things our teenagers might encounter and we panic about the big stuff. We set firm boundaries and control their exposure. Which is a good thing. But can it go too far? If we keep such tight reins on our kids, how do they handle pressure and testing?

Now, don't get me wrong. I'm not advocating that we take our hands off and let them find their own way. Not a chance. *Cue the groans from my teenagers.* We definitely need to set standards, enforce boundaries, and prepare our teens to stand up against the temptations that will come.

But while we're doing all of that, we need to look around. Look at the kids your teenagers go to school with. Teens from abusive backgrounds, homeless teenagers, teenagers who go home every day to parents addicted to drugs or alcohol. Teenagers who don't even have someone to come home to at the end of the day, or who will pray for them. Shake those blinders loose and take in the full picture.

Your teenagers are blessed to have parents who care enough to take the time to read a devotional strictly about parenting them. They are blessed to have YOU. And God will bless you for your passionate pursuit of their hearts. So don't give up when times get tough. When attitudes strike and tensions are high, just look outside the bubble. You'll surely find that it's not so bad.

## → Connection Point

*Jesus, help me be thankful in all things when it comes to my teenagers. Remind me of the blessings in our lives. Show me that tensions and relationship struggles are temporary, and help me handle them with grace and love. Amen.*

## The Purpose of Life
*Valerie Comer*

*The LORD has told you what is good, and this is what he requires of you: to do what is right, to love mercy, and to walk humbly with your God. Micah 6:8, NLT*

If you've got high-schoolers who want to follow Jesus, you'll know one of the biggest questions is, "What does God want me to do with my life?" It's so daunting to navigate the possibilities! Do you remember? How did you decide between nursing, teaching, engineering, pastoring, plumbing, or whatever options seemed appealing at the time? How did you know which career God was leading you into? How did you know which person to marry, which city to live in, which house to buy?

Your teen will make many of these choices in the next ten years, but they're not the primary decisions. God has told us how to live, and, if we choose to follow those guidelines in prayer, I believe the rest will fall into place.

Matthew 6:33 reminds us to seek God first, and the necessities of life will be taken care of. Micah 6:8 tells us to do what is right, to love mercy, and to walk humbly with God. It's a balance between remembering that salvation comes, not from our own goodness, but from Jesus' sacrifice... and reaching for a Christ-like attitude in all we do.

So when your teen asks what he or she should pursue for a career, teach a focus on doing what is right and seeking God as a foundation. When we see the world through God's eyes, He provides the details as we need them.

## → Connection Point

*Father God, help me to teach my teens to seek you before they seek their future. I believe the most important plan you have for them is to become more like Jesus. Amen.*

## Everything's "Sexy"
*Nicole O'Dell*

*Flee from sexual immorality. Every other sin a person commits is outside the body, but the sexually immoral person sins against his own body. I Cor. 6:18, NASV*

The words sex and sexuality used to make even adults blush. Now middle-schoolers describe people as sexy and hot. And Victoria hasn't kept any secrets for years now. In our sex-saturated culture, nothing is left to the imagination and everything from a song on the radio to a creative entrée at a restaurant is sexy.

It's an uphill battle to redefine sex as beautiful and mysterious and spiritual. And in a society that assumes teens will be sexual, parents are faced with more challenges than ever to inspire their teens to pursue purity. But there's one benefit Christian parents have gained in that cultural shift: the freedom to discuss issues surrounding sexuality openly and honestly, maybe even without blushing.

Purity is one of the scariest issues to face as a parent because many of us know firsthand how fleeting it is and how impossible it is to fully restore once it's been given away. Teenage sexual relationships lead down a path of pain and destroyed hearts—not to mention devastated self-esteem and, eventually, mangled marriages. No good ever comes out of two 16-year-olds taking on the adult responsibilities that come with a sexual relationship.

But what can you do to stop it? Teens are going to fall in love and lose themselves in passionate moments of desire beyond their control. Aren't they? You're powerless in the battle, so why fight it? You should just pray hard, hold on, and hope no one gets pregnant. Right?

Wrong. Parents, protecting our teen's purity shouldn't be a hope or a goal. It's not just the best-case scenario. It is a charge that we have as parents to guard our kids and protect them from the evil one who seeks to destroy their hearts and minds.

## → Connection Point

*Lord, please impart your strength and wisdom to me so I can parent my teenagers so they will treasure their purity and protect their bodies. Help me build them up with godly self-esteem so they are ready and willing to say no and mean it. Amen.*

# Hunger and Thirst
## Nicole O'Dell

*Be diligent to present yourself approved to God, a worker who does not need to be ashamed, rightly dividing the word of truth.*
*2 Tim. 2:15, NKJV*

"There are times when solitude is better than society, and silence is wiser than speech. We should be better Christians if we were alone, waiting upon God, and gathering through meditation on His word spiritual strength for labor in His service. We ought to muse upon the things of God, because we thus get the real nutriment out of them. Why is it that some Christians, although they hear many sermons, make but slow it advances in the divine life? Because they neglect their closets, and do not thoughtfully meditate on God's word." ~Charles Spurgeon

Everything we do is scheduled. Entertainment, free time, work, meals, time with friends, time with kids, even time with God. When is the last time you simply sat and pondered a truth you found in the word of God? When is the last time you questioned something you were taught and then dug deep to find out the truth?

It's time to get back to a firm foundation of scripture by diving in. Power into a deeper personal relationship with Jesus, and you will parent more effectively. Plus, it's the best way to instill a hunger in your teenagers for God's word.

Gather your study materials, or use a great online resource like blueletterbible.org which lets you easily study scripture in the original languages. Pick a favorite passage and get started. Let the Holy Spirit reveal the layers of truth within each nugget.

## → Connection Point

*Father, please fill my heart with hunger for your word. Help me learn new things that invigorate my faith so I can pass that desire onto my teenagers. Amen.*

## Lost that Loving Feeling
### Nicole O'Dell

*Love is patient, love is kind. It does not envy, it does not boast, it is not proud. I Cor. 13:4, NIV*

Okay, think back. Remember the joy you felt when that newborn baby was placed in your hands. Remember when you inhaled that sweet infant smell and vowed to cherish that baby forever. Think back to when your adorable toddler was learning how to walk, and your preschooler was learning new things and exploring interests.

I know those images are a far cry from the moody, irrational, sometimes downright annoying teenager you have living in your house. And I know it's hard to imagine that the adult-sized human you're arguing with was once that sweet little child who finger-painted you a masterpiece every day. Believe me, they can't believe it either. They are just as stunned at how quickly their lives are changing and are dismayed at the changes they see in themselves and in your relationship.

As parents, it's hard to let them grow up. It's difficult to let our expectations fall in line with their changes. But if we could somehow rekindle that wonderment we once had with our newborn babies, we would be much more gracious parents. During those early years, if someone had told you that parenting your child would be tough, you wouldn't have believed it, because your love was so deep and so strong.

Parental love is ferociously unconditional beneath the surface... under a lot of worldly things that get in the way. Let's shed all that and get back to that loving feeling.

## → Connection Point

*Dear God, help me remember the love I had when I held my baby in my arms. Remind me of those feelings when the moments get heated and my anger threatens to overflow. Help me control my reactions and give way to grace. Amen.*

# 246

## Forgiving Yourself
*Claire Culwell*

*Therefore, if anyone is in Christ, he is a new creation. The old has passed away; behold, the new has come. All this is from God, who through Christ reconciled us to himself and gave us the ministry of reconciliation. 2 Cor. 5:17-18, ESV*

Twenty-six years ago my biological mother had an abortion when she was pregnant with me. The abortion took the life of my twin but, miraculously, I survived. I know I survived so I could share love, forgiveness, and truth with people who have chosen abortion. I hold no anger toward my biological mother; I know she was doing what she had been told and thought was best. I also know that hurtful words and painful memories can keep parents who have experienced an abortion from healing and receiving forgiveness.

Whether you were the mother or the father, if you were involved in an abortion, you've likely suffered under the weight of guilt and regret. Though you can't get back the years of freedom you've missed, you can prepare for the years ahead. God doesn't want you to live in bondage.

When I think of my biological mother (whom I have met) I think of the girl who was lied to, who was treated with disrespect by doctors who saw a dollar sign on her forehead, and my heart aches for her. I wish I could have hugged her on the day of her abortion, held her hand and comforted her. I wish there were people who had told her she could do it... but the past is the past. When I see her face in a picture, I see Jesus. He created her flawlessly! He, too, has forgiven her. In fact, He no longer keeps record of the past. I see change, and I see hope. Ultimately, I see a gift from God!

A past abortion, or any kind of sin, can steal your life and render you helpless as you parent your teens through their mistakes. You have to make the decision to overcome and be free of the bondage. You can forgive yourself, and remember that you have already been forgiven.

## → Connection Point

*Dear Lord, please help me release my guilt and draw closer to you. Help me receive the forgiveness you've given me, and please help me forgive myself so I can be an effective parent. Amen.*

## Something Special
### Nicole O'Dell

*The words of Amos, one of the shepherds of Tekoa—the vision he saw concerning Israel two years before the earthquake...*
*Amos 1:1, NIV*

Parent, are you feeling a bit insignificant these days? As your teenagers get older and the end is in sight, are you worried about who you'll be when they depart your home? It's easy to feel lost in such a big and busy world, especially when your teens are facing or embarking on so many new adventures. When life gets repetitive, parenting becomes rote, and everything seems to be about them, it's normal to wonder how to really make a difference to the big picture.

Think of Amos. He was nothing special. He wasn't a powerful leader. He didn't have a big education or a prominent job. He was a lowly shepherd, just doing his work. Yet God singled him out to carry forth a vision of what was coming to Israel.

What is God looking for in those He uses? He most often chooses ordinary people to do extraordinary things. He looks for the humble and makes the insignificant into something great because it's only then He will get the credit.

It's more important to Him that you're willing to do His work and be used by Him than it is for you to have grand influence or power in the world. He will grant you the influence you need to accomplish your tasks once you surrender your willing heart. This applies to your parenting, to your personal life, and to your spiritual journey.

Be like Amos. Remain hard at work in your field, doing all that God has placed before you. He will single you out for His purposes in His timing.

### → Connection Point

*Lord please help me to be humble. Remind me that my days of doing important things are not over; in fact they've just begun. Give me a glimpse into your will for my future and help me stay the course even when it's unglamorous. Amen.*

## Sacrifice of Praise
### Nicole O'Dell

*Let us continually offer the sacrifice of praise to God.*
*Heb. 13:15, NLT*

Oh, it's easy to praise God when the bank account is cushy, your job's going well, the kid's received good report cards, everyone is healthy... But what about when the tables get turned? What happens when layoffs are looming and the bank account is draining? What if you get a poor medical report at work or a phone call from the school with bad news? It's not as easy to praise God during those times. That's when praise is truly a sacrifice. And even if you can't praise Him for it, you can praise Him through it.

Parenting is full of ups and downs. One day everything is fine, and the future looks bright. The next day you find yourself wondering how your teenager will ever get into college or hold down a job. Your heart overflows with love and admiration one day, and then you're filled with disappointment the next. It's a rollercoaster of changing emotions that leave us confused.

There is one thing that never changes. God is able. He is able to see you through the hard times. He is able to walk you through the great times. He is able to give you and your teenagers everything. He is able to do all that you can ever ask or imagine. Praise Him for who He is and put your trust in Him to work out the best outcome to any situation.

When you embrace the fullness of His character and abilities, praise doesn't feel so much like a sacrifice.

## → Connection Point

*Father God, thank you for all you've done in our lives and for all you will do. I praise you for your mighty works and trust that you desire the best for us. Help me look up with praise on my lips when tough times weigh me down. Amen.*

## 249

Powerline365

## Satan's Playground
*Nicole O'Dell*

*For all that do these things are an abomination unto the LORD: and because of these abominations the LORD thy God doth drive them out from before thee. Deut. 18:12, KJV*

The occult and all of its reachings have a big effect on our teenagers. From seemingly innocuous things like horoscopes all the way to evil practices like séances and Ouija boards, teens are exposed to the trappings of the occult on a daily basis. TV shows about witches and sorcery, horror movies about demonic activity and demon possession and more are heralded as entertainment. All of that has the effect of desensitizing our teenagers and ourselves from the evils that exist.

And this is nothing new. God has been warning His people about witchcraft and dark spiritual forces since the beginning. He warns His people to have nothing to do with any of those things. In fact, He calls all those activities and the people who perform them an abomination.

Everything related to the occult is an extension of Satan's works. Those practices are deceptive and deceitful and only for the purpose of turning eyes off of Jesus and turning hearts to a dependency on evil. He wants nothing more than to get his proverbial claws into your teenagers.

Parents, be wise about what you allow into your home and what doors you open into the spirit world. Don't dabble. Don't play around. And don't you be fooled or let your teenagers be fooled into thinking any of it is harmless fun. God has fully revealed His truth and His will for us in His word and through His Holy Spirit. There is no reason to go digging around in Satan's playground.

If you see signs that your teenager is exploring dark things, put an end to it immediately. Set rules for your home that forbids access to anything ungodly, and pray together to break any spiritual connections.

## → Connection Point

*Lord, please place your protection around my household. Guard my teenager's heart and mind from everything evil. Protect my family from Satan's touch in every way. Amen.*

## Charm is Deceitful
### Nicole O'Dell

*Charm is deceptive, and beauty is fleeting; but a woman who fears the LORD is to be praised. Prov. 31:30, NIV*

Women, this one's for you. The Proverbs 31 woman is not my favorite person. She does everything right! If she were on Facebook she would have, like, 12,000 friends. She would have perfect pictures of her children. She'd have a thriving business selling knitted scarves and hats that she couldn't keep in stock. She'd have a Pinterest page beyond compare.

But, I can honestly say that I've come to terms with my relationship with this Proverbs 31 woman. I've realized that it's not about being the most energetic, or the most determined, or even the smartest. It's not about being the most generous, or the prettiest, or the most patient. Being a Proverbs 31 woman is about setting your eyes on Jesus Christ, pursuing His will for your life with reckless abandon, and staying the course when things get tough. Everything else falls into place when those steps are ordered. When you are in pursuit of His will for you, the rest get sorted out along the way.

Living as Proverbs 31 woman is an act of worship that comes from deep within. It's not an out-of-reach status and it isn't reserved only for the perfect moms. Be there, in each moment, and recklessly pursue the path God has for you as a woman and as a parent. And if you're raising daughters, teach them to chase after God's will and to live in pursuit of Him just as the Proverbs 31 woman does.

## → Connection Point

*Jesus, thank you for the example of the Proverbs 31 woman. Help me not to hold myself to standards that I can't reach that only leave me feeling inadequate, but show me what You have for me, and help me strive for those traits and pursuits as growth, not as condemnation. Amen.*

## In Process
### Nicole O'Dell

*Now faith is the substance of things hoped for, the evidence of things not seen. Heb. 11:1, NKJV*

I don't know about you, but I was not born perfect. Babies are precious and sweet, but from day one they have physical, mental, and emotional imperfections. When I first looked at my beautiful baby girl, Emily, I was excited to see she had a cute little dimple in one of her cheeks! But the doctor swooped in and let me know that a dimple is actually a birth defect. Thanks for raining on my parade, Doc!

But like Emily's beautifully imperfect dimple, we all have flaws and issues we're dealing with, though most of them are not as cute. We are in process, which means that we will succeed, and we will fail. All of those experiences become the learning tools that shape us into who we will be as parents. And also who our teenagers will be as they grow.

Parents, don't discard your imperfections as an automatic negative. They're part of your journey and proof of your growth. They are part of the work God places in your path to make you stronger. But let your teenagers work out their own journey, too. We've talked about this a lot in this book, but I think it bears repeating. Your teens' journey is not a carbon-copy of your own. Your teens are different than you in every way, and with that comes different imperfections that lead to different struggles. Sometimes you just have to let them happen.

## → Connection Point

*Lord, give me the wisdom to see how you've already used my flaws to teach me. Help me the same potential in my teenager, so I can let those things be used by You rather than always see them as a negative. Help me be patient on this journey. Amen.*

# 252

## Labels
### Nicole O'Dell

*See what great love the Father has lavished on us, that we should be called children of God! And that is what we are! I John 3:1, NIV*

Have you ever taken an online IQ test? You answer a bunch of riddle-type questions, and it gives you a range of scores that somehow determines your intelligence quotient. A long time ago, I took it one step further and actually took a legitimate IQ test at a library. I had to pay a fee and sit for a couple of hours to hear the number that ranked my intelligence.

For what? What did that result give me? How did it change my behavior or my outlook? Maybe if the number had been higher I'd have become a molecular biologist instead of an author. Maybe if it had been lower I'd be working at a fast food restaurant because I'd have thought myself unable to reach for more. The power of a label.

I have a good friend who often speaks of the inability to read your own label from inside the bottle. We can't see what others see in us because we're in the middle of being. We feel our stress. We suffer our disappointments. We know about the incomplete items on the to-do lists in our heads. But others don't see those things when they look at us. Neither does God. So why do we allow them to define us?

Labels can be dangerous and they can stifle God's movement in our lives. Guard against letting your teenager suffocate within the confines of an identity that steers choices and limits exposure or experience. The only label that offers a limitless horizon is the one that says "child of God." With that title affixed, there is no limit.

## → Connection Point

*Dear Jesus, help my teenager embrace the only title that matters: child of the Living God. Help me discourage those limiting labels that suffocate vision and purpose. Amen.*

## Denying its Power
### Nicole O'Dell

*They will act religious, but they will reject the power that could make them godly. Stay away from people like that! 2 Tim. 3:5, ESV*

Many parents struggle over what to do about their teenager's faith walk. These are some of the things I hear:

"They're old enough to make a choice for themselves. I believe God will show them the way."

"They need to explore what's out there so they can make a firm commitment of their own."

"They have a right to question."

While those statements may be technically true, I would apply them to a college graduate, not a high-school student. We have our kids within our grasp for so short a time, and our job is to teach and guide them the best we can. Why would we pull the coach out in the last quarter of the big game?

Our enemy wants nothing more than to remove our hands from the religious training of our teens. If we do, then they are open to his lies. These days, those lies come in the form of pseudo-faiths that teach it's important to be a good person — and it is. They teach that it's righteous to help those in need — and it is. They teach honesty, morality, and general goodness. Those things are great. But they're all a form of godliness, and they deny the power of the blood of Jesus Christ and His life-giving salvation.

In this most important stage of your parenting, keep your kids in a Bible-thumping, Jesus-preaching, salvation-teaching church. Equip your teens with the tools to face the future. One day you'll have to let go, but today is not that day.

## → Connection Point

*Dear Jesus, thank you for speaking to me about this. Please forgive me for the times I've let the world water down your message and deny your power. You are mighty to save, and I will parent my teens from that message alone. Amen.*

## It's My Job
### Brenda L. Yoder, MA

*The wise woman builds her house, but with her own hands the foolish one tears hers down. Prov. 14:1, NLT*

Raising teen boys has challenges. With three of my own, I don't shy away from talking to them about hard stuff, like girls, relationships, and sex.

My sixteen-year old broke up with his first girlfriend several months ago, and recently has been informally pursuing a new girl. As he developed this new friendship, there were things I needed to talk with him about before he considered another relationship.

I carefully planned my approach and took many small opportunities to talk to him, rather than to bombard him in one conversation. Over time, I asked important questions and reminded him of relationship values and commitments he'd made as a young man walking with Christ. I finally got the, "Mom, I know!" response. His tone said enough already.

Taking his cue, I replied with a smile. "I'm just doing my job."

He didn't say anything more, in fact, not a single protest. I smiled and patted his back. My work, for the moment, was done.

I've learned teens want us to do our jobs of training, coaching, and building them to be the men and women we expect them to be. The men and women God calls them to be. Even though they might push back, they still expect it and want it.

When my teens push back and resist my efforts, my typical response is: It's my job! I've learned that though they resist, they find comfort and appreciate that I care enough to stay the course even when they think they don't need reminders. It's not always easy, but it's worth it to just do your job.

## → Connection Point

*Father, remind me not to tear down my house by giving up on the tasks that come with the job of raising my teens. Give me strength, wisdom, and encouragement to parent them until they walk out the door as adults. Thank you for not making me do this alone. Thank you for always being with me. Amen.*

Powerline365

## Drum Major
*Nicole O'Dell*

*And though a man might prevail against one who is alone, two will withstand him—a threefold cord is not quickly broken. Ecc. 4:12, ESV*

"If you want something done right, do it yourself!" Have you grumbled those words brushing past your spouse? As a sometimes-recovering type-A, control freak – I get it. I'm a "lead, follow, or get out of the way" person. Secretly, I much prefer "get out of the way" because I can get it done better, faster, and easier alone. Ugh. Just saying that sickens me. Oh, how I wish it wasn't the truth.

I'm learning (notice, I didn't say I've mastered) that God gave us unique gifts and qualities. If we discount the strengths of another, especially our spouses, we always come up short.

Once my husband created a ruckus while I was on the phone with a friend. He'd taught the triplets how to be musical instruments. One was a flute, one a trombone, and one a drum. My husband tooted the trumpet, of course. They marched around the house, having a parade. A very loud parade! "Just once I wish he'd be serious and play quietly with them," I lamented to my friend.

"Well, you've got that part covered. Can you imagine if they never got to be a parade?" Then she said, "Just once, I'd trade a lifetime of serious to see my husband play parade with my kids. Just once."

Okay, that did it. I hung up the phone and joined the parade.

Partnering with a spouse creates strength in unity. Ecclesiastes 4:12 explains two people, working together, can withstand the wilds, but, even more so those who partner with God in a three-strand cord.

God joins two people in the covenant bond of marriage because they complete each other with their strengths and gifts. When not partnered together, those two people work with half of the strengths God gave them. Rather than battling partnership, why not join your spouse as one unit, with God, to take on the world?

## → Connection Point

*Father, please forgive me for my controlling ways, for dismissing the partnership of my spouse, and doing too many things in my own strength. Help me to join together with my spouse and you as a three-strand cord that cannot be easily broken. Amen.*

## Emotional Overdrive
### Nicole O'Dell

*I therefore, a prisoner for the Lord, urge you to walk in a manner worthy of the calling to which you have been called, with all humility and gentleness, with patience, bearing with one another in love, eager to maintain the unity of the Spirit in the bond of peace.*
*Eph. 4:1-3, ESV*

I just had a conversation with a mom who is struggling with attitude. Her teenager went, seemingly overnight, from being a sweet, helpful girl who reached out to others, to being withdrawn and angry and bitter in the home. This mom is also frustrated that her daughter can be sullen and moody and angry to her, but when someone else comes along, she snaps right out of it and pastes on a big grin as though nothing was wrong.

First of all, our teens learned that from us. How many times have our kids seen us frustrated and discouraged at mounds of laundry, stacks of bills, or their own bad behavior, but then answer the phone with a bright smile and happy tone? They learned how to express their moods from us, and they learned how to turn off that expression on a moment's notice from us. So consider that as you deal with your frustration about your teenagers' ever-changing moods.

Secondly, it's safest to hurt the ones you trust. Your teenagers trust you. They know you will love them and make everything okay in the end. But they are in a hormonal tug-of-war that is a daily struggle for them. So as they work through their moods, you can expect to receive the brunt of it. That doesn't mean you should allow bad behavior or disrespect, but you should definitely consider the root of it and show some grace, which speaks loudest of all.

## → Connection Point

*Dear Lord, please help my teenagers navigate their own emotions with peace. Bring balance to their thinking. As their emotions bubble to the surface, help me show grace in my response. Amen.*

## Not My Will
### Nicole O'Dell

*Jesus walked on a little way. Then he knelt down on the ground and prayed, "Father, if it is possible, don't let this happen to me! Father, you can do anything. Don't make me suffer by having me drink from this cup. But do what you want, and not what I want."*
Mark 14:35-36, CEV

It's hard enough to deal with the daily issues that come with parenting. Schedules. Carpools. Attitudes. Did I mention attitudes?

Then there's the big stuff. The circumstances like when I had to tell my parents that I was going to be an unmarried, teen mom. Tragedies like my horrible car accident, when I fell asleep at the wheel, and my parents received a call from a police officer. Did those things happen because my parents had some kind of sin in their lives or hadn't prayed hard enough?

Some people do believe that righteousness determines whether or not prayers will be answered. Their viewpoint: it's unconfessed sin that causes hardship in life. But that ignores the truth of a God-man who prayed with deep conviction, but did not receive the answer He most desired.

Jesus had a cup of suffering to drink. He asked His Father to take it from Him, if possible – of course that'd be the preferred option. But no matter what, Jesus was going to do the will of His Father, even if He didn't like it.

As parents we can pray boldly and trust mightily, but in the end it's about surrender. We surrender our plans for our kids, our ideals for our families, and our will for the future. We pray in obedience; we surrender in obedience. Blessed be the name of the Lord.

## → Connection Point

*No matter what comes into the lives of my teenagers, I'll say, blessed be your name, Oh Lord. I'll come to you with my fears and trust in you. Help me to surrender to you, and please, always work in my kids' lives according to your perfect will. Amen.*

## Epic-Fail Parent
### Cara Putman

*My grace is sufficient for you, for my power is made perfect in weakness. Therefore I will boast all the more gladly about my weaknesses, so that Christ's power may rest on me. 2 Cor. 12:9, NIV*

Somewhere along the way someone (Nicole O'Dell) decided I was the do-it-all momma. That's fine. It was kind of flattering, until I realized how tiny that little pedestal actually is. So I find myself standing here, looking every which way... where's the staircase that spirals down from the pedestal to the reality of mothering? No matter how good some days are, others can be called nothing but (to quote my nine year-old boy) an epic-fail. Not a teeny fail. Not a small fail. Completely, utterly epic fails.

I make mistakes. I have oversights. I forget things or just plain do them wrong. And there are days when patience must have skedaddled across the ocean over night. It is nowhere to be found. Not under my bed. Not in my car. Not in my bathroom where the lock mysteriously pops out because a child has used a Lego to lever it open. Instead of being a patient, long-suffering picture of a mother who would put June Cleaver to shame, I've lost my patience so many times, I'm ready to turn in my mothering card and ask for a transfer to Siberia before I do serious harm to my children's development.

I cling to the reality that the only perfect one is Christ. While He created me with a longing for perfection, He also knows I am woefully un-up-to the task. Instead, He promises His strength is made perfect in my weakness. His strength is perfect. My weakness allows that strength to show through. Thank You, Jesus!

How about you? Do you feel like an epic-fail parent? Are you ready to fall into the arms of Jesus and let Him fill in the gaps for you? He can't wait.

### → Connection Point

*Father, please keep me from doing anything that will become a stumbling block in my children's relationship with you. Use my less-than-perfect moments as teaching opportunities for me and for them. Amen.*

## Fish Food
### Nicole O'Dell

*But my people did not listen to my voice; Israel would not submit to me. So I gave them over to their stubborn hearts, to follow their own counsels. Psalm 81:11-12, ESV*

As a parent I see my own battles of will going in three directions. There's the obvious one with my teenagers. I want what's best for them; they want what they believe is best for them... I'm right. Okay not always, but therein you see the struggle. The second kind of war is the one I have within myself. How much of what I want for my teenagers is based on their needs and their personalities and God's calling in their lives? And how much of it is based on my own past and fears of the future?

The third kind of struggle is the one between myself and God. He and I have had some pretty heated discussions over what's best. I don't know why this is such a tough one to learn, but it definitely is. How prideful it is to think God needs my opinion!

Jonah was a prophet who also had a stubborn streak and entered into many battles with God. He wanted to do things his own way, and God saw it differently. When Jonah finally resisted for the last time and fled the scene, God turned him into whale food. During the time Jonah spent in the belly of that great fish, he had time to ponder his stubbornness. Only when he agreed to do things God's way was he restored to use. The detour happened, but God's plan remained the same. He wanted to use Jonah for His purposes, but first He had to break Jonah's will.

Where are you and continuum? Are you resisting? Or maybe you're in the belly of the fish, kind of in a holding pattern, waiting for your will to break so God can really use you. Is it time to let go of control and surrender your will to the one who feeds the big fish?

## → Connection Point

*Father, please forgive me for my stubbornness. Help me surrender to your will and step aside when you're at work. Amen.*

# 260

Powerline365

## Glory to God
### Nicole O'Dell

*Sing to the LORD, all the earth; Proclaim good tidings of His salvation from day to day. Tell of His glory among the nations, His wonderful deeds among all the peoples. For great is the LORD, and greatly to be praised; He also is to be feared above all gods. I Chron. 16:23-24, NASB*

All of creation exists for one purpose. God wants to receive glory in everything we do and in who we are. But if you are like me, and I suspect you are, when you look around at your surroundings, they don't always seem very glorifying to a sovereign, Almighty God. How can piles of laundry, inch-thick dust, and a sink full of dishes bring any kind of honor to Him? In fact, when I consider the way I would like to bless Him with my life, I sometimes feel discouraged by the trappings of this world that require so much time and attention.

In order to bring glory to God, we must first understand just what that means. It happens when we praise Him with our words and when we honor Him through obedience. It happens when we point people to Jesus through our example. It happens when we raise a new generation of Christ-followers. And it also happens when we are faithful with the little things in our lives.

God isn't looking for beauty in our earthly dwellings. He isn't asking for perfection in our worldly pursuits. He wants hearts and lives and families surrendered to Him in faithful obedience and in constant pursuit of relationship with Him. That is what glorifies Him.

May your thought life be pure and lead to righteous actions. May the words that come from your mouth speak life to others. And may your deeds be as an example of His faithfulness in your life. To God be the glory.

## → Connection Point

As a parent, Lord, may I always obey you and bring honor to your name through what I say and do. May I glorify you throughout all my life. Amen.

Powerline365

# 261

## Choose Yes
### Nicole O'Dell

*May the God of hope fill you with all joy and peace in believing, so that by the power of the Holy Spirit you may abound in hope.*
*Rom. 15:13, NIV*

My grandmother was a tough, old bird. She was especially harsh with my grandfather who truly didn't deserve it. All he wanted to do was make her happy, but it was impossibility. She loved him; she just wasn't a very happy person. Every year she made lots of Christmas cookies and fudge and treats for the holidays. He looked forward to that so much, and the day she made the peanut butter fudge was always his favorite. He would do everything he could to try and sneak pieces and sometimes she even him taste it. But this one year she was feeling especially salty and told him he had to wait until Christmas. She took her trays of cookies, covered them with layers of foil, and hid them in a back bedroom.

Well, my grandpa didn't try to sneak any. He just let it go. And then he had an aneurysm and died two days later.

Those baked goods were a devastating reminder to my grandma that she'd never let him have any. She had to live with the knowledge that her harsh ways had left him wanting during his final days. She agonized over withholding the joy of those treats from him. She'd had the opportunity to be gracious and kind and loving, maybe even share a midnight snack with him. Instead she had to live with the knowledge that her last treatment of him was bitter, harsh and selfish.

Parents, I'm not saying that we have to walk around afraid that our teenagers are going to die. But we should consider the possibility that things can change in a moment. Choose joy. Choose life. Choose peace... whenever you can.

Life is short; the time you have to impact your teens is dwindling. Default to the yes instead of the no, and always choose the smile.

## → Connection Point

*Father, please help me better control my mood. Help me to automatically pull from the joy in my heart instead of my angst and pain and sadness. And help me to always remember what it is that makes me joyful so I can share it with my kids. Amen.*

# The Little Engine
## Nicole O'Dell

*Since we have the same spirit of faith according to what has been written, 'I believed, and so I spoke,' we also believe, and so we also speak. 2 Cor. 4:13, ESV*

We all know that story of the little train that got himself up the mountain fueled by the power of positive thinking. I think I can. I think I can. That little story has been motivating people for generations.

But I would like you to reconsider that outlook. I see two problems with the little engine's thinking.

"I think…" Where's the assurance? Where's the confidence? "I think" holds some hope, sure, but it also harbors doubt. There's room for failure.

"I can…" Who can? With this mentality you are solely relying on yourself. On what you can do in your own steam, with nothing but the power you have at your fingertips.

The possibility of success and the limitations of my own power isn't enough for me, and I assume it isn't good enough for you either. Nor should it be. We have access to the blessed assurance that Jesus has everything under control and is working His will in our lives. We have been promised the best possible outcome and should be confident that He'll complete the work He began in us and in our kids. We are promised that He will answer our prayers and meet our needs according to His will.

We don't have to think; we can know.

Also, not only will He make it work, but He asks us to lay down the reins and let Him do it for us. He wants us to rely on Him and let Him shoulder our burden. So change your thinking from, "I think I can," to, "I know He will."

## → Connection Point

*Lord, thank you for being at work and my life. Thank you for the way you move in our lives and empower me as a parent. Help me to trust in you when the obstacles look insurmountable. I know you can. Amen.*

## The Name of Jesus
### Nicole O'Dell

*If you declare with your mouth, "Jesus is Lord," and believe in your heart that God raised him from the dead, you will be saved.*
*Rom. 10:9, NIV*

How often is the name of Jesus spoken in your home?

This is a tragedy in our society, and if we are careful, our teenagers will be living in a world that doesn't say His name.

People believe in God, but if you ask them about Jesus they have no answer. People claim to be religious and go to church, until they have to talk about Jesus. Satan is done a great job of making it uncomfortable for most people to speak Jesus. Why? Because it's alive. It's light, and darkness does all it can to crowd out the light.

Many names claim divine power. False prophets, leaders, and others who claim to be of God will come. But it's the name of Jesus that makes the demons tremble. It's in His name that we have power over the enemy. It's in His name that we are saved.

Fill your lives and your home with the spoken name of Jesus Christ. Don't tuck it away because of societal misgivings. If people are uncomfortable when you say Jesus, they really need Him. Pray for them — don't hide the truth from them.

Unless something changes, this generation of teenagers is poised to enter an adulthood where Jesus is forbidden in every public place. Fill their lives with such regular use of His name that they crave it. As it rolls off their tongues, they will learn that it speaks healing and life.

Find ways to use the name of Jesus in your home today and every day.

## → Connection Point

*Jesus, please forgive me for letting other things crowd out your name. Help me to share your name everywhere I go and with everyone I speak to. Help my teenagers experience the gift found only in the name of Jesus. Amen.*

## Obedience is a Privilege
### Nicole O'Dell

*For this is the love of God, that we keep his commandments. And his commandments are not burdensome. I John 5:3, ESV*

Many Christians wrestle against the word obedience. They want to wave the flag of freedom and grace and forget that there are standards and rules of conduct for Christians that we must consider it and even adhere to it. Must? Or else what?

Ooh, I know. I'm turning over some age-old debates with that question. But I don't think it has to be that way. Yes, grace is the foundational element of the Christian experience. Without God's grace in our lives, there would be no hope. But as an extension of the grace and forgiveness and mercy He has shown to us, we are privileged to walk with Him in obedience.

It's much like parenting your teenagers. As a parent, you show grace on a daily basis. Your love extends beyond bad attitudes and missed curfews and bad behavior. Your mercy dictates that you provide food, shelter, clothing... and much more. Even when grades are slipping and chores aren't completed. Further, it's mercy that allows you the grace to reach your arms out and pull your teenager in for a hug when they've messed up big-time.

But even with your grace and mercy solidly in place in the relationship you have with your teenagers, you still ask for obedience. Your teenager is privileged to walk the journey you've laid out in your home. They thrive within your boundaries and excel within your rules. If you look at it that way, then obeying God really is a right not a duty. It's a natural response to His blessings and proof of our faith in His ways.

How do you need to practice obedience in your walk with Christ and your parenting relationship with your teenagers?

## → Connection Point

*Lord, please show me where I need to work on being more obedient to you and what I need to strengthen in my walk with you. Help me to sacrifice the things I want to do and embrace the things you've called me to do. Amen.*

## First Love
### Nicole O'Dell

*Go, show your love to your wife again, though she is loved by another man and is an adulteress. Love her as the LORD loves the Israelites. Hosea 3:1, NIV*

This one is for you married folks. How is it possible to have a strong marriage in this day when divorce is celebrated more frequently than a double-digit anniversary? And even if we manage to keep it together, how can we have a healthy and vibrant marriage amid the busyness of life and the distractions that hit us on all sides? Fighting, disappointments, misplaced expectations, financial stress, intimacy problems, resentment, bitterness... All of those things are very real reasons that marriages fall apart on a daily basis. If you aren't careful, prayerful, and intentional about the nurturing of your marriage, it will become one of those statistics.

That verse above is a picture of misdirected allegiance. Many marriages break up not because of a physical affair, but because of attention and attachment that gets directed at other things. You can even leave your first love and abandon your marriage by placing your children first. When our spouses get the leftovers, if there are any, they feel like an afterthought and bitterness will begin to take root. But God calls us to become one in marriage.

Consider the last time you really showed your spouse true love. What did that look like? How did it feel to you? How did it feel to your spouse? How can you take steps toward healing any damage that may exist in your marriage? Consider that your teenagers are watching and creating their own view of marriage from what they see in you.

## → Connection Point

*Father, please forgive me for the ways I've abandoned my marriage. Help me to embrace it and surrender to you. Let my marriage be an example to my teenagers that they will always strive for loving godly relationship. Amen.*

## Coffee with a Friend
### Nicole O'Dell

*Don't be afraid, for I am with you. Don't be discouraged, for I am your God. I will strengthen you and help you. I will hold you up with my victorious right hand. Isaiah 41:10, NLT*

There is nothing like spending some time with a good friend. When I'm down, all I need is to sit with someone I care about and laugh. The camaraderie of shared experiences and the banter of comparing stories always pulls me out of my funk.

This may surprise you, but I am much more of an introvert than you think. It takes a lot for me to make plans and keep them. I like being home. I like being with my family and having time to myself to think and time to study, read, and pray... and write.

But I have this other side to me that craves companionship and thrives on togetherness. When I feed that piece of my soul, I grow and I heal. A relationship with God is much the same. Often, it's seemingly easier to just continue in the daily grind and complete the tasks at hand than spend time seeking relationship with Him. Forgetting that God is near is easy because we can't see Him, so we have to experience His presence in our lives on purpose. We have to be intentional about it.

When we don't do this, we risk making bad choices in every area of our lives, including our parenting. We and our families benefit most when we are in solid relationship with God, seeking His will, and sitting at His feet. Remember, if you feel distanced from God, He hasn't pulled away from you. He's right there with you like He's always been. It is you who pulled away from Him. So be intentional today about staying near.

## → Connection Point

*Father, remind me of your presence in my life. Help me to seek you first when I am in need and in want. Give me a hunger for more relationship with you. Amen.*

# Blew It
## Nicole O'Dell

*If we confess our sins to him, he is faithful and just to forgive us our sins and to cleanse us from all wickedness. 1 John 1:9, NLT*

Have you ever blown it as a parent? Maybe the better question would be: have you blown it today as a parent? We all mess up. We're human. I usually hope and pray that my bigger mess-ups are things my kids won't remember. I have said things before and then immediately prayed, "Oh, Lord, erase that from their memory."

Sin against God, wrong attitudes, or misplaced anger toward our teenagers. In all of those circumstances, confession is key. It's our responsibility as a follower of Christ and as a parent that we confess our wrongdoings so that we can find healing for ourselves. Our confession also gives the other person the opportunity to forgive. It opens the door to restoring relationships and learning from mistakes. But without confession, the wound festers and bitterness runs deep.

As a parent, continually examine your heart and your actions to ensure there's no unrevealed sin or damage taking place. When you recognize something you need to address, do it right away. Don't put it off until later; that time may never come. And when you're forgiven, accept that forgiveness and walk in it.

You will teach your teenager more through the example of your confession, accepting forgiveness, and walking in renewal than any verbal lesson you could spout.

## → Connection Point

*Jesus, please show me the areas of my heart that need to be renewed. Help me see the things I need to confess either to you or to my teenagers... or to anyone. Please give me the words to say and a heart that is pure as I confess. Amen.*

# 268

Powerline365

## What you Make
*Nicole O'Dell*

*Be very careful, then, how you live—not as unwise but as wise, making the most of every opportunity [make it count], because the days are evil. Therefore do not be foolish, but understand what the Lord's will is. Eph. 5:15-17, NIV*

Life is what you make it. Your relationships are only ever what you make of them. Even your relationship with God is the sum of what you put in and take out of it. Being a Christian means living for Christ, not for money, ambition, or any other worldly substitute. Jesus Christ should be the focus of our thoughts, words, and actions. Our reach should be for relationship and eternity.

However, we spend so much time and effort striving. We strive for things. We strive for position. We strive for perfection. And then when we have our share, we strive for more.

The apostle Paul was example of living for eternity. He understood the temporary nature of our human existence, and he lived in such a way that pointed others toward the cross and eternity with Christ. Paul said that for him to live was Christ, and to die was gain. In other words, the life he lived on this earth was only for the purpose of furthering the cause of Christ, and death only brought his reward that much sooner. He understood that he could get out of his life and his relationships what he put into them, and he chose to focus on the only things that would matter for all of eternity.

It's time to embrace that attitude at home, to put priorities in order, and focus most on the things that will last. How would refocusing change your parenting? How about your outlook on your teenagers? Think about some changes you can make and some ways you can impress on your teens the importance of living for eternity even now.

## → Connection Point

*Heavenly Father, please help me present a clear view of heaven. Help me raise my teenagers to have an eye on the prize and live each day for you, not for earthly gain. Let me be a model of temperance and grace, not of endless pursuit. Amen.*

## It's not Fair!
*Nicole O'Dell*

*For God made Christ, who never sinned, to be the offering for our sin, so that we could be made right with God through Christ.*
*1 Cor. 5:21 NTL*

It was like my brother and I were raised in two different homes. I had a strictly enforced curfew, but my brother didn't. "It's not fair!" Sometimes I had to stay home to do homework; my brother could go wherever he wanted. "It's not fair!" I had to clean the bathrooms on Saturday morning while my brother slept in. "It's not fair!"

Okay, lest you think my parents were brutally unfair, let's unpack that a bit. I had a curfew because I tested my boundaries every chance I got. My brother didn't have a curfew because he rarely stayed out late enough to require one. I was forced to stay home and work on homework because my grades were slipping as I placed socializing ahead of schoolwork. My brother could seemingly go anywhere because my parents desperately wanted him to make some friends. I had to get up on Saturday mornings to clean the bathrooms while my brother slept in, because he did the dishes all week while I was at swim practice. Wait a second. I had swim practice on Saturday mornings, too. Maybe I'm remembering the bathroom thing wrong.

See how that fairness thing works? It's often one-sided in a skewed, selfish light. Looking back, I can see my parents agonized over the disparity between my social life and my brother's. I understand some of their choices. But it's hard to see and accept it in the moment.

When your teenager bellows, "It's not fair!" use my story to paint a picture of the misperceived fairness. Better yet, use the story of Jesus in the scripture above, to show things may not always seem fair, but fairness isn't the goal of a parent. The goal is to point to growth and righteousness. It doesn't have to be fair.

## → Connection Point

*Jesus, thank you for walking such an unfair road out of love for us. Would you help me do what's right for my teenagers even though it may not seem fair? Help me explain my parenting choices without arguing and let my motives come across to my kids. Thank you. Amen.*

## Raising Teens the Joyful Way
### Sherri Wilson Johnson

*You make known to me the path of life; you will fill me with joy in your presence, with eternal pleasures at your right hand.*
*Psalm 16:11, NIV*

Screaming down a roller coaster, surfing the waves, skiing on the slopes, or sitting by the fire putting together a jigsaw puzzle... when the family is all peacefully together, anything is great. When you take the time to have a family outing, and your teens are agreeable with the adventure, you forget about most of your troubles. Too bad every day can't be like that.

Raising teens is hard. Your house erupts with emotions, and you don't even know what caused the eruption. As parents, we face emotional times ourselves. Times when we're exhausted, sick, lonely and overwhelmed. We have to drag our feet just to move one step forward. When you add the challenges of raising teens, sometimes it's almost unbearable.

The Lord desires for us to have joy — a deep-down, overpowering, soul-filling kind of joy. A joy that doesn't come from any possession, event or location. The joy to make it through the days that wear us out and drain every ounce of energy and patience from our bodies. He tells us that every day with Him is sweeter than the day before. All we have to do is ask Him to give it to us and trust that He will.

If you're having one of those times where you can barely function — where the call God has put on your life seems to be too much, lean on Him. Trust Him to pull you through this time and to give you back the joy for which you so long. After all, when you're raising teens, it takes a renewed strength and joy daily. In fact, parenting teens is what helps parents earn jewels in their crowns — if they survive the experience, that is. With the Lord's helps, you will.

## → Connection Point

*Dear Lord, will you help me be joyful with my teenager? Help me to look like you. Give me joy to get through the challenges we face. Help me to be a shining example to other parents who may be struggling, as well. Amen.*

## Flexible Priorities
*Nicole O'Dell*

*Everyone has heard about your obedience, so I am full of joy over you; but I want you to be wise about what is good, and innocent about what is evil. Rom. 16:19, NIV*

In the shuffling of a bunch of family get-togethers and outings, I had shifted a promise I made to my littles one too many times. I'd told them I would make a bowl of popcorn and sit with them on the couch and watch their favorite movie. Logan asked, "Without your computer?" Ouch! Yes, son, without my computer.

But with my oldest son home on leave and my brother in from Alabama, we had one activity after another, and movie time had gotten squeezed out repeatedly. It isn't only my computer that robs my kids of my attention, it's other people, plans, and priorities, too. None of those things are bad. I do good things for people with my computer. And time with family is always important. So where was the mistake? Some would say I shouldn't have made the promise if I couldn't keep it. Or that I should have kept my word no matter what.

But I think somewhere in the middle is the right thing. Kids need to learn flexibility. They need to learn they aren't always the priority; they need to learn to put others first. But we are also their best example of honesty and trustworthiness. So I used the frustration my little ones felt to teach them about choices by asking questions like:

- Did it frustrate you that it seemed like I broke my promise?
- What should Mom have done differently?
- How could you have responded differently?
- How can we make it better next time?

We have choices to make, and it's up to us to teach our teens to keep their word while being flexible enough to enable good prioritizing. In the end, my kids agreed that it was much better to spend time with family they rarely get to see than it was to hold me to a promise to sit in front of the television. Plus I gave them a dollar.

## → Connection Point

*Father of time, please help me prioritize the very best for myself and my family. Open my teenagers' eyes so they would learn how important it is to cling to the precious moments we have. Amen.*

## Feeling Guilty?
### Nicole O'Dell

*The child will not share the guilt of the parent, nor will the parent share the guilt of the child. Ezekiel 18:20b NIV*

My mother's face blanched as the news of my pregnancy sank in. After all, I was nineteen and unmarried. In fear of her reaction, I'd chosen the church sanctuary at the end of a church service to tell her. Maybe not my best choice, but I figured she wouldn't get too angry right after a worship service – connected to God and all those people around. Well, I was wrong. Of course.

In the days following my announcement my mom struggled with anger, but I also know feelings of guilt were in the mix. Thoughts like: Did I fail as a mom? What could I have done differently? Does God hold me accountable for my teenager's sin?

That last one is a heavy question, and one you might not have considered it if doesn't apply yet. But something could happen down the road, and I want you to be assured. God asks you to do your best as a parent. To lead and guide your children in the Word and live as an example of God's grace and righteousness as best you can. Our children are a reflection on us, especially when they are young. But God says we are each accountable for ourselves. Was the father held accountable for the choices of the Prodigal Son? No, he wasn't. He'd raised and tried to guide him, but ultimately he couldn't make the choices for him.

Being absolved of the guilt of your older teen's choices may be of little comfort when your heart aches at the mistakes, hardship, and pain your child self-inflicts. Allow the absence of fault to bring rest and comfort so you can pray in faith and peace.

## → Connection Point

*Heavenly Father, it's so hard to let go of control. It's so difficult to know I can't make all the choices for my kids. And to watch them make destructive choices — it grieves my heart like it does yours. Would you help me rest in your truth and feel the comfort of your loving arms? Would you help me trust in the promise you're always at work and never giving up? Please be with my teenagers, and guide them to good choices. Amen.*

## Take Inventory
### Nicole O'Dell

*So we must not grow weary in doing good, for in due time we will reap a harvest if we do not give up. Gal. 6:9 NIV*

Things can turn on a dime in the lives of our teenagers. We think everything is going well and something happens to upset the delicate balance of peaceful co-existence. Maybe there's a break-up and your teen sullenly nurses a broken heart. Maybe there's a falling out among friends and your teen spends too much time alone at home, moping. Or maybe hormones kicked in and it's the only explanation for a rotten attitude or sad mood.

Since things change so fast, take inventory regularly. Here are some questions to help determine if you're at a trouble spot.

- Does your teen worry about what peers think?
- Has there been a change in boyfriend or girlfriend status?
- Has your teen expressed concern in changing popularity?
- Is there a change in focus on trendy clothing?
- Any physical changes that may cause struggles? (Weight gain or loss, acne, braces, glasses, etc.)
- Could a change in eating habits signal eating disorders?
- Has your teen or pre-teen experienced bullying? (Hot Buttons: Bullying Edition has more help on this one.)

It's vital to take all of those changes or struggles seriously and lay them out in the open. Your teens will likely resist at first. It's uncomfortable, and they'd rather retreat into their thoughts... and their bedrooms... to deal with it alone. But this is when it's most important to press in. Keep at it. Show your teenagers you don't have a limit. You're not going to give up until you've connected. Eventually they'll know you're for real and they'll let you in.

## → Connection Point

*Heavenly Father, you know what's going on in the heart, mind, and life of my teen far better than I. Please give me your discernment when something is wrong and the wisdom to address it effectively. Help me break down the walls that rise up between my teen and I with consistent, loving, godly counsel that makes a difference. Amen.*

## Sacred Moments
*Brenda Yoder, MA*

*There is a time for everything. Ecc. 3:1a NIV*

"Hey mom, can we go?" My middle-schooler was dying to go to a Christian rock/rap concert during an already busy week. I couldn't add one more thing to my plate. But I remembered taking his older siblings to similar concerts at the same age. I knew what my answer would be, even though I was already exhausted.

Teens don't often ask for time with you. When they do, you need to take the opportunity. Most important conversations I've had with my teens have been in the car to or from activities we've gone to together...shopping, rock concerts, and weekend get-aways. During these midnight car-rides, we've talked about friendships, God, and sex. I've asked and have been asked personal questions that God gave supernatural answers to. It's during those times when I've been able to learn more about my children and help them understand me better.

I've learned moments when teens listen to you about significant topics usually don't happen around the dinner table. But the opportunities often occur — or would occur — during moments we let pass by because we're too busy.

The next time your teen asks to do something with you, don't miss the opportunity. And then take the reins. Don't be afraid to ask questions you may otherwise be afraid to ask. And be willing to answer their questions, too. You'll be surprised at the results.

## → Connection Point

*Lord Jesus, help us not to miss important moments you ordain with our teens. Equip us to be present with them and to have your ears and eyes for what their needs are. Thank you.*

Powerline365

# Praying for your Teens
### Nicole O'Dell

*Be assured that from the first day we heard of you, we haven't stopped praying for you, asking God to give you wise minds and spirits attuned to his will, and so acquire a thorough understanding of the ways in which God works. Col. 1:9, MSG*

Do you pray for your teenagers throughout the day? Do you imagine what their day is like and the types of challenges they encounter as they walk the halls at school or spend their free time? Do you pray they would feel God's presence? I'm actually surprised by the numbers of parents who admit they seldom actually pray for their kids during the day. They might say some bedtime prayers and name their kids on a list, but for many parents, there are no fervent prayers storming the throne room of Heaven on a regular basis.

One of my favorite movies, Facing the Giants, shows the character of Mr. Bridges walking along the corridor of the school, touching each locker as he prays for the student whose things are inside. Mr. Bridges knows the importance of regular warfare on behalf of our kids.

Our teens are pelted with temptations and pressures on a moment-by-moment basis. They deal with ungodly people and situations. They are pressured and often tempted to sin. At any given moment, they can go from being at ease to having a major temptation right in front of their faces. If we believe God's Word, then we need to be obedient to the call to prayer. We need to pray for our teenagers constantly.

You can pray for physical safety, for peace of mind, for spiritual protection, for strength to withstand temptation, and for a happy heart. You can pray your teens will be good leaders and good role models to their peers. You can pray they would learn more about Jesus every day. Lifting your teenagers up in prayer over the daily things of life is the best support you can offer.

## → Connection Point

*Father, please lead my teens in the paths of righteousness and help them to withstand temptation and peer pressure. Right now, wherever they are, would you make Your presence known to them? Amen.*

## Praying with your Teens
### Nicole O'Dell

*Confess [your] faults one to another, and pray one for another, that ye may be healed. The effectual fervent prayer of a righteous man availeth much. James 5:6, KJV*

I don't remember my parents praying with me very much even though we were a very committed Christian family. I remember praying over dinner sometimes, and I think my mom prayed with us when we were little. I also remember them talking about prayer, especially my mom, but I don't remember turning right to prayer if I got hurt or went into surgery unless the pastor was there to do it. It wasn't until I was a parent myself that I realized my kids would learn their prayer life from my example, and that I would have a much greater impact if I modeled surrender and faith through prayer.

Do your teenagers see you pray? Do they know that you retreat to a quiet place to get alone with Jesus and work out your fears and surrender your needs? If not, how will they know to do that for themselves?

Taking it one step further, are your teenagers used to you going into prayer when they express a need or a fear? Why not? Think of how many battles could be won if you surrendered to Jesus before they escalated to a conflict. Think of how many hours of conversation and worry could be handled with a joint prayer of faith. And think of the love your teenagers would feel as the sound of their name rolled off your tongue in prayer?

Praying individually with your teen is vital, but family prayer is another way to go to new depths. Pray together for safety, for the salvation of loved ones, for guidance in the unknown, and for deeper relationships with God and each other.

## → Connection Point

Jesus, please help me develop a stronger prayer life with my teens. Open their eyes to the value of prayer and give me the words to say to make a deep impact. Amen.

Powerline365

# Good Fences
### Nicole O'Dell

*Devote yourselves to prayer, being watchful and thankful.*
*Col. 4:2, NIV*

I often talk with parents who are worried about their teenagers' online activity. I thought it would be helpful if I shared some best practices for parenting today's data-driven teens. You would guard against danger in public places. It's even more important online where the dangers are global and anonymous.

**Monitor online activity.** Do an Internet search for instructions about how to view the history of use for your Internet browser, and then monitor your teens' search habits and traffic patterns. Savvy teens will know how to delete some or all of their Internet history, so you want to keep an eye out for that too.

**Check chat histories.** If your teen uses a chat program, you should check up on these logs, too. Again, it's possible to delete these histories, so it's best to check often and watch out for large gaps of time with no conversation. Let your teen know that if the histories are ever erased, Internet access is over for a while.

**Install filtering software** to block undesirable Web content. This is one safeguard against pornography, but it shouldn't replace open dialogue.

**Use reporting software** that tells you where your teens have been online. I let my teens know that they are submitting to those kinds of guards and checks if they use my Internet. They are free to stay offline if they don't want to be monitored.

**Communicate. Communicate. Communicate.** The key to all of these protective procedures is communication. Let your teens know what the rules are and why they're necessary. Communicate the consequences for broken rules and then stick with them. In the end you are looking out for their best interests and one day, I promise, they will thank you for it.

## → Connection Point

*Father, please protect my teenagers from the dangers that lurk online. Help them make good choices and interact with honesty and integrity. Give me wisdom to keep them safe. Amen.*

## Black Tie, Optional
### Nicole O'Dell

*But what things were gain to me, these I have counted loss for Christ... for whom I have suffered the loss of all things, and count them as rubbish, that I may gain Christ. Phil. 3:7-8, NKJV*

I don't know about you, but over my years as a parent of six kids, I've gotten fewer and fewer invitations embossed with those three elegant words: Black Tie, Optional. Life as a parent is a lot different than life as a single adult, or as a young married couple without kids. Parties have evolved (or devolved, depending on how you see it) from elegant, black-tie affairs, to pizza parties with dancing mice and then later to teenage bashes with blaring music. As parents of teens, we no longer host the parties; we do our best to stay hidden while we keep a careful eye on our young revelers. We no longer make toasts — instead we toast marshmallows over backyard bonfires.

And it's not just the details that have changed; the meaning has, too. Are these things we should lament or changes we should celebrate?  When I think back to my single days, I can barely remember the names of the people who were so important to me at that time. But think of the eternal impact we can have on our teenage guests-of-honor as we open our homes and our hearts to show them the love of Jesus.

If you're casting a longing look backward at a comparatively meaningless history, consider the future and let the weight of eternal glory win over the pull of the past. Press on to the high calling of Christ as you parent teenagers whose names you will never forget and whose friends need to see Jesus in you. Now that's a party.

## → Connection Point

*Jesus, I eagerly let go of the life I once had and embrace the joys of parenting teens. Let me be an extension of you in their eyes and allow me to have an impact of their friends. Grant me a full measure of your grace and wisdom as we celebrate their lives together. Amen.*

Powerline365

## In Good Company
*Nicole O'Dell*

*Do not be misled: "Bad company corrupts good character."*
*I Cor. 15:33, NIV*

Our teens spend more time alone now than ever in history. Parents are working overtime. Church demands and community needs press in. Sports and other commitments take parents away from the home more often than not. So, our teens are lonely, bored, and vulnerable to the schemes of the enemy who seeks to tempt them with all the world has to offer. When teens feel the need to be accepted by their peers, it's easy for them to be led down a path of experimentation, and they easily fall prey to peer pressure from all sides.

It's important that you're close to your teens and that you limit their alone time whenever possible. But just as important is that you know their friends and ensure that your kids are spending time with friends you've approved. Get involved in actively helping your teens build quality friendships with teenagers from Christian homes, families who share your value system, and teens whose parents will partner with you in providing safe places to hang out.

Yes, it's important that your teen also reach out to friends who are struggling and falling into bad choices. After all, your teenager is a missionary at school. But that focus should come after a deep circle of Christ-honoring relationships is established. Those friends will provide accountability and strength to stand against peer pressure and temptation.

How well do you know your teenager's friends and their families? How comfortable do those kids feel with you? It's time to step into a new role as your teens build different kinds of friendships and face this critical time. Make an impact by encouraging relationships that will help develop good character in your kids.

## → Connection Point

*Lord, help me encourage my teenagers to build good relationships. I pray against the enemy's lies and destructive pull. Please help my teens reach for your best in all things, especially their friendships, and give them good accountability partners. Amen.*

## God's Type
### Nicole O'Dell

*God does not see as man sees; for man looks at the outward appearance, but God looks at the heart. I Sam. 16:7, KJV*

When it comes to dating or choosing a spouse, everyone has a list of physical, spiritual, and emotional traits that stand out as most important. Some of them are wish-list types of preferences, but others are non-negotiables. Maybe you find you're most attracted to a certain hair color, but you're flexible on that. However, you were raised in a home where finances were always a big source of argument so you won't settle for being someone who doesn't place a big importance on having a balanced budget.

That's all well and good if you're really able to get to the bottom of those things before marriage, but sometimes that's just not possible. It's hard to really know how someone will react to life's challenges until they go through them.

It's the same with parenting. When God places children in our arms, do you think He looks at the fullness of our current capabilities? Heavens no. If He did, none of us would ever have children. Instead, He looks at what He'll be able to do through us if we surrender to Him. Then, as we experience life, make mistakes, and parent through our flaws, He teaches us how to do better next time.

Many parents make a lot of money, take their teenagers on fancy trips, and send them to private schools. Many parents stay very busy with extra-curricular activities, church involvement, and community efforts. And many are what their teens would consider "cool." And while those things aren't bad in themselves, they aren't part of God's wish-list of parenting traits. God's type of parent, the qualities He desires in us, include a patient spirit, a surrendered will, and a sacrificial heart. With those traits in place, He can do amazing things. If you struggle in those areas, make them your prayer focus this week.

## → Connection Point

*Father please help me develop the qualities of a parent that you value, not the ones the world has declared as important. Help me to be patient with my teenagers and always surrendered to your will and to what you would teach me through life's lessons. Amen.*

## Dating School
### *Nicole O'Dell*

*Start children off on the way they should go, and even when they are old they will not turn from it. Prov. 22:6, NIV*

Teenagers are not born with dating skills. They learn most everything they can from watching people around them. The problem is, their friends have no idea what they're doing either, so that can't be the best way to learn how to be in a relationship.

Another alternative is a sort of trial-and-error, on-the-job training approach. But putting them on a date with someone who may or may not have your teenager's best interests at heart might be a bit shortsighted.

Instead, the best dating school around is the education they can get from you. Teens whose parents are open with them and really talk to them about dating make better choices, have happier relationships, and are more confident to defend their values.

You can begin by asking questions to help your teenager identify some important things:

- What qualities are important to you in someone you may wish to date?
- What qualities would be sure signs it's not the right person to date?
- What are your goals for a potential dating relationship?
- What steps can you take now to ensure that God is in charge?

For more help with this, check out my book Hot Buttons Dating Edition. It will help you guide your teens through their relationships.

## → Connection Point

*Dear God, teen dating is a scary thing. Please give me wisdom as I set boundaries and help my teens make good choices. Give me the words to say to impress the importance of choosing the right people, protecting purity, and honoring you in all things. Amen.*

## Will not Spirit
### Nicole O'Dell

*Fathers, do not provoke your children to anger by the way you treat them. Rather, bring them up with the discipline and instruction that comes from the Lord. Ephesians 6:4, NLT*

My mom read a book by Dr. James Dobson that talked about needing to break the will of a child, not his spirit. I overheard her going on and on about that quote to her friends, but I didn't understand what it meant. I didn't get it, that is, until I looked in the eyes of my defiant son. He was about 13, and he was very good at it. He glared at me, the dare evident in his eyes. I knew that my reaction would be a defining moment that would set the stage for his teen years. In that moment I understood what Dr. Dobson had meant. I needed to break his will, not his spirit.

Discipline, done correctly, consistently, and controlled, will shape your teenager's will into one that seeks to please you and God. But punishment done in anger and desperation will only make them angry, drive wedges between you, and push them away from you and God. This is done when a child has no idea what is expected of him. Most of us have been in situations at work or school when we are unsure what is expected of us. It is frustrating when the boss allows one behavior one day, but then says you will be disciplined the next day for the same actions. The lack of consistency is frustrating. Don't do that to your child.

Proper discipline takes a lot of prep work. Your teenager should know what is expected and what will happen if those expectations aren't met. They should know you'll react the same way every time, and your consistency will reinforce that. Good discipline also requires regular follow-up. Be sure to use every tool you have to reinforce godly lessons.

## → Connection Point

Jesus, please help me control my reactions. Give me self-control so I can live out the difference between punishment and discipline. Help me know how to turn my teenagers' will toward you. Amen.

## A Rules Diet
*Nicole O'Dell*

*I am the good shepherd. The good shepherd lays down his life for the sheep. John 10:11, ESV*

The fewer rules, the better. Now, there are definitely some expectations that go without saying, but when it comes to some of the other things, I try to be as hands-off as I can be.

Would you believe my teens don't have a curfew? Why give them a curfew if I have every intention of knowing where they are at all times? A curfew suggests they can run around at will until the clock strikes a certain time. A curfew doesn't keep them out of trouble; it only gives trouble a time limit. And if they started acting out, it wouldn't be the time of day I adjusted, it would be everything else.

Would you believe that I don't hover over my teens while they do their homework or prepare for exams? They get excellent grades, and I love that I can give them the credit for it. They don't need me to push them or micro-manage their work. They do just fine on their own. And if their grades started to fall or they began to struggle, I would try hard to find ways to empower them to fix the problem. (While I prayed they didn't ask me for math help!)

I don't make requirements for how they manage their money. I teach them the value of saving and the blessing of giving, and I model it for them. But that's another one I let them work out for themselves. Imagine my joy when I see my teenager consistently and quietly dropping her envelope into the offering bucket at church!

What I love about the gentle shepherding and the minimal rules is that they can claim these victories for themselves. They know how to make good choices no matter what time of day it is because they've done it. They know they have success at their fingertips because they've proved it to themselves. They know what it feels like to be obedient to God without being forced. They are empowered.

## → Connection Point

*Father, will you help me become a shepherd instead of a rule master? Would you teach me how to be a gentle guide to my teens, to empower them to make good choices? Please give me wisdom to see where I need to let go. Amen.*

## Grape Juice
### Nicole O'Dell

*The Lord meant that when you eat this bread and drink from this cup, you tell about his death until he comes. I Cor. 11:26, CEV*

What is communion and why is it important to the church today? Communion is an act of worship and obedience. It's an opportunity for the church to gather together in unity in remembrance of the sacrifice Jesus made. We do it because He first did it as an example and then instructed us that it would be the way we could remember Him. It is not meant to be a tradition or a ritual that we perform. It's meant to be a meaningful experience in which we remember our Savior.

Another important aspect to communion is the idea of getting centered, getting your heart right before God. Use the moments before the bread and cup are passed to examine your heart and clear up any blocks that might be between you and good fellowship with God.

What do our teens see when they participate in communion? How have we prepared them or helped them understand what it is? I remember one specific time when I arrived at church blustered, flustered, and angry. I had had a rough morning getting everyone out of the house. People were arguing, and I was not in the right frame of mind. By the time the communion part of the service came around, I had released a lot of my stress through worship and was feeling more centered, but I knew there was an issue between myself and my teenagers. I had to clear that up before I participated in communion so they could see the importance of forgiveness and relationship restoration before approaching the communion table. So I reached over and squeezed their hands. I smiled at them, winked, and mouthed a simple apology. They smiled and nodded. I could sense the sigh of relief. They understood that we needed to acknowledge the division between us and deal with it so we could celebrate Jesus. We were then able to enjoy the communion moments with a clear path to Christ.

## → Connection Point

*Father, would you show me the ways that I need to clear the way for my teenager? Reach them through the act of communion and show them what it means to remember the sacrifice you made. Thank you for dying for our sins. May we always be grateful. Amen.*

# Hide and Seek
## Nicole O'Dell

*But the LORD God called to the man, "Where are you?"*
Gen. 3:9, NIV

I always kind of thought it was funny how Adam and Eve hid from God when they were ashamed of their sin. I mean, did they really think He didn't know where they were or what they'd done? It reminds me of when we catch a child with a hand in the cookie jar and crumbs all over. "I didn't eat a cookie! No way. Not me."

We chuckle. It is funny. But in reality it shows a misunderstanding of who we are as parents. If our kids really don't think that we're smart enough to know the truth or can't figure out the truth from the clues, or if they really think they've done such a good job of hiding the truth, then they're not in tune with reality.

The same thing is true with our relationship with God. Do we not fully grasp how deep His love is for us? Do we not understand that His love will drive Him to pursue us in the depths of our sin and challenge us to do better every step of the way? That He can see our hidden places and understands the cries of our heart and the longings we feel? Why, then, do we live in any way that's not transparent before him? What are we trying to hide?

This week take some time to talk with your teenager about transparency. Use the examples above to have an honest dialogue about what God sees, what He knows, and what He expects from us. Ask your teenager for ways you can help extend a spirit of authenticity in your home.

## → Connection Point

*Father, before I approach my teenager about being more authentic, help me to examine my own heart. Show me the places where I'm hiding the truth even from myself, and help me to walk in truth and sincerity. Amen.*

## S-U-C-C-E-S-S
### Wendy Fitzgerald

*Study this Book of Instruction continually. Meditate on it day and night so you will be sure to obey everything written in it. Only then will you prosper and succeed in all you do. Josh. 1:8, NLT*

If your teenager were kidnapped into slavery, is there enough faith already built that it would grow to maturity? If you were killed in a car accident, would your teen's faith withstand without you there to teach?

As parents, one of our biggest fears is losing contact with our children. It is truly every parent's worst nightmare. And yet, there are at least two examples of this early separation from family in the Bible: Joseph and Daniel. Both young men, during their teen years, were taken as slaves into foreign countries never to return to their homeland. What makes both men stand out is their unwavering faith in God. How did their young faith endure the trials and temptations of a foreign land? It was only possible because they already had a firm foundation built on the strength of God's Word.

As parents, we have only a few short years to instill a faith in our kids that will be strong enough to withstand the constant barrage of the world's temptations. How do we ensure that our children, like Joseph and Daniel, know how to stand when they leave our home? We must teach them to study, memorize, defend, and obey God's Word. The truth of God's Word is the only way that our children will be able to succeed in a world of lies.

## → Connection Point

*Father, help me understand how to pass on the knowledge and application of your Word to my children. Help me teach them to conform to your ways, your will, and your Word through my own example. Amen.*

Powerline365

# Armor of God
### Nicole O'Dell

*Therefore put on the full armor of God, so that when the day of evil comes, you may be able to stand your ground, and after you have done everything, to stand. Eph. 6:13, NIV*

A soldier wears armor into battle as a protection against the enemy's weapons. It blocks the arrows, bullets, swords, and physical attacks so the soldier can defend his position.

God gave us a picture of the battle we fight against our enemy, Satan, who seeks to destroy us, our families, and our faith. He uses every weapon he can against us: deceit, temptation, jealousy, anger, and so many other things that can drive a wedge between us and God, and between us and our teens.

The armor of God is both defensive and offensive. It's designed to protect us from the enemy, but it also equips us to fight back. With the armor of God in place, Satan is ultimately powerless against you and, by extension, your teens.

Parents, even though the battle gets heavy at times, we're assured victory! We've read the end of the Book, and we know how the story ends: we win! But though the ultimate victory is assured, we may feel like we lose some of the battles along the way when our teens go against our wishes or talk to us like someone else has taken over their mouths. We might get discouraged at times, like when they question their faith or make scary statements about their future. That's when we need to rest in God's power, rely on His promises, and stand firm without fear.

Today and every day, pray the armor of God onto your teenager. Imagine the breastplate of righteousness firmly in place. Visualize the sword of the Spirit (God's Word) filling your teenager's heard and mind. Read Ephesians 6:10-20 to find the rest of the armor and read it aloud, in a prayerful manner, each morning as you send your teen out into the world.

## → Connection Point

*Jesus, with my armor in place, I stand proud as a soldier fighting for my family. I visualize the armor covering my teen's head, heart, and soul. I stand confident in your promises. Amen.*

## Casual Fridays
### Nicole O'Dell

*So then, brothers, stand firm and hold to the traditions that you were taught by us, either by our spoken word or by our letter.*
*2 Thess. 2:15, ESV*

When I was just starting out in the job market, there was such a thing as casual Fridays. We looked forward to those days because it meant we could wear denim or other comfy clothes and had nothing to iron. But it seems like today's focus is on casual everything, every day.

Do your teenagers even know how to write a professional business letter? Are they being taught how to communicate effectively with proper grammar in a respectful and complete manner? Or is everything text-message based and abbreviated as much as possible? Do they even know how to spell abbreviate without abbreviating it? Would they instinctively know how to dress for an interview?

Today's efficient methods of communication are valuable in some ways, but if we don't instill the importance of protocol and etiquette into our teens, it will disappear. And what about the next generation?

Pay attention to whom your teenager is addressing and guide them to proper protocol. If they're sending email to a teacher, instruct them to use properly formatted documents. If they're shooting a quick text to a friend, it's okay to relax the approach. And when your teens are actually participating in a business activity such as applying for a job or creating a resume, spend a lot of time showing them how to research and create a quality document and how to act professionally.

Have conversations about the value of taking a few extra minutes to do it right. Sometimes you may even want to ask them to revise or rewrite an email or text they sent to you. This is a good way to get them in the habit of thinking before they press the send button. You can also practice interviewing skills and work on professional comportment until it becomes natural.

## → Connection Point

*Lord, help me guide me teenager even in areas of professionalism in business activities. Help me prepare my teens to enter the workforce or communicate with professionals in a proper manner. Amen.*

## Martha, Martha
*Nicole O'Dell*

> But Martha was distracted with much serving. And she went up to him and said, "Lord, do you not care that my sister has left me to serve alone? Tell her then to help me." But the Lord answered her, "Martha, Martha, you are anxious and troubled about many things, but one thing is necessary. Mary has chosen the good portion, which will not be taken away from her." Luke 10:40-42, ESV

Martha was busy taking care of other people and Mary was busy being in relationship with Jesus. Martha complained that she wasn't getting much help, but Jesus praised Mary for choosing the best thing.

This is a hard lesson to learn. Prioritizing, resting, following Jesus instead of what others demand, setting personal goals aside, and more. It also has implications for parenting. If you're like me, you find yourself living much like Martha. Busy, busy, busy making sure everyone has what they need. In fact many of your tasks are so that others can have time so they can seek relationship and rest. But when we live opposite of what we teach, what will our teens actually learn from us? Will our sons and daughters grow up to be people who sit at the feet of Jesus, or will they be busy about all the tasks that life throws at them? More often than not, they will follow our example.

Are we so busy doing the stuff that we have no time to simply be? When is the last time you sat and made eye contact with your teenagers and just talked?

Don't let this day pass without doing that. One at a time, take your teenagers by the hand, pull them into a kitchen chair, and just look into their eyes. Ask them how they are. Ask them how they feel. Ask them what they would change about their day if they could go back and do it all over again. These questions will open the doors to the opportunity of knowing your teenagers well and to set an example of relationship-focused parenting.

## → Connection Point

*Jesus, please remind me to put my relationship with my kids and with you before all the tasks. Show me what I need to cut out of my schedule and where I need to say 'no' so I have more time for what is most important. Thank you for the blessing of relationship. Amen.*

## Credit Cards
*Steve Repak, CFP®*

The rich rule over the poor, and the borrower is slave to the lender.
*Prov. 22:7 NIV*

The use of credit and credit cards is one of those things you don't want your children to learn about from their friends or from the school of hard knocks. I know firsthand of the dangers! Upon graduating from high school I decided to enlist in the Army. After about a year, I obtained my first credit card. I thought it was so cool that someone was giving me money that I could spend on anything I wanted. That was my first mistake. I wasn't given anything, instead I was on my way to becoming a slave to my lender.

Each time I was promoted I made more money. That sounds like a good thing but the problem was that I was also offered more credit. More credit meant I would get further and further into debt. Ultimately, I left the Army after 12 years of service with over $32,000 of credit card debt.

See, I didn't have much when I was growing up so I thought having a bunch of stuff when I was older would make up for the things I had to go without when I was a child. I thought that buying things would make me happy, and I tried to buy a whole bunch of happiness. I once read "The happiest people don't always have the best of everything, they just make the best of everything they have." It took me a long time to figure that out.

Is all debt bad? No, but there is no such thing as good debt. Getting an education, buying a house or starting a business are three endeavors that can be beneficial uses of debt if undertaken thoughtfully, but trying to buy happiness on credit can be hazardous to your financial health, and your teen needs to learn this from you rather than the school of hard knocks.

## → Connection Point

*Heavenly Father, grant my children wisdom, which is more valuable than gold and crystal. Please provide them with the understanding that happiness is not the byproduct of having stuff but of a life well lived, full of blessings from you. Amen.*

Powerline365

## Breaking Up is Hard to Do
### Nicole O'Dell

*What shall we then say to these things? If God [be] for us, who [can be] against us? Rom. 8:31, KJV*

A break up is among the most difficult things your teenager will experience. Not only is it embarrassing if your teen is the dumpee, but it can be an overwhelming pressure if your teenager is the one who ends things. No matter who does the dumping, there is disappointment and loneliness along with a sense of hopelessness for many teens.

If/when your teenager goes through a break-up, be sure to keep an eye on things while giving enough space to the situation. Allow a certain level of sadness and let your teen work through the changing emotions. But watch for despair that gets darker rather than lighter.

Be present more than ever when your teen is in the throes of this kind of grief. Be a listening ear, offering little advice. Let your teen talk it out, and don't turn the subject around to your own experiences unless specifically asked about them. Save your nuggets of wisdom for reminders to turn to Jesus. Pray with and for your teenager, and guide the prayer to areas of future, hope, and peace.

Another important, but difficult, way you can be a good role model in your teenager's break-up is to resist the urge to bad-mouth the ex. Focus on the good things that came out of the relationship and keep your mudslinging to yourself.

Sooner or later your teen is going to want to date again, just make sure that there has been evidence of growth through the rough experiences and that you are both seeking God's will for any future dating relationships.

## → Connection Point

*Father, I'd love to spare my teenagers from the pain of breaking up. But if they should face that experience, please help me know how to handle it. Above all, let it bring them closer to you. Amen.*

## Sticky Notes of Faith
*Nicole O'Dell*

*So I will always remind you of these things, even though you know them and are firmly established in the truth you now have.*
*2 Pet. 1:12, NIV*

Do you ever feel like a broken record? Constantly telling your teenagers to pick that up, put that way, don't do that, take your feet off the furniture, close the door, turn off the lights... it never ends. They need constant (though hopefully not nagging) reminders of how to behave, how to respect things, and how to live in a way that respects the people around them. Why do we not naturally assume they need those kinds of reminders related to their faith in God?

In the verse above, Peter said he would always remind us about these things because he knew that his task as an apostle of Jesus Christ was to keep Christians focused on Jesus and why they were following Him. We all need those constant reminders lest we forget what God has done for us and why we serve Him as we do. How much more so, then, do our teenagers, who do not have the experiences we have or the foundations we have, need reminders, too? They need reminders of when to turn to God in prayer, of what He has done for them, of what He promises for their future, and of how He expects them to live. Reminders like those should be flowing from our lips as often as the reminders of putting socks in the hamper and bringing in the mail after school.

Make a promise to yourself and your teenager that you will fill your communications with gentle proddings and reminders of God's faithfulness, love, mercy every single day. Let your home be filled with proverbial sticky notes of faith that show up at every turn.

## → Connection Point

*Jesus, please forgive me for letting the mundane crowd out the holy. Fill my lips with the things you would have me say to my teenager about you. Let me be an extension of your heart in outreach to them as a constant reminder of your grace. Amen.*

Powerline365

## Can I Get a Witness?
*Nicole O'Dell*

*Then Jesus said to them, "So wherever you go in the world, tell everyone the Good News." Mark 16:14, GWT*

Have you ever had the great joy of sharing the Gospel with someone and seeing the light dawn? There's nothing like being used by God to fill in the gaps of someone's faith struggle and seeing the twinkle in their eyes as they realize the truth. Partnering with the Holy Spirit in that way is such a gift to every believer, and it's one we're instructed to seek. God wants us to share His truth with others.

What about your teenagers? I think sometimes we get so focused on teaching them the Word that we forget to teach them to teach others. We want to make sure they are equipped with truth and lifestyle skills. We work hard to teach them how to study the Bible or what it means to pray. But if we aren't setting the stage with our own example and following that up with practical coaching on how to share the Gospel with others, we are keeping them from one of the greatest joys they'll ever experience as a Christian.

Sharing your faith with others is a daunting mission. But if you train your teens now and help them develop the skills and the confidence it takes to be a fearless and relentless sharer of the gospel, it will carry with them through life. What better trait could you impart to your teenagers?

Why not make this your focus today? The first thing you should do is talk about your teens' questions and fears about sharing the Gospel with others. Go through the book of Romans together, and make sure they understand the plan of salvation, have a good grasp on truth, and know where to find answers to tough questions. But also let them know that leading someone to Christ is ultimately the work of the Holy Spirit. He uses us as participants in his work for our benefit and to build relationships in the body of Christ, so there's no pressure. Then pray together for divine opportunities to reach out to others.

## → Connection Point

*Father, I'm excited about the prospect of raising a teenager with a mission. Open doors for sharing, and open hearts to receive. Please embolden my teenager to be a dynamic witness for you. Amen.*

## Teen Trouble
*Nicole O'Dell*

*For all have sinned and fall short of the glory of God.*
*Rom. 3:23, ESV*

Has your teenager been getting into some trouble lately? Many of you reading this may be dealing with that, or it may be something you'll soon face. First, I want to encourage you that your teenagers choices are not your own. They don't necessarily reflect bad parenting, so set the guilt aside while you deal with the reality of parenting. Your teenager has a free will and will make choices you disagree with over and over. When mistakes, sin, disobedience, or other choices spring from a simple human desire to experiment or experience, we need to react swiftly and consistently. Our teenagers need to know that there are consequences for their bad choices. Always.

Other times they may be reacting to some other kind of outside pressure or stress. Maybe grief or loss has left them feeling hopeless. Fear and loneliness cause many teenagers to give in to peer pressure. And disillusionment can make them angry enough to lash out in all kinds of ways. Examine the possibilities, and consider the basis of your teenagers' actions before you react to them. If the issue is rooted in something deep below the surface, be prepared to deal with that first. Get to the heart of the why, and then address the what. If counseling is needed, seek it. If confrontation is needed, facilitate it. If forgiveness is needed, offer it.

When your teenager feels like more than a balance sheet of rights and wrongs, you'll find your relationship will strengthen and confidence will rise. Just like the mercy God pours on all of us, it's not always about what they do. Sin is a symptom of some other kind of problem — fear, disbelief, low self-esteem, etc — and you'll see much greater results if you get to the heart of it rather than only addressing the surface of it.

## → Connection Point

*Lord, please give me wisdom. Show me the truth of what's driving my teenager's behavior and recognize exactly what I need to do to address it. Help my teenager have an open heart to my correction and a desire to grow in you at all times. Amen.*

## Poor Me
### Nicole O'Dell

*Do all things without grumbling or questioning. Phil.2:14, ESV*

Lately, in my prayer time, God is dealing with me about a spirit of complaining. I have realized that I tend to default to a complaint. Someone else is wrong. Someone isn't helping enough. Someone is expecting too much. I've got it hard because... The list never seems to end. But will it ever?

Complaints are rooted in dissatisfaction and misplaced expectations, not in reality. The reality of my situation is that I'm so very blessed in every possible way. My children are healthy. My finances are in order at least compared to a global condition of poverty and wealth. I have a home. My children are able to go to school, and we are able to serve God as a family and as individuals. And most of all, we are saved from our sins by loving, gracious, merciful God. We have eternity as our promise.

What on earth is there to complain about? Complaining is so shortsighted. It's focusing on the temporary, the things that will rust and fade and disintegrate while we ignore the blessings all around.

My goal is to learn to default to the positive. To seek things to praise God for instead of to complain about others. I challenge you to do the same thing. Tell your teenagers how great things are instead of how much better you wish they were. Focus on the joys and blessings instead of the longings of the strivings. You will raise much more satisfied, confident, and grateful human beings.

## → Connection Point

*Lord, forgive me for overlooking your hand of blessing so many times and complaining about others. Forgive me for my shortsighted look at what I deserve and what I should expect in my life in from other people. Help me to convey to my teenagers just how beautiful our lives are because of you. Amen.*

# Teen Trouble
## Nicole O'Dell

*Whoever scorns instruction will pay for it, but whoever respects a command is rewarded. Prov. 13:13, NIV*

Has your teenager been getting into some trouble lately? First I want to encourage you that your teenagers' choices are not your own, and they don't necessarily reflect bad parenting. Free will is a tough reality when raising kids. We can't always stop them from taking the wrong path.

When mistakes, sin, and disobedience come from a basic desire to experiment or experience, we need to react swiftly and consistently to show there is no gain to such choices. Our teens need to know that there are consequences for their actions. Always. It's our responsibility as parents to address everything that comes up and not overlook anything, even what might seem minor. They're all teaching moments and an opportunity to instruct our teenagers while we still can.

However, there may be times that their behavior is in response to something else like an outside pressure or stress like grief or loss. Consider the basis of your teenager's actions before you react to them. It doesn't mean you overlook anything; it's just important that you understand the root of the problem so you can address it well. If the issue is rooted in a need of some kind, deal with that first. Get to the heart of the why, and then address the what. If counseling is needed, seek that. If confrontation is needed, facilitate that. If forgiveness is needed, offer that. Then you're free from those constraints so you can address the sin appropriately.

In the end, your teen should feel disciplined, but loved. Your goal is to raise healthy, wise, godly teens. You definitely want great behavior from them, but only as a result of deep spiritual convictions, strong parental training, and wise reactions to tough situations.

## → Connection Point

*Lord, please give me wisdom. Help me see the truth of what's driving my teenagers' behavior and help me recognize exactly what I need to do to address it. Convict my teens to run from sin. Give them open hearts to my correction and a desire to grow in you at all times. Amen.*

# One Word
## Nicole O'Dell

*So teach us to number our days, that we may present to you a heart of wisdom. Psalm 90:12, NASB*

What is your "one word" parenting focus this month?

My friend Rachel Olson, along with Mike Ashcraft, wrote My One Word to help us sweep aside the long to-do lists, failing resolutions, and unattainable goals in favor of a one-word focus. One at a time. The goal is to do something about one thing instead of nothing about everything. It is believed that choosing a word that represents what God wants to do in you, and focusing on that specific thing will offer clarity as you concentrate your efforts. You'll position yourself for God to form your character at a deep, sustainable level.

I like doing this each year for myself. I prayerfully seek that one focus I need to have for the year. Serenity was my word two years ago, and Focus was last year's word.

But parenting teens is an ever-changing proposition, so I see nothing wrong with looking for a one-word focus for that endeavor each month or each quarter. Here are some ideas for words related to parenting; consider what you might choose.

Wisdom
Peace
Joy
Patience
Prayerful
Worship
Discipline
Lifestyle
Balance

Whatever you choose, make it your daily prayer theme and look for ways to exercise new skills and see growth in that area.

## → Connection Point

*Jesus, please show me what my One Word is for a renewed parenting focus. Help me to grow in that area as I surrender to you, and show me what I need to do to make sustainable changes. Amen.*

## Get Engaged
### Mary DeMuth

*I want to see you and share with you the same blessings that God's Spirit has given me. Then you will grow stronger in your faith.*
*Rom. 1:11, CEV*

In the instant world of iPhones, social media, and the Internet, how do parents strategically engage tuned-out kids? How can we create the kinds of homes that are irresistible to our children, enticing enough to make them tune-out from games, media and texting and tune-in to the rhythms of family life? Here are five failsafe ways I've discovered.

Give them something better. The most enticing thing to a kid is community—real, authentic, God-breathed community. Spend time together. Enjoy each other. Listen. Pray.

If you can't beat them, join them. Instead of always pushing against television and movies, sit down next to your child and watch them together. Then use the time afterwards to discuss the important elements. This shows your teens you want to spend time with them and prepares them to better discern movies and media they watch.

Create Sabbath. Taking time away from the crazy rush-rush of a media-saturated world is a counter-cultural move your family can take. Choose a day or afternoon for rest. Limit media in favor of creativity.

Go outside. Dare to open the front door and walk out. Take walks together. Find a local park or wilderness preserve to visit. Feed the ducks. Launch rockets. Play Frisbee. Breathe.

Focus outward. Sponsor a child in a third-world country. Go on a mission trip as a family. Find a cause to support—like digging wells in Africa. Volunteer at a nursing home. Muddying our feet and hands in the real needs of the world gives kids a greater picture of the world and pulls them away from the artificial, often narcissistic world they live in.

It is possible to re-engage your disengaged child. It takes effort, creativity and pluck, but it can be done. The reward? A rejuvenated, connected relationship with your child that no gadget can compare to.

### → Connection Point

*Father, please open my eyes to the best ways to engage my teens. And make them receptive to my efforts. Please make our family and home irresistible to my kids. Amen.*

Powerline365

# I Corinthians 13
## Nicole O'Dell

*(very loosely paraphrased)*

If I instruct my teens and lecture them about right and wrong, but don't show them love in the process, the words from my mouth sound like nothing more than a ringing bell. If I spend all kinds of time on my knees in prayer, and if I have a powerful personal relationship with God and understand His Word, but don't laugh with my teens, or pull them close for a hug, my parenting is wasted. If I am generous, hospitable, and sacrificial, but don't take the time to sit and talk with my teens about their needs, none of it means anything.

A loving parenting is patient in stressful times and kind when it's difficult. A loving parent isn't jealous of outsiders, boastful about personal accomplishments, or proud about material possessions. A loving parenting doesn't gossip or disparage others, and never manipulates circumstances for selfish gain. A loving parent finds joy in God's ways and runs from the things that dishonor Him.

A loving parent always protects the family, always trusts in God, always hopes in truth, and always perseveres through the hard times.

Everything else will fade away, but love never fails. And though we've been confused as we've walked this parenting journey, one day we'll get it. It will all make sense as we see God's final purposes.

And now these three remain: faith, hope and love.

But the greatest of these is love.

## → Connection Point

*Loving heavenly Father, you're my example of what it means to truly love another. Help me to be that example to my teens. As you love them through me. Amen.*

## Reclaiming Purity
### *Nicole O'Dell*

*"Come now, let us settle the matter," says the LORD. "Though your sins are like scarlet, they shall be as white as snow." Isa. 1:18a, NIV*

...Adapted from Hot Buttons Sexuality Edition

Sexual intimacy outside of marriage gets its claws into the hearts and minds of its victims and never lets go. Teens might dabble with some sins and find they can leave them behind once they find forgiveness. But once they have sex, they will be affected by it forever. Why? Because that's how God made us. Christians, as Christ's Bride, are to be pure, and sexual intimacy was intended for marriage. Anything short of that will leave the believer feeling empty, broken, and unclean. Teens find it especially difficult to put it behind them and move forward as a new, clean creature in Christ. They feel soiled, dirty, used up, and the enemy screams at them that they're unworthy of God's favor. That lie keeps them mired in the wrong crowd, chasing after the ex with whom they've been intimate. It keeps them searching.

Prevention is the best plan, but what if it's too late for prevention? I'm sure for many of you it is. At least half of the parents who read these words have a teenager who has already had sex. Are you one of them? If you say no, are you sure?

Really search your heart on this is because if your teen has had sex or some level of sexual impurity, healing must take place before the wound festers and sin grows. Through your counsel and understanding, and with the grace of God, you can help your teen get back on the right path before things spiral out of control.

Forgiveness and restoration are gifts from God but it is an ongoing struggle to protect purity. It's important for your teens to reaffirm the purity commitment regularly, claiming it anew with each new relationship. The race toward purity is won with every single step.

## → Connection Point

*Lord, if there is anything that I need to have my eyes opened to, would you please remove the scales? I want to know. I want to walk fully aware of whatever it is I need to know, especially in the area of my teens' purity. Amen.*

## Carbon Copy
### Nicole O'Dell

*For as in one body we have many members, and the members do not all have the same function, so we, though many, are one body in Christ, and individually members one of another. Rom. 12:4-5, ESV*

No two children are the same. As a parent of triplets, I know this very well! I have six kids, and each one of them is as different from the others as you and I are from each other. I thought my triplets would have a unique unity that would make them a lot more alike than my other kids. But they don't. They are brothers and sisters; they share the same parents and live in the same home. That's as far as their similarities extend. One of them is a natural leader and a worrier. The other is silly and a bit of a mischievous, artistic type. And the third is a snuggler yet very particular and systematic. They've been parented exactly the same way. They were born on the same day into the same circumstances. And they have rarely spent time apart. Yet I could tell you story after story after story of how they approach situations differently and make different choices as a result.

Whether you're parenting one teenager or four, this should be a freeing realization for you. Let this reality free you from some of the pressure you feel to exact certain responses or behaviors from your teenagers. As mentioned in previous devotions, they have a free will and they will become very good at utilizing it. So, instead of trying to get them to behave exactly the same as siblings do or even as other teenagers around, find what is unique about your teenager and embrace it. Find ways to capitalize on special skills or talents in order to build character individually.

In the end, we are the training ground and the Holy Spirit does the work. Don't spend so much time focused on what you see in the moment, and look ahead to what God is calling your teenager to become. Many times that route is circuitous; sometimes it's a direct line. Either way, the end result is what we seek.

### → Connection Point

*Father, thank you for making me a partner in the work you're doing in my teenagers. Help me to see them as individuals and to inspire them uniquely as you have a special calling for each one. Amen.*

# 302

## Group Project
### *Nicole O'Dell*

> And let us consider how to stir up one another to love and good works, not neglecting to meet together, as is the habit of some, but encouraging one another, and all the more as you see the Day drawing near. Heb. 10:24-25, ESV

I have said many times that I am not a fan of group projects. I never liked it in school when we had to partner up, share work, delegate, and divide responsibilities. I always ended up doing more than my share of the work and ended up annoyed and resentful. But don't worry, I've since found ways to play well with others.

I've found that teenagers much prefer "group projects" at home to individual assignments. They are much more likely to do the dishes happily if we jump in and dry or put away. They are much more likely to have a good attitude about folding laundry if we're there helping them. After all, isn't it about much more than the laundry?

On a much more important scale, Bible study, daily devotions, and prayer should be group activities in your home. If you've never done a joint Bible study with your teenagers outside of any church structure, you definitely need to give it a try. There's nothing like digging into the Bible, and it's such an awesome feeling to see your teens grapple with questions and find answers in scripture.

My teens and I are going through the entire Bible in a year using the free YouVersion Bible app (YouVersion.com). It has a daily reading plan and it offers prompts to make sure you stay on track. With my teens as my "friends" I can see their progress, and they can check up on me. I can give reminders toward the end of the day about their daily reading, and you can bet they are sure to catch me if I'm running a little behind. Why not give it a try? At the end of the year you and your teens will all have read the entire Bible. Together.

## → Connection Point

*Lord, thank you for your Word. I want to draw closer to my teens while helping them draw closer to you. Please open their hearts and minds to doing Bible study with me and help me stick with it—showing them that there's nothing more important that coming together with them while learning about you. Amen.*

## Failure is an Option
*Nicole O'Dell*

*But he said to me, "My grace is sufficient for you, for my power is made perfect in weakness." Therefore I will boast all the more gladly of my weaknesses, so that the power of Christ may rest upon me. For the sake of Christ, then, I am content with weaknesses, insults, hardships, persecutions, and calamities. For when I am weak, then I am strong. 2 Cor. 12:9-10, ESV*

Not only is failure an option, it's inevitable. If you are always succeeding, whether at work or in personal pursuits, or even in your parenting, it means you're not reaching far enough or pushing hard enough. It means you're settling for the status quo. Failing is nothing more than evidence of your effort to stretch and grow.

Winston Churchill lost all of his money more than one time. He tried and failed politically many times. It's recorded that his failures led him to define success as nothing more than going from one failure to the next without losing enthusiasm.

When it comes to parenting your teenagers, it takes a lot of trial and error to figure out how to get through to each individual. It takes a lot of outreach and conversation starters and bridge mending to figure out the step you need to take to get over the most recent hump in your relationship. You will try, and you will fail. But ultimately it's the effort that counts. The rest is up to God.

So let's reframe our viewpoint. What if we accept or even embrace our failures as part of our journey? Part of our growth process. Part of what God is trying to teach us and teach others through us. In that way each failure is a steppingstone to ultimate, godly success.

## → Connection Point

*Jesus, thank you for walking with me as I parent by trial and error. I trust you to use my mistakes as a means to your successes. Teach me through them and guide me according to your will. Amen.*

## Words of Life
### Nicole O'Dell

*I tell you, on the day of judgment people will give account for every careless word they speak. Matt. 12:36 ESV*

"You'll never amount to anything!" "You're lazy!" "You're stupid!" "You're so negative." "Will you ever make it through high school?" "If only they knew the truth about your behavior at home!"

The single most important and powerful tool every parent possesses – a mouth. Words that come from our mouths have the power to bring life or speak death. They build up; they tear down. They encourage or impart hopelessness. Words are everything.

Young children and teens look to parents to define themselves. They find that definition in the spoken word. What identity label have your words affixed to your teen's heart? How can you reshape your language to invigorate rather than disintegrate the vibrancy and joy in your teen?

"You're so lazy! Would you get out of bed and do something for once?"

Compare that to: "Yeah, I understand teenagers need extra sleep, and I know your bed feels great. But I believe in your abilities and ambition. So, how about we work on the garage today? Let's see what we can accomplish together."

The first one would have any teenager pulling the pillow tight to drown out the sounds of failure. There's no concrete way to accomplish the "do something" plea in open-ended criticism. Some components of the second statement are validation, encouragement, and specific direction. The second one gives a specific goal. The words may not be the way your teen wants to spend a Saturday morning, but they are empowering. Consider your words. They are so very powerful — they will affect your teenagers forever. A heavy burden, but the truth. Use word power for God's best purposes.

## → Connection Point

*Holy Spirit, I surrender my tongue to you, but you're going to have to help me out. In my own strength, I say some dumb things. But if you'll be ever-present and convicting, I believe my words can do some great things in the life of my teenager. Please help me. Amen.*

## Home Improvement
### *Nicole O'Dell*

*No temptation has overtaken you that is not common to man. God is faithful, and he will not let you be tempted beyond your ability, but with the temptation he will also provide the way of escape, that you may be able to endure it. I Cor. 10:13, ESV*

Will I be dating myself if I bring up the television show Home Improvement? Remember Tim the Tool-man Taylor and his wife Jill? But my favorite character was the next-door neighbor. Remember Wilson? He never showed his entire face on the show, and spent his involvement in the Taylors' lives as a wise counselor. He always had some nugget of wisdom to share, mainly with Tim, but he did it in such a way that Tim always thought it was his own idea. Somehow Wilson was able to pull the best out of people.

Who is Wilson in your life? Do you have a mentor who strives to help you along on your parenting journey, someone who stays out of focus, but gently guides you to the answers you need? This kind of relationship isn't easy to come by, but it's worth all the effort it takes to find. If you don't have someone like this in your life, pray that God will bring someone along. My husband went to the counseling pastor of our church and asked that he help find a mentor. This pastor prayed about it, and then helped establish a real mentoring relationship for my husband. They've been meeting weekly for about six months and it's been an invaluable thing in my husband's spiritual walk, his parenting, and our marriage.

Next, who is your Tim? We all need mentors, but we also need to be mentors to the people coming up behind us. Who would God have you reach out to in mentorship? Be sure to take your cues from Wilson as you open your heart and offer advice.

## → Connection Point

*Dear God, please bring me a mentor. Point me to someone who's ahead of me on this parenting experience. Let me learn from someone who is wise, and give me the wisdom and grace to take their advice and learn from them. Amen.*

## 'Fess Up
### Cassie Beck

*Therefore, confess your sins to one another. James 5.16a, ESV*

Think about the number of times in your life that someone has apologized to you. Now, compare it with the number of times when you felt an apology was warranted but never given.

Why is it so difficult for people to apologize? Because it requires a deliberate act of the will, the laying down of ones' pride...HUMILITY above all! As parents we know there is no such thing as a perfect parent. Yet, when it comes to confessing to our own children that we have wronged them, we flinch – we duck and cover. We can internalize our error—stuff it down and keep it hidden—but it is just too hard to 'fess up and admit to our own children that we are not perfect. This merely sends a message to our teens that we think we are without fault, arrogant, and incapable of admitting our own mistakes.

How did your own parents model humility in the act of apologizing to you? Has their example affected your ability to admit when you have wronged your own teen? Is there a situation lingering that you need to apologize to your teen for? Remember, humility mends relationships.

Humility is the peacemaker that has the ability to mend relationships. Now it's time to put it into practice. Listen to that feeling in your gut that tells you when you need to apologize... that's the Holy Spirit! Take advantage of every opportunity to confess your wrong and use it as a teachable moment with your children. In doing so, you are modeling the character of Christ, and encouraging them to do likewise!

*"If it is possible, as far as it depends on YOU, live at peace with everyone." Romans 12:18*

## → Connection Point

Lord, please forgive me for the times when I've been angry and arrogant. Help me to show more grace to others, especially my teens, by admitting my own faults. Amen.

## Who's the Boss?
### Nicole O'Dell

*For in Him all the fullness of Deity dwells in bodily form, and in Him you have been made complete, and He is the head over all rule and authority. Col. 2:9-10, NASB*

There's a natural hierarchy in a family. Parents are in charge, and kids obey. Except, of course, in unbalanced homes where order is flipped upside down, and kids rule the roost, but that's a devotion for another day. One thing to point out, though, is that even though Mom and Dad are in charge of the daily workings of the home, Jesus Christ is head over all. Are you raising your teenagers with a proper understanding of the authority of Jesus?

It's hard enough to teach our kids moral absolutes when society, even our government, fights against those absolutes in the name of tolerance. Our culture is warring against us for the attention of our kids. This culture stands up and boldly proclaims that we are wrong for setting boundaries and calling "choice" sin. And what is missing, both in our homes and in our society as a whole, is a proper allegiance to the true head, the One who sits on the throne.

Allow me to challenge you to have a talk with your teenagers. Ask them who is in charge of their lives. Ask them about some moral absolutes and issues of sin that plague this culture. Do they understand consequences and submission to God? It's time that we practice unadulterated intolerance of attitudes that usurp the authority of God in our homes.

## → Connection Point

*Father, please forgive me for overlooking or overshadowing your true authority. Help me to display humility as I serve you through my parenting. Teach my teenagers a healthy respect for your rulership in their lives and in our home. Amen.*

## Boredom vs. Busyness
### Nicole O'Dell

*Idle hands are the devil's workshop. Prov. 16:27, TLB*

I often counsel parents against too much busyness. Running here and there from one activity to the next is not good for a teenager. They need time to imagine, to explore, to think, and to pray. But that doesn't mean that having no activities or commitments is a good idea, either. There should be a healthy balance between busyness and boredom.

Boredom is just as unhealthy as busyness. An idle teen will experiment with dangerous things, make bad choices in efforts to get attention, and take up with the wrong kids who are also bored. There are so many negative outcomes that can happen when teens are bored and unsupervised.

Being busy just for the sake of filling all the time possible or exposing your teenagers to everything that exists is not healthy. However, to avoid boredom and idle hands, involve your teens in enough things to stretch their growth and engage their minds. Help them find a sport or a club. Encourage them to get more involved in youth group. Maybe they could join a community activity or get a part-time job.

Fulfillment is important, just be sure to guard against busyness. If you're confused about when to push ahead and when to pull back, ask yourself these questions.

- Does my teenager have at least an hour of peace and quiet each day?
- Is my teenager over-extended and tired?
- Is my teen exhibiting signs of boredom like a bad attitude or sluggishness?
- Am I worried about my teenager's schedule?

Your answers to those questions will point you in the right direction; trust your instinct. And, as always, pray for guidance.

## → Connection Point

Jesus, please give me wisdom to know just how to fill the time. Give me insight into ways to engage my teenager in things that will be productive and develop healthy habits and long-term interests. Amen.

Powerline365

# Thanksgiving Every Day
## Nicole O'Dell

*Give thanks to the Lord for he is good; his love endures forever.*
*Psalm 107:1, NIV*

There's a big turkey on the table and there are trimmings all around. Everyone takes a turn to mention something they're thankful for this year. That's great for a holiday, once a year. But what about every day? Why would we practice thankfulness only once a year when we have so much to be thankful for?

Most of us don't take the time to stop and think about what we've got to be grateful for. We're so concerned with our worries and the pursuits we have in this life, that it chokes our gratitude from ourselves—let alone from our parenting. Thankfulness can only come from a true understanding of the gifts we've been given. And teaching thankfulness to our kids can only be effective if we are authentic.

I think it would be a safe bet to say that if you did a 360-degree turn right now everything your eyes took in, including your own body, are worthy of gratitude. Your life, everything you own, even your children are precious gifts from God. Your salvation is a gift from God.

My challenge to you this week is to sit with your teens and make a list of 100 things you're thankful for. It will get easier the further you go down the list as your heart begins to open to the goodness in your life, and you'll have no trouble completing the list. Then, I'd like you to read it out loud together expressing thanks to God for those things on that list. Working together on this will give you unity as you express gratitude to God.

## → Connection Point

*Father, will you help me turn my Thanksgiving from a holiday I celebrate to an attitude that springs from my heart? And will you help me cultivate a thankful heart in my teenagers? Amen.*

## Final Words
### *Nicole O'Dell*

*"Yes, I am coming soon." Rev. 22:20, NIV*

I've thought a lot about what my final words might be. It's not really something we can control, since we can't control the day we leave this earth or how we make our departure. We could come up with some gloriously memorable phrase or comment to be like President Cleveland who said, "I have tried so hard to do right," just before he took his last breath. We could create our own perfect closing statement and set it aside until the perfect moment. But you and I both know it's unlikely that the circumstances of our last days will be so elegant.

In relationships, scripture advises us not to allow the sun to go down on anger. In other words, we're to solve conflict before the day ends. And that's vital, truly, but I am also going to suggest that there is nothing more important than the very last words, the most recent words, you've uttered to your teens. They are the gasoline in their tank as they leave your presence. Those last words are the fuel that will motivate them to make good choices or bad choices. They shape the way they see themselves and the way they look at you until the next time. They even affect the way they see God. You are that important to them. Consider that as you choose your words and be careful that your words uplift and exhort even in correction and discipline.

Jesus chose His last words carefully. He said, "Yes, I am coming soon." He left us with the promise of hope and the assurance of His return. Let's make sure our teenagers can cling to the same type of hope, love, and peace from us.

## → Connection Point

*Father would you teach me how to be like you as I counsel, discipline, and parent my teenagers? Give me the graciousness I need to correct with love. And help my teen see the intent behind my words and forgive me for my sometimes-sharp tongue and hastily spoken thoughts. Amen.*

## 311

## A Mountain Hike
### Nicole O'Dell

*I press toward the mark for the prize of the high calling of God in Christ Jesus. Phil. 3:14, KJV*

Have you ever read *Hinds' Feet on High Places*, the allegory by Hannah Hurnard? It's told from the point of view of Much-Afraid who served the Chief Shepherd whose flocks were pastured down in the Valley of Humiliation. Much-Afraid lived with her friends and co-laborers Mercy and Peace in the village of Much-Trembling. And though she loved her work, Much-Afraid was hindered by secret distress and shame. Sound familiar? The allegory is a beautiful depiction of the hills and valleys we face in life, the mountaintop experiences and bottom-of-the-pit despair moments we go through as Christians and as parents.

Where are you on your hike right now? Are you just clipping along at a healthy pace, moving forward through the beautiful forest? Or are you fighting an uphill battle, struggling to get one foot in front of the other and grabbing onto nearby branches for support?

No matter what it's like right now, the best part is that you are moving. Each choice and each step you take is a move toward newness. Focus your eyes on the sun (Son) and press forward on your journey. Let the streams of Living Water refresh you moment by moment.

I know. That's all a little flowery for this devotional book. We like practical, don't we? So here it is: Whatever it is you're doing today will look and feel completely different tomorrow. Slough off the stress you feel and drop whatever encumbers you. Keep your eyes forward so you don't miss out on the beauty along the way.

## → Connection Point

*Father, we talk so much about this being a journey, but it really is. Help me see the light at the end of the path, the light that you shine on my way. Help me shed my troubles and all that burdens me. Give me strength for my journey and show me your beauty all around me. Amen.*

## Salt and Light
*Nicole O'Dell*

*You are the salt of the earth. But what good is salt if it has lost its flavor? Can you make it salty again? It will be thrown out and trampled underfoot as worthless. Matt. 5:13, NLT*

Just as salt seasons our food, God calls us to season the world with truth. He wants us to shine His light into dark places, and sprinkle His Word on fear, doubt, and pain. As parents, we are to be salt and light in our homes. Our teens get no benefit from us if we are bland and used up. There are three very important things we need to remember as parents in specific and as Christians in general.

We are zesty. We cannot blend in with the world and taste, look, and sound like everyone else. We need to be a haven for our teens, a place where they can find the flavor of truth consistently.

We have a job. I often have to take stock of my intentions and my schedule. Am I making am impact by being available? Am I reaching out to my teens and to others? If we hide away and isolate ourselves, or if we stay so busy that we're out of reach, we're just like that bland, used up salt the verse above warns about. It's worthless to have such a gift and then hide it away.

We are important. No matter what message your teenagers seem to be sending, they are looking to you to learn how to influence others. They are watching how you interact with people, and they are taking cues from how you teach them through your words and your lifestyle. The life of a follower of Christ should be exciting, joyous and powerful. Salt their world!

## → Connection Point

*Jesus, please use me to flavor my home into somewhere exciting and powerful for you to move. Let my salt and light perk up my teenagers so that they can be seasoning to the world around them outside our home. Amen.*

## His, Hers, and Ours
*Nicole O'Dell*

*Work willingly at whatever you do, as though you were working for the Lord rather than for people. Col. 3:23, NLT*

We are in a culture of blended families. More often than not there is some version of a stepchild arrangement, visitation schedule, or blended circumstance. It's not easy.

My family is a blended one. I entered my marriage with three kids, and then we had three more. There are big problems in every family. Financial concerns, employment needs, household issues, and parenting struggles top the list, but I don't think anything is as difficult as the angst that arises in a stepparent/stepchild situation.

One of the biggest issues seems to be dual rules. Certain rules for the home, except when other kids are visiting. Different rules for visiting kids. Different rules for stepparents in the way they treat the stepkids. All that tells me is that we are missing the point.

The point isn't an issue of who's right or who's wrong, or who's more in charge, or who is more or less respected. The point is that we must do the work God has set before us and brings honor and glory to Him. What kind of parent has He called you to be?

Blood related or not, the children that are in your home whether permanent, temporary, or intermittent, are a challenge entrusted to you by God. It's a calling God has placed on your life—to parent those teenagers no matter the circumstances. We don't get to talk back to God with excuses about our limitations or our roles. He already considered those issues before He charged us with the task.

Whether it's boundaries you set, the lifestyle you live, or the way you speak up about the Lord—do it with all your heart as unto the Lord. The results don't matter because they are up to God. What matters is that you move and work and love those teenagers as if they are Jesus. What you do for them is just as if you're doing it for Him.

## → Connection Point

*Lord, please help me in my blended family. Help me to know when to speak up and when to keep quiet. Give me influence and impact with my teenagers and with the other parents involved. Use me and help me to work at this parenting call you placed on my life. Amen.*

## Building Bridges
### Amy Joob

*Those from among you shall build the old waste places; you shall raise up the foundations of many generations; And you shall be called The Repairer of The Breach, The Restorer of Streets to Dwell In. Isaiah 58:12, NKJV*

London Bridge is falling down? Do you wish your teenager was still a cooing toddler on your lap bouncing as you sang that song? Is the bridge between you and your teen broken or teetering on the verge of collapse. Or maybe your bridge is still there, but it's not getting the mileage it used to. While those early days of parenting, when bonding seemed magically easy, are over, it's never too late to build or repair a bridge between you and your teen.

According to Webster's Dictionary one meaning for breach is "a gap (as in a wall) made by battering." While that may not refer to physical battering in this case, perhaps our words have pummeled a hole that caused the breach. Even though these can be challenging years, have our responses and reactions to our teen been hurtful, nagging or scolding? Perhaps our kids have retreated not only into their rooms but into a shell due to our harsh words and criticisms. How do we restore a right relationship and build a bridge once again?

First of all, God gave us His digits. We can call Him anytime…Jeremiah 33:3 says, "Call to Me, and I will answer you and show you great and mighty things, which you do not know." And secondly, He encourages us through James 1:5 "If any of you lacks wisdom, let him ask of God, who gives to all liberally and without reproach and it will be given to him." It's actually pretty simple. God called us to repair our broken relationships, and He would never ask us to do something that was impossible for us to do! And when you are building bridges of communication and forgiveness between you and your own child, you are paving the way for future generations.

## → Connection Point

*Father God, I ask you to help me today to rebuild the bridge between me and my loved one. Show me ways I can repair and restore that which is broken. I thank you in advance that you are repairing the breach between me and my teen today. In Jesus' name I pray, Amen.*

Powerline365

# Identity Crisis?
### Nicole O'Dell

*For we are his workmanship, created in Christ Jesus for good works, which God prepared beforehand, that we should walk in them.*
*Eph. 2:10 ESV*

Who am I?

Assume your teenager asks that question on a regular basis. My teenage self stared into the mirror until my vision swam in front of me, trying to see through my pupils into my soul. I wanted the answer so badly. Who am I? Over the years I've learned that question means: What space will I take up while I'm here on Earth and what impact will I have? Within the context of that exploration, teenagers imagine all sorts of different roles and different people around them.

In that construct, I don't believe it's an identity crisis, but a healthy way to try on different hats and see how they fit. The world places superficial value on success, charm, beauty, and material possessions. But all those things are fleeting. God encourages us to be individuals, uniquely created with certain skills, and a style just our own. If we parents encourage a healthy exploration of our teenager's identity, as God intended it, we're making an investment in enduring qualities.

Have simple conversations that begin with questions like:
- What do you think it would be like to be a doctor, teacher, missionary, etc?
- Do you like to teach?
- What do you like to learn most?
- If you could be any movie or book character, who would it be?

The idea is to explore, freely discuss, and express without expectations. Leave parental judgment out even if the conversation feels unfinished. You're trying to open doors of thought for your teenager, but you never know what you might learn about your teen – or about yourself.

## → Connection Point

*Thank you, Jesus, for my teenager's true identity in you. Please help me to nurture the qualities that will endure and not get caught up in the unimportant things that will fade. Give us all a healthy perspective for the future. Amen.*

# 316

## Made to Crave
### Nicole O'Dell

*Yet God has made everything beautiful for its own time. He has planted eternity in the human heart, but even so, people cannot see the whole scope of God's work from beginning to end. Ecc. 3:11, NLT*

Have you had a craving for chocolate lately? Or maybe you're a salt-lover and recently had a hard time getting potato chips off your mind. You probably tried to eat a healthier substitute first, but, if you're like me, until you satisfy the actual craving, it doesn't let up.

God has planted eternity in the human heart. I love that concept. He had made us to long for eternity. He has caused us to search for it, to seek to understand it. To find the path to it. To crave it.

You were made to crave a relationship with God. You were made to crave His presence and His guidance and even His approval. Thankfully His approval is offered freely, along with His love, and everything you need is right there for you to claim.

If you feel lonely today as a parent, or really in any walk of your life, consider that your soul, your deepest self, longs for closer unity with Jesus and no substitute will do. If you're feeling down or afraid, maybe it's because you're not pressing in enough. You were made to crave a holy God. You were made to pursue a relationship with Him, but like any relationship, it takes effort. He wants to guide you as you parent your teenagers, but He can't affect your actions and your choices unless you're listening to Him.

Take some extra time today to just sit quietly and let the Holy Spirit speak to your heart. Put on some worship music while you're cleaning the house or driving to work, and reflect on who God is to you. Let your relationship with Him grow to new heights as you fill that craving deep in your soul. The natural effects, the outpouring of that effort, will flow over everything you touch, including your teenagers.

## → Connection Point

*Father, I want to know you more. I crave your presence and I long for your peace in my life. Please show yourself to me in a new and deeper way. Amen.*

# The Marks of Maturity
### *Nicole O'Dell*

*Then we will no longer be immature like children. We won't be tossed and blown about by every wind of new teaching. We will not be influenced when people try to trick us with lies so clever they sound like the truth. Instead, we will speak the truth in love, growing in every way more and more like Christ, who is the head of his body, the church. Eph. 4:14-15, NLT*

Teenagers are somewhere on the continuum of maturity. They haven't arrived yet, but they are farther along than they once were. Physically, they may already look quite like an adult, but for the most part, they have a long way to go mentally, spiritually, and emotionally. As they continue to grow in those areas, you'll hopefully see them make better choices as they learn from their mistakes, adopt personal responsibility in areas like their health and fitness, and advance in their intellect as they seek higher levels of education.

If you look back over your own journey, do you feel as though you've arrived at the end of your maturing process? Are you complete? I sure hope I'm not! The truth is, we never fully finish the process until we're completed in Christ one day. That's a good thing. It means we (and our teenagers) get to grow and learn more and more. We get do-overs and fresh starts each day, and we get to pursue God daily. But sometimes it seems like our teens want to camp on the fresh starts and never quite grab hold of the growing part. So, if you're looking for clues that your teenagers are moving along, watch for these:

- Self control over emotions and rash judgments
- Compassion toward others in need
- Digging into God's Word
- Asking hard questions and really wanting the answers
- Practicing patience

When you begin to see some of these examples or others you might encounter, encourage your teen by acknowledging the growth.

## → Connection Point

*Jesus, is my teenager maturing? Sometimes it doesn't seem like it at all. Please help me see the areas where you're working in my teen. Use me as an encouragement to that growth. Amen.*

# 318

## Costly Value
*Nicole O'Dell*

*Don't store up treasures here on earth, where moths eat them and rust destroys them, and where thieves break in and steal. Store your treasures in heaven, where moths and rust cannot destroy, and thieves do not break in and steal. Wherever your treasure is, there the desires of your heart will also be. Matt. 6: 19-21, NLT*

Everything has a cost. Every material possession, thought, choice, and activity... they all cost something of you, good or bad, big or small. That cost is whatever it is you must give up (time, money, integrity, etc) to obtain or keep that thing. You must weigh your options and make decisions about the cost of everything.

Value is completely different than cost.

Let me tell you what I know about value! I recently joined Weight Watchers, which asks me to measure everything that goes into my mouth and give it a point value. Not everything that shares the same cost has the same value. I could eat a single cookie for four points or a huge bowl full of Brussels sprouts for zero. Which is better for me? Which tastes better? Who gets to decide if the value is worth the cost?

Cost is objective. It's a price, and emotions don't change it. But value is often buoyed or weighed down by a subjective opinion or emotional response.

Being an effective, disciplined, and consistent parent is costly. It can't be swayed by emotions. You need to determine that the value of having God-honoring teenagers and a respectful home is worth the price of the time it takes to do the training and teaching. You can also use the cost/value analogy to teach your teenagers about making good choices. There's a big cost to disobedience and disrespect, and the cost far outweighs the value of self-expression and perceived freedom. When you approach it objectively like that, it's difficult to argue.

## → Connection Point

Jesus, all value is found in you, and following you is worth any cost. Help me to convey that truth to my teenagers and to give them an understanding of cost and value so they will make good choices for the right reasons. Amen.

## Sex Sells
### Nicole O'Dell

*Young women of Jerusalem, swear to me by the gazelles or by the does in the field that you will not awaken love or arouse love before its proper time. Sol. 2:7, GWT*

Sex abounds. Whether it be in movies, music, TV shows, or books, our teenagers are bombarded with sex on a moment-by-moment basis. It's inescapable. Our teenagers are being sold all the hype and taught that they are powerless against the pull of physical desire. It's expected that they will succumb to it, so many choose not to bother even fighting it. People will even use the Bible, specifically the Song of Solomon, to argue that sex is naturally God ordained.

Yes, the Bible talks about desire and sexuality, but the Song of Solomon portrays the beauty of love in a convent union. Marriage. The words of the verse quoted above appear two more times in the book of Solomon, showing how important it is to remain vigilant toward purity, to wait until marriage for sex and even for that spark of physical desire. In chapter two they discuss their attraction for one another in honest, open, but guarded ways that show restraint and warn of the power and intensity of physical attraction in love. They know their limits and they recognize them and live within those boundaries.

Walk your teenager right to the Song of Solomon and circumvent the warped teachings of the world with the truth in scripture. Talk about desire and physicality, explain what happens when feelings are awakened, and discuss tools to avoid those situations.

God did ordain sex within the marital union and He did create desire. It's a good thing in the right way at the right time. Don't be afraid to have this talk with your kids until they understand God's plan and purpose for sex and the importance of waiting. Don't shy away from it, and use the Bible itself to support this position.

## → Connection Point

*Father please help me to have the words to say to show my teenagers that their physical desire and sexuality is natural, but that restraint is possible. Help protect them from the lies of the enemy that would pull them down the slippery slope of sexuality. Amen.*

## College Bound?
### Nicole O'Dell

*If we confess our sins, he is faithful and just to forgive us our sins and to cleanse us from all unrighteousness. I John 1:9, ESV*

My hope is that you're reading this with a little bit of time left before those milestone moments happen. As early as middle school — well, even earlier than that, but middle school is a really good time to start thinking about that leapfrog into the future. Once you have your sights set on the end goal, you're better able to make intentional progress along the way. What do you want to equip your teenager with before he or she leaves your home? What kind of adult do you hope to launch into the world?

1. Does your teen have a thriving relationship with God? Many Christian families raise their kids wonderfully well by keeping them in church and teaching them the Bible, but they miss the part of identifying and eradicating personal sin. That is something you can begin to address and fix immediately.

2. Is your teen beginning to move on from childish things and making mature decisions? This isn't to say that your 17-year old won't be silly or make rash decisions sometimes. But it is to say that he or she may be considering what it takes to balance a budget and save for the future. Maybe talks of car repairs have replaced the conversations about boy bands or video games.

3. Is your teenager developing good friendships and choosing wisely when it comes to dating? Recognizing the importance of quality, godly relationships is a big step toward a successful future. You can begin to shape those choices now.

Is the conversation about personal success, ambition, and freedom? Or is it about serving God with specific gifts and talents, changing lives for the Kingdom, and finding personal fulfillment along the way? Beginning to shape your conversations along those lines will help your teenager on the jet-fueled blast toward the future.

## → Connection Point

Please show me where we are in the maturing process. Help me know how to steer and prepare my teenager for the future and not miss the most important things. Amen.

# Fix-It Conversation
## Nicole O'Dell

*My dear brothers and sisters, take note of this: Everyone should be quick to listen, slow to speak and slow to become angry.*
*James 1:19, NIV*

Have you ever read a formulaic romance novel and gripped it in irritation as an entire web of destruction unfolds in the lives and relationships of the main characters, all of which could have been fixed with nothing more than a simple conversation?

You already know what's going to happen, but you're powerless to stop it. As the story continues, all you want is for the characters to talk it out. If they would listen to each other, you know they'd understand. If they pushed past the misunderstanding, they'd find the truth. Instead, the confusion and resentment builds until the destruction hits. When does the fix-it conversation happen? At the very end of the book, just in time for happily ever after. The End.

It's so often like that in our parent-teen relationships, isn't it? We mean well. We do our best, often acting based on limited information, but usually with the best of intentions. Then assumptions and misunderstandings weave into the fray and we're left doubting each other and closed off to the possibility of repair.

We let pride, jealousy, doubt, insecurities, and whatever else our enemy can use against us creep in among us and divide us as we assume the worst in a person's motives, instead of the best. What plotlines of misunderstanding do you have unfolding in your parent-teen relationships? What wrong assumptions have laid the foundation for your enemy to heap on doubt and insecurity, which gives way to distrust and anger?

Miscommunication. No communication. Poor communication. It all causes division. Look through your teenagers' words and seek to understand their hearts.

## → Connection Point

*Jesus, please help me see the truth clearly and not let misunderstandings or assumptions darken my view. Help me and my teens see through words into the truth of intentions. Amen.*

## Closed Doors
*Vicki Tiede*

*For once you were full of darkness, but now you have light from the Lord. So live as people of light! For this light within you produces only what is good and right and true. Eph. 5:8-9, NLT*

There was a time in my life when I was a fan of closed doors. A closed door offered privacy, security, and a haven where I could be me and not worry about living up to the standards of others. There came another season, however, when the closed door was hiding greater shame than just being true to myself.

Do you remember when your kids would hide by covering their eyes? That used to crack me up. Likewise, I wonder if God shakes His head and laughs when He sees our pitiful attempts to hide things behind closed doors?

God sees what's done behind closed doors just as clearly as what's done in broad daylight with the door standing wide open for the world to see. What's more, He not only sees me when I have an epic parenting failure, but He also sees my heart and knows my motives. Not only that, but God also sees when I'm wrestling in the dark night of my soul with Him, with confusion, with fear, with uncertainty, with unfaithfulness and self-righteousness. He sees.

Here's the sad reality: When God shines His light into darkness, shadows of sin are often cast. When my first husband's addiction to pornography came to light, that light also revealed my propensity for sarcasm and disrespect toward him, which was growing in the shadow. Left in the dark, it continued to grow like black mold.

We must embrace light and walk in authenticity so our teenagers can come out from behind closed doors and live in truth. Shine the light in the dark places of your home, and live in freedom.

## → Connection Point

*Jesus, please illuminate the sin and hidden things in my family. Help me to walk in brightness, confident in who I am, exposing the truth of my heart in order to draw others to You. Help my teenagers learn that living in the light of your truth is the only way to truly walk with you. Amen.*

## Tune In
### Nicole O'Dell

*And let them offer sacrifices of thanksgiving, and tell of his deeds in songs of joy! Psalm 107:22, ESV*

When I was a teenager and decided to get my life together, one of the steps I took toward that goal was a music purge. I went through my cassette tapes, my concert t-shirts, and my pre-set stations on the radio, and rid myself of anything that detracted from my pursuit. To me, music that turned my attention off of God, and caused me to feel anger, lust, jealousy, or doubt had no place in my life.

I remember looking at my pile of trash and wondering what my mom would say if she really knew the lyrics of the stuff I'd been listening to. The secular music industry exists for one reason: to make money. Today's culture rewards the most outrageous with the highest sales and accolades. And if you're like my parents were, you may be unaware of the extent of filth and violence being marketed to your kids. Albums featuring themes of drugs, sex, rape, abuse, and suicide routinely take number one on the chart and sell millions of copies. Is your teenager among those millions of teens who are listening?

Music, like little else, is so powerful it can get its claws into the hearts and minds of young people to either pull them away from God or draw them to Him. But you can use your influence to keep dangerous music out of your home and, instead, fill it with praise and music that tells of the goodness and glory of God. Ask yourself:

- What is on my teenagers' playlist?
- What impact does it have?
- Does it glorify God and encourage greater intimacy with Him?

## → Connection Point

*Father, music is a gift from you and it has such impact. Please reveal any lurking dangers related to the music my family is listening to. Birth a new desire in my teens to draw closer to you in praise and worship. Amen.*

## Bad Habits
### Nicole O'Dell

*Not neglecting to meet together, as is the habit of some, but encouraging one another, and all the more as you see the Day drawing near. Heb. 10:25, ESV*

Bad habits are sneaky. They start off innocently enough, but they cling on long and hard until it's nearly impossible to get back on track. Let's look at three examples.

Family dinner. Maybe you've had dinner together for years, but a few months ago, something changed. Schedules just don't quite line up and people are coming and going at odd hours. Dinner has become a heat-it-up-when-you-can affair.

Good nights. As teenagers get older, they want more and more time alone. Have they begun escaping to their bedrooms to do homework and be alone and stopped coming back to visit before falling asleep for the night? This can reduce your daily contact a lot.

Devotional time. Let's face it, it's hard enough to get our teens to tell us about their day, let alone sit with us and talk about the Word of God. At some point, maybe it just became easier to let it slide. Maybe the conflict in trying to have daily devotions became too great, and you chose to keep the peace. But once the priority of studying the Word slips from your grasp, it's very hard to get it back.

What other bad habits have crept in lately? Can you think of ways to get back on track? First, you need to have a conversation with your teens. Let them know that you were wrong for letting the bad crowd out the good, but that you are now committed to making it right. Second, ask them for help. Ask them to think of a few ways to guard against a future slip-up. They'll love to be counted on for something like that. And lastly, pray regularly that God would show you the areas in your life and in the workings of your family that have slipped into a danger zone, and ask Him for help in getting back on track.

## → Connection Point

*Dear God, I can identify several bad habits already, are there others you'd like to reveal to me? Please help me see the needs and commit to making a change. Help my teens receive the change eagerly and supportively. Amen.*

Powerline365

## Too Young?
*Nicole O'Dell*

*He will keep the temptation from becoming so strong that you can't stand up against it. When you are tempted, he will show you a way out so that you will not give in to it. I Cor. 10:13b NLT*

Since society throws pressure and unrealistic ideals at incredibly young ages, you need to go after those peer-pressure points even earlier than you think. You have to be willing to tackle tough issues like modesty, body image, celebrity influences, and self-esteem openly – before problems arise.

One day my eight-year old daughter played quietly in her bedroom with her BFF. I happened by and noticed they had about a dozen Barbies sitting in a circle. Aww, a nice little game of Barbie duck-duck-goose, right? Not quite.

My daughter said they were playing The Bachelor, and the Barbies were in the hot tub. Of course, there was only one Ken in the circle. My daughter had never seen The Bachelor in my house. How did she know about the hot tub? Had she seen it at a friend's home, or had the pop-culture phenomenon of reality TV found the elementary school?

Regardless of how, the exposure had happened, and there was nothing I could do to get in front of it. Foundational work about God's plan for relationships and self-respect would have been so much more effective, but the time for that was gone, and I had damage to control.

Your pre-teen or teenager is NOT too young. The exposure is happening on a daily basis. Get there first with truth about consequences, understanding about temptation, and concrete steps for avoidance. But if you're late, it's even more important not to let another day pass before you begin to hit the issues head on. You can also check out my Focus on the Family approved Hot Buttons series that guides you through the tough talks in a way that ensures your teens and pre-teens will respond.

## → Connection Point

*Lord, please shield my teen, and help me to be a barricade between our home and the world. And please give me the words to say and the insight to know just when to say them, and let them reach the heart of my teen. Amen.*

## Mistakes are Allowed
### Jill Hart

*"For my thoughts are not your thoughts, neither are your ways my ways," declares the Lord. Isaiah 55:8, NIV*

If there is anything I'm learning as my children turn into teenagers, it's the need to be flexible. So often I have an idea of how I want to do things and they have their own idea. It can be hard to let go and allow them to do things their way, especially if I see trouble on the horizon. However, one of the best things that we can do for our kids is to allow them to make some of their own mistakes.

Of course we want to protect them from major disaster, but it may benefit them to learn from making some of their own minor mistakes. Think back to a minor (or even major) mistake you made during your teen years. Did it shape you?

I know that some of the dumb decisions that I made as a teenager, and the resulting consequences, are some of the reasons that I am who I am today. I needed to assert my independence, needed to try out being the decision-maker in my own life.

There are things I regret doing my teen years, but seeing how God continues to use them gives me the freedom to release my children to His care. We know that He is a personal God and that He adores our children even more than we do. We also know that He can see the big picture of their lives while we can only see the present. He knows what our children need and He can be trusted with their futures.

Next time to see your child stepping out to make a decision, allow them the freedom to do so, if it's possible in the situation. Trust that God will guide and direct them, even if that means allowing a mistake or two to be made in their lives.

None of us are mistake-free and this may be a mistake that God uses to bring your child closer to Him.

## → Connection Point

*Dear God, please help me to hand control of my teens over to you. Help me to know when to step in and when to allow my kids to make their own mistakes. Watch over my children and surround them with others who love you, who can also help guide them and point them to you. Amen.*

## 327

## Outdoing Respect
### Nicole O'Dell

*Love one another with brotherly affection. Outdo one another in showing honor. Rom. 12:10, ESV*

It can be maddening when you have to partner with someone who doesn't see things the way you do. Especially when it's something so important as your parenting. Seldom are spouses on the same page 100% of the time. It's very difficult to blend two backgrounds and two personalities into one parenting method and mechanism and have it flow effortlessly into a picture-perfect home.

No one knows this better than my husband and me. We are the most different people who come from the most opposite backgrounds... more different than you can imagine! And we come at things with different viewpoints and framework. Sometimes it can be very difficult to arrive at the same goal.

We have agreed on a couple of things when it comes to raising our kids. We have agreed that the no always wins. If I want to allow something that he doesn't, the no wins. If he is being too free with the kids, and I'm trying to crack down on something, the no wins. We've also agreed to support each other in front of the kids when it comes to our reactions and discipline and whatever else happens in the home, but then talk about things privately so we're on the same page.

Does that always work? I'm not going to lie to you and tell you that we haven't failed at the above. We fail all the time because both of us are stubborn and have difficulty not saying what we're thinking all the time. But restraint is necessary when you're parenting in a partnership. Without restraint you will inevitably disrespect each other and this can be devastating to your parenting goals. Instead, as quoted from Romans 12, outdo each other with respect.

## → Connection Point

*Dear God, sometimes I wonder if my spouse and I will ever make it through these years. Please be our glue. Remind us daily that our partnership is more valuable to our family than gold. Give me enough humility to hold my tongue and let go of my prideful insistence that my way is the right way. Amen.*

## Reality Culture
*Nicole O'Dell*

*Finally, brothers, whatever is true, whatever is honorable, whatever is just, whatever is pure, whatever is lovely, whatever is commendable, if there is any excellence, if there is anything worthy of praise, think about these things. Phil. 4:8, ESV*

Are you a reality TV addict? I have to admit that some of my favorite television programs are reality shows. I love the singing and dancing competitions. I really enjoy the cooking shows and watching people excel at other things, too, like fashion design or home decorating. I particularly love seeing teamwork and support in the midst of competition like on a select few of those TV shows. But, for the most part, reality television is not reality.

What are our teenagers learning and how is this affecting what they expect from the world and their future? Do they expect to live like a real housewife? Or do they understand what it really means to be a housewife? Do they expect to live like a bachelor or bachelorette and have 30 beautiful specimens of human beings paraded before them for their selection? Do they expect to take the world by storm with some incredible talent that sets them apart from everyone else as they sail through the competition?

Parents, we need to consider how we are teaching reality versus the reality they're seeing portrayed in Hollywood. I have a challenge for you this week. Have some specific conversations about reality television. Take a program or two, the ones your teenager has watched and ask for a list of flaws in the expectations the show establishes. What does that show portray that is different than real life or contrary to God's plan for the family and God's reality in the church? Have conversations about what the future might hold and what reality God has in store for your teenager. Then talk about ways to take the attention off the fake and bring about that beautiful reality.

## → Connection Point

*Jesus, thank you for the beauty you've created in the plans you've prepared. Help me to get my teenager to embrace the future you have laid out, and help me guide the way toward it. Amen.*

Powerline365

# 329

## Critical Thinking
### Nicole O'Dell

*Do your best to present yourself to God as one approved, a worker who does not need to be ashamed and who correctly handles the word of truth. 2 Tim. 2:15, NIV*

There are two very important things when it comes to doing good research. First, you have to know your source. It doesn't matter how shocking the news item is or how juicy the tidbit of gossip is, if the source is flawed, the information is worthless. Check and double check the source before you use the data.

In educational and scientific research, it's necessary to use the primary source. In other words if you're going to quote someone, quote them from the original work, not from a work where they are being quoted by someone else. That's called a secondary source, and the further you get from the original the harder it is to ensure accuracy. Plus, the original source deserves the credit.

When it comes to studying and teaching the word of God, it's vital that you practice critical thinking. Consider the source of any teaching you might embrace and pass on to your kids. And use your primary reference. There's so much out there that waters down the Gospel. Why not go right to the source when you're trying to teach your kids, answer their questions, or offer advice? I remember when the Left Behind books were very popular. It was a book series that offered a fictional viewpoint of possibilities that might occur at the fulfillment of the prophecies recorded in the book of Revelation. I know the author of those books, and he would be the first to tell you that though he did portray his best effort at a depiction of prophecy, they were works of fiction and never intended to replace Bible study. Yet people quoted it to me as if they'd read it straight from Scripture.

You want to get your teenagers started with a solid foundation. Drive your teenager to the Word of God as your primary source.

## → Connection Point

*Father please illuminate Your Word to me, and help me be a teacher and sharer of your Word. Help me to learn Scripture so well that it flows from my lips. Amen.*

## Picky People
### Nicole O'Dell

*Let no corrupt speech proceed out of your mouth, but such as is good for edifying as the need may be, that it may give grace to them that hear. Eph. 4:29, ASV*

Do you deal with someone who has a critical spirit? Or maybe it's you who seems to find the negative or the flaw in everyone. It is draining when everything you do is put through the filter of blame and negativity. With my teens I am most critical when I'm afraid, which is usually rooted in a lack of control. Other times I'm critical because I feel guilt over something I've said or done, and I'm afraid that I'll be judged harshly unless I get there first with my own finger-pointing.

Whatever the conscious or subconscious reasons for heaping criticism on others, we are warned against having that kind of nature. Yes, we are to test the spirits and question biblical teaching. We are to judge the fruits of others to determine whether they stand up to the test of scripture. We are to watch our teenagers closely and parent them well, which means discipline and sometimes even snap judgments. But there's a difference between doing all of those things while standing firm in Scripture, and simply being critical.

Does it really matter how your teenager makes her bed as long as there's an attempt at obedience? Does it really matter if the recipe is followed exactly the way you would do it or the poster is colored exactly as you would have done it? How about conflict in friendships? Does it matter if your teen goes about things differently than you would but still achieves good results? In fact, wouldn't that be better?

As parents and as spouses (if applicable) we need to check a critical spirit at the door. It has no room in the home. The home should be a haven, a place to explore new things and test interests and possibilities without the stress of potential negativity. Support your teens even when they aren't just like you.

### → Connection Point

*Father, please forgive me for the times when I have been critical. Help me to be kindhearted and open to new things even with these teenagers who are so different than me. And please help me to raise a kind-spirited teenager. Amen.*

# 331

Powerline365

## Compartmentalize
*Nicole O'Dell*

*I can do all things through him who strengthens me. Phil. 4:13, ESV*

If you're like me, an emotional person, it can be difficult to do the basics and keep a smile on your face when you're in the middle of a personal crisis. Some people are better at compartmentalizing and setting aside issues and conflicts that are weighing heavily on them; others wear their emotions on their sleeve.

People will let you down. Whether your spouse, your best friend, or even your teenagers, people will disappoint and even hurt you time and time again. But you still have to function as a parent and do your duties with joy while you're struggling to wade through whatever personal issue you're facing. How is that possible?

Teenagers get to stomp off to their rooms to brood and mope, maybe even put headphones on and listen to loud music. They get to call their friends on the phone and dish about the bully at school or the relationship drama they're suffering. They can cop an attitude with you (somewhat) and can shut down while they find a way to cope. Not so with parents. Here are three ways to ensure that you're equipped to press on in the face of pain:

1. Plan ahead—Know when your kids are going to come home and prepare yourself. Dry your eyes and paste on that smile so you don't cause them needless stress.

2. Prepare an answer—If they ask you what's wrong, have an answer prepared that makes sense, isn't gossipy, and isn't something you'll regret later. Don't throw your spouse under the bus!

3. Pray hard—Knowing you're about to step back in your parenting shoes, give it over to God. Ask Him to carry it for a while. Who knows, when you have your next moment alone to take it back, you might be ready to let it go forever.

## → Connection Point

*Jesus, thank you for being faithful, for being the One who never fails me. Please help me to surrender life's issues to you so I can parent with all my heart. Amen.*

# 332

## New Car Smell
### Nicole O'Dell

> *Do not seek what you should eat or what you should drink, nor have an anxious mind. For all these things the nations of the world seek after, and your father knows that you need these things. But seek the kingdom of God, and all these things shall be added to you.*
> Luke 12:29-31, NKJV

Have you ever bought a brand new car? The very best thing about buying a new car is the smell! However, the car depreciates the moment you drive away from the car lot. It's no longer new. But we want the newest, the best, the fastest, the biggest everything. More, more, more. This clamoring to acquire everything the world has to offer at the moment it's available, is keeping our families slaves to commercialism. Slaves to a paycheck and work hours, even slaves to our cell phone plans. Always trying to have the latest gadget leaves us unsatisfied most of the time because the newest is only new for about a week before it's obsolete.

If we follow Jesus, our striving needs to be toward Him. We strive for relationship. We strive to understand His will and implement it in our lives. We strive to parent our teenagers to seek Him with all their hearts. When we busy ourselves with all the other reaching, how much time is left to chase after what is good and right in the sight of God? Seek first the kingdom of God, and lead your teens to do the same thing. Keep them from becoming enslaved to the trappings of the world by modeling pursuit of the kingdom of God in your own life.

We don't have to waste time chasing the things that will rot and rust and pass away. We can turn our eyes on Jesus and let Him change us into a reflection of Him. But this requires a heart that longs for eternity and understands what is righteous and what is valuable. A passionate heart that longs for Jesus will never lose that new car smell.

## → Connection Point

*I want to know you more. I want to seek your kingdom first, and I want to teach my teens to strive hard after you, to chase all that you have to offer and abandon the glitz and glitter of this world. Thank You for providing for our needs so we can focus on what is richest in this life and for all of eternity. Amen.*

## Forgive and Forget
### Nicole O'Dell

*Bear with each other and forgive one another if any of you has a grievance against someone. Forgive as the Lord forgave you.*
Col. 3:13, NIV

As I look back on the landscape of my life I can see a few deep valleys of offense where someone hurt me deeply. They're there. I've managed to forgive, sometimes over and over, but I haven't managed to fill those valleys so they don't mar my view.

Relationships are one of the biggest blessings in our lives, but they are also the source of the greatest possible hurt. People say damaging things. People are disloyal. People break trust. And in response we harbor resentment, jealousy, bitterness, rage. You fill in the blank. We put up walls, and we shut people out because we can't get hurt if we don't let them back in. Yet God calls us to forgive.

I have found it difficult to parent effectively when it comes to issues related to those deep valleys in my life. I realized that when I have not fully forgiven, or when I have forgiven and then grabbed the offense right back, I cannot live authentically in front of my teenagers. How can I teach them God's economy of forgiveness if I can't live it?

Does forgive mean forget? Of course not. We aren't capable of fully forgetting. And that means triggers will bring the offense to the surface from time to time. That's why we must keep careful watch and be ready, at all times, to revisit the need to forgive.

But how can I forgive? Truth is, you can't. Forgiveness is an extension of the expression of forgiveness we are shown by God. When you are at the end of yourself and unable to forgive people who have hurt you, revisit that place where you first felt bathed in God's loving embrace and ask Him to flow His forgiveness through you as you reach out to others.

## → Connection Point

*Lord, anger and pain threaten to overtake me sometimes. Yet, I've been forgiven so much. I get it; I need to show others the forgiveness you've shown me, but the fact is, I'm weak. Please work in me, soften my heart, and let me be a living expression of your mercy. Amen.*

# Risk Taker
## Nicole O'Dell

*So be strong and courageous! Do not be afraid and do not panic before them. For the LORD your God will personally go ahead of you. He will neither fail you nor abandon you. Deut. 31:6, NLT*

Do you take chances, or do you prefer to keep it safe? Trials and choices and temptations are thrown at us on a daily basis. We have to make decisions for ourselves and for teenagers; sometimes it's good to make the safe decisions, and sometimes it's important to take a risk.

I think of Peter (Matthew 14) when Jesus called him to climb out of his boat and step into the sea. Was Peter taking a risk when he obeyed? Of course he was. It would've been much easier and safer to stay in the boat where he had no risk of sinking or looking like a fool. But what if he hadn't followed Jesus' command?

You're in a boat today, and Jesus is calling you to some action, some courageous step. Are you afraid to take it? Maybe you're afraid to fail. Maybe it feels like too much is at risk. Maybe you don't want to be embarrassed. But it's time to slough off the burden of fear and take on the cloak of courage.

God tells us to be strong and courageous, not because we are mighty, but because He is. If worry has you frozen as you face the challenge to step out of your boat, find that quiet peaceful place to turn your focus onto God. Let Him guide you, and let Him fill you with the courage you need to do what He's called you to do.

Further, consider that He wants to use you to call your teenagers from the safety of their boats. Don't let them grow so comfortable there that they miss the voice of God calling them to join Him in the water.

## → Connection Point

*God, thank you for always being with me and providing the strength I need to do what you've called me to do. Please give me the faith I need to trust in you no matter what. And please help me stir my teenagers to step from their safety into your will. Amen.*

## Hunger and Thirst
### Nicole O'Dell

*Blessed are those who hunger and thirst for righteousness, for they will be filled. Matt. 5:6, NIV*

What does real hunger feel like? Most of us in first-world living conditions don't know what true hunger is. The minute we feel that rumbling in our belly, we fill it. We are so blessed to have our physical needs satisfied on a moment-to-moment basis, but in order to understand spiritual hunger, we have to first understand physical hunger.

Physical hunger comes about when your body is depleted of the food stores it needs to function at efficient and effective levels. Proper nutrients are the fuel that your body needs to operate as a fully functioning machine. We have the same need spiritually. Prayer, studying the word of God, fellowship with believers–those are the nutrients that fuel the spiritual walk of the believer.

Has regular church attendance, a full treasure trove of Christian friends, a few Bible study groups, and a bookshelf full of material kept you just short of the rumbling in your belly and kept you from experiencing what it means to be spiritually hungry? Sure, when something goes wrong you run right to your resources, but what about when everything is going right? Do you feel that hunger and thirst for more of God?

If you are feeling dormant, it will spill over into your parenting. How can you parent with power if you're not desperately seeking more of it? Ask yourself what happened to your appetite for God? What is filling your time and your attention? When you choose to fill your belly with more and more of Him, you will see that He is good. Be invigorated to seek and tap into the power of God.

## → Connection Point

*Father God, only you can truly feel my empty soul, but I do know that I am not feeling the hunger pangs that drive me to your Word these days. Please make my belly rumble for more and more of you. Amen.*

## Power in Prayer
### Nicole O'Dell

*Be joyful in hope, patient in affliction, faithful in prayer.*
*Rom. 12:12, NIV*

A lot of people pray when they have needs, but a faithful pray-er understands the power in prayer and can't live without it.

We spend a lot of time in these devotions praying. I recommend praying as one of the most important steps in dealing with any issue as a parent or in any area of life. I provide a prayer for you to use at the end of each devotion. A while back, I even provided a list of scriptures to pray for your teens. That's how important I believe it is.

Prayer is the way we surrender our will and our needs to God, and it's also the way He advances His purposes on this earth. We were intended to be in fellowship with God. He communicates with us, teaches us, and bathes us in His love when we spend time with Him in prayer. God knows that we need to connect with Him; that's why Jesus taught us how He talks to His father.

It's not intended to be a habit or a to-do list item to check off every day as you say your prayers. It's meant to be a lifeline, a tether between your heart and God's.

What does it look like when a parent is faithful in prayer? It means that your relationship with God is intimate enough that when you're in need, rather than reaching for your cell phone or some kind of comfort item or habit, you immediately turn to communicate with God. A faithful pray-er craves quiet time alone with God, and the day doesn't have the right tone without it.

It's not always easy to find those quiet moments. So if it's not a part of your routine yet, start with just a few minutes. Even if it's on your drive to work or in the few minutes before the kids come home from school. Talk to God like He's your best friend, because He is.

## → Connection Point

*Jesus, help me to be faithful in prayer. Remind me that you do hear me and answer my prayers. Show me your presence when I spend time with you. Amen.*

Powerline365

# Strength for the Journey
## Nicole O'Dell

*Come to me, all of you who are weary and burdened, and I will give you rest. Matt. 11:28, NLT*

Elijah experienced an amazing triumph on Mount Carmel, but it left him completely emptied of mental, physical, and spiritual strength. And the enemy loves to strike when God's people are weak. He went after a vulnerable Elijah through threats of murder and more. Elijah had had enough; he was done. As recorded in I Kings 19, he prayed, "I have had enough, Lord. Take my life."

Are your parenting energy stores all used up? Are you feeling lonely or discouraged as you parent your teens? Maybe life has pressed in on all sides and you're like Elijah, beaten down physically, mentally, and spiritually. I hate to tell you, but these are the moments your enemy sees an opportunity and wages another attack. He knows that, in your weakened state, you are more likely to hang your head in despair and give up the fight, and far less likely to turn to God.

But God heard Elijah's plea and sent an angel to minister to Elijah's most basic needs, food and water, that gave him just enough strength to face another day.

What are you facing as you parent your teens? Don't give up. It's okay to feel like you're at the end of your rope, but look up. Pray for strength and wait to see how God will minister to you. He will lighten your load and give you rest.

## → Connection Point

*Jesus, thank you for shouldering my burdens and standing with me in the battle. Please give me the strength I need to keep up the fight against our enemy. He has no place in my life or in my home, and with you on my side, I know he doesn't stand a chance. In your name, amen.*

## Sabbath Siblings
*Amber Frank*

*Then Jesus said to them, "The Sabbath was made to meet the needs of people, and not people to meet the requirements of the Sabbath." Mark 2:27, NLT*

It's Sunday morning. You're worn out from your week, and the thought of battling with your teenager to get out of bed, get dressed, and get to church on time is just too much. Sunday is a day of rest, right? Maybe you can just sleep in and skip church just this once. You do need your rest. God even said so! Sabbath was made for man, not man for the Sabbath... right?

Yeah, we have all been there. I know the feeling. Sometimes it's tougher to get your teen to church on time on Sunday morning than it would be to get a tortoise to cross a finish line. But church is much more than just going to sing a few songs that make us feel good and to hear what someone else thinks about a Bible verse.

Church is family, our family, the family we have been given through our faith in Jesus Christ. Just like you wouldn't want your teen to miss a family outing, an important holiday, or a reunion, you shouldn't let them miss out on meeting with their brothers and sisters in Christ. They need to encourage each other in the faith, to pray for one another, to see their siblings in the Lord on a regular basis and know that they are there for each other. It's one thing to hear another adult tell them why we need Jesus, but another thing entirely to have another teen speak that into their life by either word or example.

We must be enthusiastic about church ourselves, and even when our teens want to pull the covers over their heads, we need to make them understand it isn't about what they want, it's about what is good for them and for their siblings in Jesus.

## → Connection Point

*Father, please help me be enthusiastic about going to church and to set a good example for my teens. Help me show the importance of meeting together, and the value of encouraging our Christian brothers and sisters, and being encouraged by them. Let my kids be drawn to you and to their church family. Amen.*

## Parenting Fruits
*Nicole O'Dell*

*But the fruit of the Spirit is love, joy, peace, patience, kindness, goodness, faithfulness, gentleness, self-control; against such things there is no law. Gal 5:22-23, NASB*

It's really easy to search out the "fruits of the Spirit" in others. Are they loving? Are they good and kind? Do they exercise self-control? It's easy to measure others against those standards, but is that God's intention with that scripture?

Galatians chapter 5 is all about the freedom we have in Christ and how He wants us to live and thrive in that freedom. The fruits of the Spirit are simply a list of the things that should be evident in a follower of Christ; they are the fruits of that relationship and the effect of the influence of the Holy Spirit. They are meant to be a way to examine ourselves first and foremost.

In what ways can the fruits of Christ in us affect our parenting? We can love our teens as Jesus has loved us. We can parent with a spirit of joy and a heart of peace and overcome frustration in favor of patience. We can offer a gentle touch and soft words, and we can be an example by practicing self-discipline.

It's not easy to force those traits to the fore by sheer will. It takes unity and intimacy with the Holy Spirit so that He will flow through us, and the fruit of that relationship will be a blessing in our homes. Press into a new level of intimacy with God through prayer and worship. Let the Holy Spirit of God bathe you with the evidence of Himself in you.

## → Connection Point

*Lord, please show me where I need to focus and grow so the fruits of the Holy Spirit will be evident in my parenting and in my life. Please help me to grow into the parent you have called me to be. Amen.*

# 340

## When They Hurt
*Nicole O'Dell*

*Rejoice with those who rejoice, weep with those who weep.*
*Rom. 12:15, ESV*

Empathy is a missing factor in a lot of homes. People are so busy trying to make a way for themselves they lose sight of what other people are dealing with and what they really feel. Plus families are running at such high speed it's hard to slow down enough to feel with hurting loved ones.

It was very painful when I lost my grandpa. I had never felt hurt and loss like that before, and I didn't think something could hurt more. That is until I looked into the eyes of my son as I told him of our loss.

My boy had struggles in his early years. For a lot of reasons, he harbored intense anger and felt a lot of loneliness. But Erik and Papaw shared a bond that healed so much of the pain that Erik suffered. My grandfather was his constant, his best friend, his proof that God the Father could really love him the way we said He did.

When I sat Erik down and told him that his Papaw had passed away the night before, I saw fear in his eyes. Instantly, he felt alone in the world. He'd lost his advocate and his protector. He'd lost the one person who understood him. And he was afraid.

To be honest, as a parent, I was afraid, too. How could I fill the sudden vacuum Erik felt in his life? So I held him, and we cried. Sometimes there are no words to make it better. Sometimes no piece of advice will solve the problems our teenagers face. Sometimes the best we can do is to feel with them and let them know we're on their side.

And it's enough.

## → Connection Point

*Father, please help me to really feel what my teenagers are going through, and then show me what I need to do to respond to their needs. May I never be so busy that I can't slow down and feel with my teens. Amen.*

# My Way
## Nicole O'Dell

*For we are his workmanship, created in Christ Jesus for good works, which God prepared beforehand, that we should walk in them.*
*Eph. 2:10, ESV*

Before I became a parent, I made all sorts of declarations about how I'd do things. I'd never do certain things like my mom. I'd never be like my dad. I'd let my kids do the things my parents wouldn't allow me to do. In fact, we'd do them together! Most of all, I'd be their friend. We'd talk openly and honestly about everything because I'd understand. And the list went on and on.

And most of all, I believed it wouldn't be difficult. I thought that somehow my kids would just get it. They'd naturally do the right things. They'd find success whether they wanted to or not. All the best of life would fall from the sky like rain, and we'd have no stress.

Then I had kids. It wasn't long before I understood my parents, and not much longer before I realized I was becoming them — and worse!

When I looked into the eyes of my babies and as I've watched them grow into children, teenagers, and even one an adult, I've been overcome with the realization that they are men or women who will one day become the pillars of Christ's church. Yes, that young boy who ate dirt and the little girl who flushed the remote control — they had a calling by God to serve His kingdom and affect people for all of eternity.

Suddenly, being their friend was not my priority. It no longer mattered if they approved of my boundaries or discipline. It only mattered that through those things, they saw Jesus at work.

In what ways can you tighten up your focus and motivations to ensure you're parenting with an eye on God's future for your teens?

## → Connection Point

*Dear God, it amazes me that You've got a special calling for these teens that can't even remember to close the front door. Help me to be faithful to uncover and nurture the gifts you have instilled in them and to parent them as an extension of you. Amen.*

## Greener-Grass Syndrome
*Nicole O'Dell*

Why do you fight and argue with each other? Isn't it because you are full of selfish desires that fight to control your body? You want something you don't have, and you will do anything to get it. James 4:1-2, CEV

The grass is always greener on the other side — or so we're told. When your teenagers stomp around with a bad attitude but their friends always have a smile for you, the grass looks greener over there. When you get a call from the principal who tells you your teenager has been skipping school on the same day that your Facebook news feed is full of honor roll bragging and college scholarship announcements, the grass looks greener in someone else's yard. When your teens have nothing but grunts or two word answers to every question and you have to find out from a friend about a new crush or major decision, the grass looks greener anywhere else.

It's easy to look at the seemingly perfect families and teenagers around you and want what they have. The truth is, there are no perfect families. We all have grass, and sometimes yours looks appealing to the rest of us! And even if you could trade teens for a while, you'd soon discover that your problems weren't necessarily all that bad.

The problem is that it is our selfish desires that cause us to rebel against what we have rather than accept and appreciate our blessings. Constant comparison with other marriages, families, and teenagers will only lead to dissatisfaction as we wish for something other than or more than we have. Our enemy wants to keep us looking outward with longing rather than inward with passionate commitment.

Instead, focus on the life and beauty that God speaks into your family as He reveals the gifts He has given to you through the blessing of your teenagers.

## → Connection Point

*Jesus, thank you for these awesome teenagers! Please reveal all the special qualities you see in my teens so I can cling to those during the rough times. Help me to keep my eyes on my own blessings rather than comparing and striving for what I see in others. Amen.*

## Can't Buy Me Love
*Nicole O'Dell*

Are you humming the bars to that old song? As the Beatles recognized, money can buy a lot of things, but it can't buy love. This concept shows itself in dating relationships and marriage, but I think parents, more than anyone, fall into the trap of trying to make their teenagers happy by throwing money at the problems.

Do any of these sound familiar?

- My teenager isn't doing well in school, so I'll hire an expensive tutor.
- My teenager is bored, so I'll sign her up for a bunch of expensive sports and clubs.
- My teenager feels unpopular, so if I buy a bunch of trendy clothes she'll be more confident and get more friends.
- My teenager is angry with me, so maybe the newest iPhone or computer device will cover over those feelings.

Trust me, we've all done it. It's human nature to want to find a solution to a problem. And sometimes solutions cost money. But I want to encourage you to first get to the root of the issues. Every one of those things mentioned above could be addressed more effectively without money. Problems in school? Maybe the schedule needs to be lightened and more study time made available, or maybe they need your help. Anger issues? What's at the root of it? Because I guarantee that your teenager, in five years, won't remember the trinket you bought, but she will remember why she's angry if it's not addressed.

In order to root out the foundation of any relationship struggle, you first need to communicate. Ask your teenager what he or she thinks is the main problem. Listen to the answers and work together to find a solution. Most of all, pray over the problem and pray together. Let your teenager know that no problem is too big or too small, and that you know where to go for healing. Run to the foot of the cross, not your checkbook.

## → Connection Point

*Father, please forgive me for looking in the wrong places to solve problems. Please convict my spirit when I'm trying to take the easy way out and remind me of the steps I need to take to ensure a positive and lasting effect on the relationship I have with my teen. Amen.*

## Blended Talk
*Nicole O'Dell*

*He was oppressed and afflicted, yet he did not open his mouth; he was led like a lamb to the slaughter, and as a sheep before its shearers is silent, so he did not open his mouth. Isaiah 53:7*

Communication in families is difficult enough without the added stress of divorce and co-parenting and all the iterations of those family situations. Not only is it necessary to communicate with the people in your home, but there's often another parent out there who has input into decisions you make with and for your kids. In a stepparent situation, that creates a culture of confusion and often leads to arguments, defensiveness, and withdrawal. The kids see and hear it all, or at least sense it. When they feel pulled and confused, that's often when they shut down or act out.

Try to look at it as a business situation. In the workplace, you've likely dealt with all sorts of people. You've had bosses who drove you nuts. You've had co-workers who stabbed you in the back. You've had customers or clients who got on every last nerve. But, in order to be successful in that job, you had to find a way to approach conflict in a civil way. You had to compromise in order to settle a storm. You had to give in and lose battles in order to stay ahead in the war. Aren't your kids worth at least that much effort?

Set aside the battles that only defend your rights. Who cares if you have to drive a little farther or lose a few minutes of time? Who cares if you could probably go back to court for this or that? Who cares if your teens don't really know the whole truth about your ex? Who cares if his/her new spouse badmouths you? All of those things are focused on you, not on your kids. For your sake, you want to fight back, but for their sake, you need to be at peace. Pride is your biggest enemy, and peace is one of the greatest gifts you can offer your teens.

## → Connection Point

Father, please surround these readers with your grace and strength. Squelch the spirit of pride in these homes. Raise up a confidence in each parent that seeks your approval, your justice, and your grace above all else. Please grant wisdom and perseverance to these moms and dads. Amen.

## Weebles Wobble
### Nicole O'Dell

*Though he may stumble, he will not fall, for the LORD upholds him with his hand. Psalm 37:24, NIV*

Were you a weeble wobbler when you were younger? I sure was. I had the treehouse and the cars and all sorts of accessories. I loved pushing on the Weeble people and watching them spring back up to life no matter how hard they were knocked around. If you don't know what they are, then I have sufficiently dated myself and you should run to Google and see what you've been missing. The best part was the slogan: "Weebles wobble but they don't fall down!"

As a child of God and a parent of Kingdom kids, you are assured ultimate victory over this world. No matter what comes your way, you can stand tall and face it. A check bounces. The washing machine is on the fritz. Your teenager comes home with a failing test grade for you to sign. Your spouse becomes unemployed. Bam! Bam! Bam! But Psalm 37:24 tells us that even though we may stumble, He upholds us with His own hand and we will not fall.

You wobble and it seems like you're about to collapse, but no matter what, if you claim God's promises for yourself and your family, you can spring right back to life. Face the day like a Weeble. Smile and stand firm no matter what happens knowing that there's no force strong enough to keep you down.

*Blessed is the man who remains steadfast under trial, for when he has stood the test he will receive the crown of life, which God has promised to those who love him. James 1:12, ESV*

## → Connection Point

*Jesus, thank you for being so faithful and for being my strength in the tough times. Please help me remember that I am a Weeble; I may wobble, but I won't fall down. Amen.*

## Conquering Victor
### Nicole O'Dell

*Who shall separate us from the love of Christ? Shall trouble or hardship or persecution or famine or nakedness or danger or sword? No, in all these things we are more than conquerors through him who loved us. Rom. 8:35, 37, NIV*

I've been down with a back injury and a dear friend texted to ask me if I had enough help. I replied, "It's all good. I'm pretty much a do-it-myself'er anyway." Hmm. As I said that I realized that even though it's true, maybe it's not the best way to approach hardship. The Apostle Paul had his share of burdens to bear, but, rather than crumbling under the weight of them, he decided that he need not endure them alone. He realized it was only through Christ that he would find the strength to endure the challenges of life. (Philippians 4:13) That very same truth exists for you.

Maybe there's no one close by (in either geography or experience) to help you through these years of parenting teens. Maybe you and your spouse are experiencing some distance in your relationship (there are other devotional books to help with that!). Maybe you are just putting your hand to the plow and doing the hard work of parenting on your own.

But don't lose sight of the fact that Jesus Christ will gird you up with every bit of strength that you need to endure each facet of whatever challenge you face. Not only will He get you through it, but, if you will allow Him to, He will bring you through it as the conquering victor. Being more than a conqueror means that you won't simply "get through" what you face; you will enjoy a far-surpassing victory through Christ.

### → Connection Point

*Lord, sometimes I feel as though I can't possibly stand up under the pressure that I feel. Please help me remember that you will give me all the might I need to do all you've called me to do. I want to be a victorious conqueror through you, so please be my strength today and every day. Amen.*

## Rocky Teens?
### Mary DeMuth

*The seed on the rocky soil represents those who hear the message and immediately receive it with joy. But since they don't have deep roots, they don't last long. They fall away as soon as they have problems or are persecuted for believing God's word. Matt. 13:20-21, NLT*

It's not simply a life-management program. It shouldn't be the crutch we fall on when life gets ugly. It should be the legs we walk on, the air we breathe. When I read the book of Acts, I'm humbled and a little scared too. Why? Because I don't resemble those folks. I certainly don't think like them. My inner transformation hasn't looked so dynamic, so entirely world-changing. I don't often suffer for the sake of the Gospel. I haven't counted all things loss. Instead, I cling to my possessions, relish my comfort, and spend a lot of time seeking earthly peace.

The Gospel they shared was simple, but it earthquaked the foundations of people's lives. It called for allegiance, total adherence, but it promised the Holy Spirit, the One who would empower them to live out that kind of commitment.

Unfortunately, the Gospel we hear most often in our pulpits or even friend-to-friend, looks nothing like this. It sounds more like platitudes and self-help manuals.

- Meet Jesus and your life will improve.
- Jesus will save your marriage! Your kids! Your life!
- Jesus will forgive you of all that awful stuff you did. Now you have a clean slate and can live the best life you can imagine!

It's not that these things aren't true—to some extent they are—but they are wholly incomplete. Those things, though true, miss the need to die to your own desires and embrace Jesus' lordship.

The gospel isn't a list of self-improvement tactics. We do our teens a disservice if we assign a list steps that rest on a simple prayer and skip the part about surrender. What happens when all the pretty things we share about the gospel seem untrue because reality interrupts?

## → Connection Point

*Jesus, please keep my teens from rocky soil. Let them grow rooted in your truth and surrendered to your lordship. Help me teach them about you so they will not overlook the fullness of who you are. Amen.*

# 348

## Perfect Plan
### Nicole O'Dell

*For you created my inmost being; you knit me together in my mother's womb. I praise you because I am fearfully and wonderfully made; your works are wonderful, I know that full well.*
*Psalm 139: 13-14, NIV*

God, the Creator of all, the One who holds the universe in His hands, created you perfectly according to plan. And before He created you, He already knew your children and created them with the same value and intention as every other soul that ever has or will walk this planet. Your messy, smelly, argumentative, and sometimes downright annoying teenager is just as important to Almighty God as Billy Graham and Mother Theresa.

Then, while all that planning and creating was going on, He selected you for this very moment in history to be the parent of those precious creations you call your kids. What a truly humbling and wonderful thought to know that He ordained you to carry the torch of salvation and the light of ministry into their lives.

Is that freeing or daunting? To be honest, one day that's the most liberating thought to me, but the next day, maybe when I feel like I'm not doing such a great job, it's crippling. Please don't allow Satan to feed you the lie that you can't measure up. Trust in the promises of God (who longs for your victory) and not in the lies of Satan (who only wants you to fail). When Mary was fearful at the news that she was to have a baby, the angel told her that nothing is impossible with God. (Luke 1:37) That truth gave her the confidence she needed to face her future. She knew that she would never be alone, and neither will you.

So, instead of second-guessing the God who spun it all into being, maybe you can assume He might know what He's doing.

## → Connection Point

*Thank you, Father, for your knowing hand that has been on us, with us, and FOR us since the beginning of time. Help me to rest in the knowledge that you're in control. Amen.*

Powerline365

# 349

# Throne of Grace
## Nicole O'Dell

*Let us then approach the throne of grace with confidence, so that we may receive mercy and find grace to help us in our time of need.*
*Heb. 4:16, NIV*

We're nearing the end of our year together, and I find myself feeling like I have so much more to say. There are some biblical concepts that have really left an impression on me over the years and have truly shaped my parenting. One is this verse from Hebrews. This is one of my favorite scriptures. You see, back in Old Testament times, the high priest went into God's presence to appeal for God's favor and make atonement for sin for the people. They couldn't approach God for themselves because they would be found unworthy and struck dead immediately. In fact, even the high priest was taking such a risk that they tied a rope to his ankle in case he didn't make it out of God's presence alive.

But Jesus made a way so that everyone could be cleansed of sin and could therefore enter into the presence of God. In other words, as Hebrew 4 indicates, we can go before the throne of God confidently and with the assurance that He will move and work on our behalf. Think about that and, if it hasn't sunk in, read it one more time and consider the full implication of complete and immediate access to the King of Kings and Lord of Lords.

As our loving Father, He not only allows us to approach Him, He longs for it. He truly longs for us to open ourselves to Him so that He can fully work out His purposes in us and through us for our good and to further the Kingdom.

How does that truth impact your faith walk? How does it impact your parenting?

## → Connection Point

*Jesus, I come into your presence with thanksgiving. I am so comforted and secured by the fact that I can approach you and appeal for mercy and help, but even more so that you know my needs before I ask. Thank you for being my partner in this parenting thing. Amen.*

## More Than No
### Nicole O'Dell

*He who walks with the wise grows wise, but a companion of fools suffers harm. Prov, 13:20, NIV*

Remember Nancy Reagan's campaign slogan, "Just say no"? Those three little words gave voice to the concept of personal choice and standing for truth in the face of temptation, and the statement sent the message that all we needed was a little resolve and confidence in order to stand up for what was right. If we said no and meant it, we'd be fine in the face of pressure. It sounds great. And most of us are raising our teenagers to approach peer pressure and temptation with the same mindset: Just say no.

In truth though, it takes much more than uttering a word to avoid sin. Just saying no out of rote obedience without understanding the reason for the sacrifice is nothing more than legalism. So, there is a lot of prep work required before teens are ready to say no. Nancy Reagan might have had more success if her slogan recommended that parents Just Talk, or for teenagers to Just Plan Ahead.

Peer pressure is daunting and it's daily. Our teens have to be armed with the words to say and the confidence to say them before they're faced with the peer pressure. Just saying no isn't enough. Train your teens to reject sin, of course, but also to be ready to defend their reasons. They need to know when, they need to know how, and they need to know why they should stand against sin.

## → Connection Point

*Jesus, please help my teenagers have a divine wisdom about their own strength in the face of peer pressure. Help them avoid dangerous situations, and give them the confidence to defend their choices. And please give me wisdom to prepare them effectively for all they'll face. Amen.*

## They'll Figure it Out
### Brenda Yoder, MA

*Like arrows in the hands of a warrior are children born in one's youth. Psalm 127:4, NLT*

"It's time for them to go," I told my husband in reference to the college students spending the summer at our house.

Ahem. They were our own kids, and it was time for them to go.

It wasn't that I didn't enjoy them being home, and it certainly wasn't that I didn't love them...or even like them. But young adults living at home is a hard phase.

The same day I said that to my husband, a friend had to tell her twenty-one-year-old daughter she had to move out because she was causing havoc in their home. She couldn't hold a job, she stayed out until morning, and she did nothing to help out at home.

The mom felt guilty. So did I when I verbalized my feelings to my spouse.

Then I realized there's a reason kids are released when they're adults. Like arrows in the hands of a warrior, children are sent into their lives once they're adults. Though they may not act adult-like or live how we'd want them to all the time, they're capable of finding out what their life and faith looks like.

They have to figure it out.

There's time for everything as it says in Ecclesiastes 3. For young adults, there is a time for them to go. For parents of those young adults, it's okay to let go. It's okay to be ready for that. It's okay to say so. You're not alone.

When kids are no longer teens, they can figure out life on their own. They may have to struggle, but God's got them.

## → Connection Point

*Father, thank you for having a hand on our kids even when we don't see it. Thank you for helping them figure it out. Please help me know when it's time to hold tight and when it's time to let go. Amen.*

## Daniel's Compromise
### Nicole O'Dell

*To these four young men God gave knowledge and understanding of all kinds of literature and learning. And Daniel could understand visions and dreams of all kinds. Daniel 1:17, NIV*

Sometimes we have to pick our battles in order to win the war. That rubs some parents wrong because they worry that it looks a bit like they're giving in and letting their teenagers win. But I ask you, is that so bad?

Daniel was a big compromiser. He was taken from Jerusalem into captivity in Babylon. He was separated from his family, forced into slavery, and required to worship their gods. You would think Daniel would have stood firm and refused to obey his new masters in all things, but that's not at all what he did. He assimilated into Babylonian culture in almost every way, except for a few areas. He would not bow down and worship any other God, and he would not eat food sacrificed to idols. Otherwise, he obeyed his masters, and he lived within the culture.

Our teenagers are surrounded by all kinds of cultural things and even customs that we don't understand because they are different than what we experienced at their age. Battling over the minutia will only serve to keep us busy when we need to have our eyes on the front lines. So, instead, let's choose our battles wisely as Daniel did. Focus on the things that have eternal, Kingdom impact and let your teenagers be a light in their culture just as Daniel was—and still is today.

## → Connection Point

*Father, please show me which battles to fight and which to lay down. Help me be wise and discerning as I defend you in my home and help my teenagers fight their battles in this world. Amen.*

## Just As If
### Nicole O'Dell

*Being justified [forgiven and made righteous] by faith, we have peace with God through our Lord Jesus Christ. Rom. 5:1, NIV*

When I was young and learning about matters of faith and scripture, I was taught that the word "justified" meant "just as if I'd never sinned." Wow. What a concept. Really, it's so much bigger than forgiveness. Being forgiven means being free from the penalty, but there can still be baggage to carry associated with memories and natural consequences. But God not only forgives, He also justifies — He restores us back to the beginning with a truly fresh start. Over and over.

I remember struggling with this as a teenager. I never really felt forgiven for my mistakes (whether that was my fault or my parents, it was how I felt). I constantly worked to overcome my failures. I certainly never felt "justified" in my parents' eyes, so I had a hard time understanding what that meant related to my relationship with God.

We worry about being naïve and allowing our teens too much freedom, but as parents, there's a fine line between turning a blind eye to risk and offering grace freely. You need to use your teens' history to help you avoid dangers and mistakes for the future, but you should also strive for a forgiving nature like the one Jesus has offered you. Does forgiving always mean forgetting? Well, we're human, so unfortunately, it does not. But we need to do all we can to keep our teens from staying mired in their mistakes. We need to foster freedom and growth, and offer a fresh start. Over and over.

## → Connection Point

*Father, thank you for your grace. I don't know where I'd be without an incalculable number of fresh starts. Would you empower me with a nature of grace so I can parent my teens with a heart of restoration? Help me to walk in freedom as I parent. Amen.*

## Blurt Not
### Nicole O'Dell

*Where words are many, sin is not absent, but he who holds his tongue is wise. Prov. 10:19, NIV*

When I was young I had to fight the urge to say everything on my mind. It didn't matter what my thought was about — the color of a half-eaten M&M or the way the wind sounds if you press your ear against the car window — I couldn't stop myself from saying it, and it didn't matter who was around or what they were doing. Note to self: Go a little easier on Megan when she interrupts, the poor kid comes by it honestly. There were times when I literally bit my lip to try to keep from blurting out. It would work for a minute or two, but all the while I'd be collecting more thoughts. Just when I felt I would explode, they'd all come tumbling out. Over time, I had to learn restraint, but it's not always easy.

When our teens make mistakes or face confusing decisions, we instantly have a lot to say. Sage advice. Brilliant anecdotes. Thoughtful challenges. But our words often have a different effect than we intended and there's usually only one reason why. Timing.

When our words fail to bring about the result we'd hoped, it's most often because our teens weren't ready to act upon our advice, or their hearts weren't yet softened to realize their own need. So we either have to repeat ourselves the next day if we're blessed with another shot at it, or we lose our voice into the problem completely.

If you find yourself talking more and your teenager listening less, consider your timing. Are you rushing to blurt out everything you think the moment you think it, or are you prayerfully considering what to say and when to say it? Let your words come from a patient heart that is moved by God, and watch what happens as your teens hear you.

## → Connection Point

*Jesus, please help me to be more restful with my words. Help me trust your timing and get out of the way of your work. Please use me in the right moments to have impact on my teens. Amen.*

Powerline365

## The One You Feed
### Nicole O'Dell

*Among whom we all once lived in the passions of our flesh, carrying out the desires of the body and the mind, and were by nature children of wrath, like the rest of mankind. Eph. 2:3, ESV*

I just finished editing my book, The Shadowed Onyx, for its rerelease. This book looks deeply in to the topics of spiritual warfare and its effects. In it, a wise counselor shares this story:

 An old Cherokee once told his grandson about a battle that rages inside every person, no matter their age, ethnicity, or lot in life. Even their sex, their financial status, their heritage— none of it matters in this battle for souls.

 That old Cherokee said, "My son, there is a battle between two wolves that exists inside every one of us."

 The little boy leaned in and listened closely, as he tended to do when Grandfather spoke.

 "One of those wolves is Evil. It is everything bad in a person: anger, envy, greed, arrogance, self-pity, guilt, and lies… all lies. The other is Good. It is joy, peace, love, hope, serenity, humility, kindness, benevolence, empathy, generosity, truth, compassion, and faith."

 The grandson pondered the concept for a moment. Then he turned his concerned gaze up to his grandfather's aged face, so full of wisdom, and he asked: "Which wolf wins?"

 The old Cherokee simply replied, "The one you feed."

Which wolf are you feeding as you parent your teens? You can feed the evil wolf with tasty arguments, gossip, sin, criticism, and anger. You can feed that good wolf with wholesome talk, good fun, family times, honesty, and faith. Our nature gravitates toward the evil wolf and all he wants to devour, but with the power of God, we can turn our focus and nourish the life within ourselves and within our teens.

## → Connection Point

*Lord, thank you for redeeming our sinful nature and making it possible for me to nurture the good in my home. Please show me what I need to do to put that evil wolf to death in my teenager's lives. Amen.*

## Captive Thoughts
### Nicole O'Dell

*Set your minds and keep them set on what is above (the higher things) the earth. Col. 3:2, AMP*

I often say that my brain reminds me of the stock and news ticker screens that constantly run in New York in Times Square. I get pelted by my schedule, to-do list, worries about the future, and concerns about my kids. It's tough to sort out my thoughts sometimes, let alone understand them. But I know I'm not alone.

Have you ever stopped to examine your thinking? Your thoughts come and go easily; you don't have to force them to the surface because your brain is constantly working. But even though thinking is natural, God wants us to be conscious about what we let enter our minds and in control about how we let our thoughts consume us. A wild Times Square ticker scene is not His idea of a calm, faith-filled approach to life. He wants us to be ordered, in control of our thinking, and focused on the good stuff He has brought into our lives.

Think about it. If we don't aim our thought focus, we can stumble into a pattern of disillusionment, dissatisfaction, resentment, blame... the list goes on and on. But when we choose to steer our minds to the things of God, He can use our intellect for His purposes. When it comes to parenting your teens, it's easy to get to discouraged. If you're having trouble directing your thoughts, turn to Scripture. It's very difficult to interrupt God when He speaks to you through His Word.

## → Connection Point

*Father, please forgive me for being so wrapped up in my way of thinking that I've lost sight of Yours at times. Help direct my thought patterns to healthy effective things. Please use my mind for your purposes in my home and outside of it. Amen.*

# 357

Powerline365

## Sing Over You
### Nicole O'Dell

*He will take delight in you with gladness. With his love, he will calm your fears. He will rejoice over you with joyful songs. Zeph. 3:17, NLT*

*Since you are like lukewarm water, neither hot nor cold, I will spit you out of my mouth! Rev. 3:16, NLT*

Since we are so close to being out of time in this year of devotions, I feel an urgency to get back to some possible harsh basics. I would like you to imagine an overview of your home and what it contains. Look at your possessions, your bank account, your work ethic, your interpersonal family relationships, and your entertainment choices, as well as your parenting methods including the time and communication you offer your teenagers.

Which verse would apply to what Jesus sees from that same view? Is He rejoicing over you and your household with joyful songs? Or does He find you to be lukewarm? Parents, you only have a little time to get this right. Your salvation may not be about works, but your parenting is. It's about putting in the time and the miles. It's about having the long talks and setting a great example. It's about surrendering to God in faithfulness and enduring hardship and sacrifice for your children. It's about proverbially blistering your knees as you spend time in prayer for and with your teens.

That doesn't mean your teenagers will always make the perfect choice. They have free will too. You are only responsible for what you bring to the equation. So, how can you turn the tables and shake things up? What can you change right now to begin to change the spiritual tone in your home? It's time to cast aside any tendency toward being lukewarm and run for God's absolute best.

## → Connection Point

*Father, please forgive me for the ways I've been lukewarm in my parenting and in my walk with you. Convict my heart to do whatever is necessary to get things on the right track. Guide me as I parent these teenagers in a way that will lead you to sing joyful songs over our household. Amen.*

# 358

## Whale Song
*Valerie Comer*

*All creatures in heaven, on earth, under the earth, and on the sea, and all that is in them, were singing. I heard them say, "May praise and honor for ever and ever be given to the One who sits on the throne and to the Lamb! Give them glory and power forever and ever!" Rev. 5:13, NIRV*

This past week I've been blessed to vacation in Port McNeill along the coast of British Columbia. The beauty of creation is so evident in this place and I'm reminded of just how majestic our God is. I set off on a whale-watching expedition this morning and we saw so many whales. In fact, we were privileged to see some before we even left the dock.

Over the years I've learned that whales communicate with clicks and sounds. They use echolocation to send messages to other whales and to find their way. Different species of whales use various forms of communication, and this pattern is evident to those who study whales.

A beautiful fact of God's design is that whales sing! It has been studied and recorded that they sing in a pattern that sounds lyrical and unique to them. These songs can be up to 30 minutes long, are repeatable, and can travel as far as 100 miles from the singing whale.

Whales form pods and their communications are specific to their family groups. Some believe that whales convey their health and security through their songs, which is most evident in the disparity between the communications of whales in captivity to those who are free.

The Lord hears our songs as a unique offering to Him. He knows our hearts and sees our needs. Your family has a song all your own. One the Lord craves to hear.

Whether you sing, pray, or worship in some other way, take a cue from the whales, draw your family together and worship your Creator.

## → Connection Point

*Lord, thank you for hearing our prayers and knowing us so specially that you recognize us even by our sounds. Unite my family with hearts to worship you. Amen.*

# Powerline365

# 359

## To Serve
### Nicole O'Dell

*Therefore, as we have opportunity, let us do good to all, especially to those who are of the household of faith. Gal. 6:10, NIV*

Our society is in trouble. We have needs on every street corner — people of God, and others who need Him, are suffering and lonely. With the vast amount of needs all around, we have so many opportunities to do good for others and to teach our teenagers to serve.

But where do we start? Paul offers the advice to look first into the household of faith. Does your church have a soup kitchen or young moms' support group? Is there a single parent's ministry that could use some help? How about a meals program for the sick and needy in your congregation? Those are all great places to start with your teens. It will give them the chance to serve in a safe environment and to fulfill needs that exist near them.

Serving others is also a great way to combat entitlement in our children and foster a thankful attitude. Most importantly, when you serve others as a family unit, everyone is blessed. So find a place where your family can serve together on a consistent basis and make sure your local church is included if possible. But don't be surprised that once they get a taste of the blessing that comes from serving, your teens will want more. They'll bring ideas and opportunities to you.

Make your family culture one of service. Jesus had the ultimate servant's heart, so teach your teens that reaching others in His name is just like being an extension of His hand.

## → Connection Point

*Jesus, thank you for teaching us that the least is the greatest and that a person who shows compassion and generosity to others is near to your heart. Please help me teach that to my teens in ways that light a fire in them to reach others in your name. Amen.*

## Mistakes Do Happen
### J. Alden Hall

*Therefore, confess your sins to each other and pray for one another, that you may be healed. James 5:15, ESV*

Don't let this alarm you... but we are human. But there seems to be something that happens to us when we give birth. We find it difficult to admit we make mistakes. When the children are little, we can get away with it. It's like our superhero status makes it easy for them to overlook our blunders.

"My daddy is bigger than yours!" "My mom's the prettiest!" In their young eyes, we were invincible, we could do no wrong. Then the teenage years arrive. Their rose-colored glasses are exchanged for laser-like eyes that watch and wait for our slip-ups.

Years ago, the editor of The Indianapolis News angrily confronted his staff. "Who spelled height as hight? I will not allow grammatical errors in my newspaper." The employees frantically searched through the original copies and found the one responsible – the editor. They sheepishly slipped the proof to him.

After a slight pause, he replied, "Well, if that's the way I spelled it, it has to be right." For the next thirty years, The Indianapolis News misspelled the word.

We parents sometimes fear that admitting mistakes will devalue our authority. But teens don't want their parents to be perfect. They want to trust us. If they witness you handling your blunders with humility and truth, then they will much more likely respond in kind when they fail. They need to learn that making mistakes is okay, that it's part of being human.

It may shock you, but they already know you make mistakes. That's okay, but the next time you blow it, try something different...be honest about it.

Ask yourself, "Why am I hesitant to admit my mistakes?"

## → Connection Point

*Dear God, I desperately want my teenager to trust me. Give me the attitude of humility. May I have the grace to share my blunders and may my teen learn that they too can share their mistakes with me. Amen.*

## Lift Your Eyes
### Nicole O'Dell

*I lift up my eyes to the mountains—where does my help come from? My help comes from the Lord, the Maker of heaven and earth.*
*Psalm 121:1-2, NIV*

Our days are busy. Our steps are deliberate. Our schedules are jam-packed. Where are your eyes focused in the mayhem? Downward for the next place to plant your foot? Are you focused on the next item on the to-do list or the next scheduled event so intently you approach everything in your own strength?

I've put myself through that misery many times. It's a personality flaw of mine that drives me to stay so busy my schedule has little room. Granted, what I fill my time with is worthwhile. And I'm not a procrastinator or a quitter. But I'm too busy most of the time. I've explored my processes to find a reason why I do that. Is it a self-worth issue? Is it an organization issue? Is there a reason I can't rest? But that self-exploration always leads me back to the same point: It's how God made me.

I'm goal-oriented and results-driven. I have ideas I strive to accomplish. The busy-ness isn't necessarily the problem. The problem is that I rely too heavily on my own strength and forget I don't have to go it alone. When do you forget to look to the Lord for help?

When parenting our teenagers, it's even more important to lift our eyes up to the hills. That means looking ahead into the future, over the horizon, beyond what we can see and watching God's work in our teens' lives and in our own. It means trusting things God put right in front of us and knowing what's over the next rise is going to be good because it's of Him.

It's a matter of trust. Now continue your journey forward – it's a good journey – but be sure you're looking ahead of you, over the hills, and beyond the obvious ... to where your help comes from.

## → Connection Point

*Father, please forgive me for the times when I've overlooked your help. Would you lift my face and lock eyes with me when I get too focused on my work that I forget about my Master? Please guide me and help me on this parenting journey. Amen.*

# 362

Powerline365

## Little Faith
*Nicole O'Dell*

*Jesus said to his disciples, "Why are you so afraid? Do you still have no faith?" Mark 4:40, NIV*

Wow, we've been through a lot together over this year of seeking God about parenting our teenagers. We've dealt with the specifics of peer pressure, the preparation needed to go into the world to defend the gospel, the struggles that come with parenting, and faith issues related to our personal walks as parents and how we relate to and train our teenagers. But, like Jesus asked His disciples who had woken Him, afraid of the storm, do you still have little faith?

Trust me, you're not alone. I ping-pong my way from faith to doubt to confidence to fear and back to faith again. It's difficult to stay centered in trust when storms hit and the evidence convinces us that fear is warranted.

Jesus' disciples really should have known Him well enough by that boat ride to trust in His provision for them in all circumstances. Yet there they were, in His very presence, afraid.

To be at peace, we have to be confident that God can and will calm the storms we face. Can we shift our reactions and assumptions so we can approach life that way? Can we be so confident in who Jesus is — assured that He will protect us and our teenagers — and walk solidly forward, even into the storms?

When we truly believe that He will show us what we need, and that He will provide for every need, only then can we have personal mastery over the fear and doubt that creeps into our lives. Let Jesus calm the storm in your heart, and trust Him to be all He's promised to be to you and your teens.

## → Connection Point

*Jesus, I thank you for being who you are. I thank you for showing me time after time that you are the master of the storms. Help me to put my faith in you at all times. Amen.*

## Soldier On
*Nicole O'Dell*

*For the eyes of the Lord range throughout the earth to strengthen those whose hearts are fully committed to him. 2 Chron. 16:9, NIV*

There is a great spiritual battle raging all around us. The host of Heaven and the armies of our enemies are at war for the souls of mankind — and for our teens. Long ago, God declared war on Satan, and He chose people like us as His soldiers. At the moment of salvation — when we turn our hearts over to Jesus and pledge allegiance to Him — we become His soldiers.

What strength do I have? How can I fight a spiritual battle? I know it seems odd, but God loves to use the weak to shame the strong and to bring glory to His name. God has used the meek to do mighty things through all of history. He used young David's sling to slay the giant and a teenage virgin to birth the Savior. In fact, instead of appearing as a great warrior on the earth, Jesus came as a humble man, a servant.

Your teens are also in the midst of this great spiritual battle and your enemy wants nothing more than to keep them from fully surrendering to God. So, this is when you need to soldier on more than ever. Fight this battle on your knees and look to your Commander and His words for instruction.

Remember, you are a soldier in the mightiest army ever assembled, and you serve One who delights in you when you rely on Him. And every knee will bow, and every tongue will confess that He is Lord. We wear the victor's crown.

## → Connection Point

*Mighty God, please strengthen me for the fight. Help me see into the spiritual realm so that I can know the battles being waged for my teens. Help me to remain faithful in prayer. Thank you for hearing my prayers and for standing with me in battle. Amen.*

## Best Defense
### Nicole O'Dell

*How can a young person live a clean life? By carefully reading the map of your word. Psalm 119:9 MSG*

Our kids are bombarded. Their minds are assaulted with images of sexuality and perversion. They're tempted in every area of sin in this sex-crazed culture that demands personal satisfaction above all else. How can they possibly stay strong and avoid sin in this society?

Have you ever read Psalm 119 in its entirety and thought about it in light of your teenagers? It emphasizes God's word as a cleansing, powerful tool. It lays out a foundation of truth and sets the course for the future. It's a call to study God's word, but more than that, it shows us why we need the Word of God in our lives.

Listen, teenagers are tempted because the world makes promises — promises of fulfillment and success, of popularity and happiness — but it can't keep those promises. Sadly, our teenagers discover that through trauma and deep hurt.

Instead, by teaching them to pour themselves into scripture and devote themselves to knowing it, we are equipping them to stand firm against sin and temptation and whatever enticing thing it is the world [can't even] offer.

I had a friend who memorized the entire chapter of Psalm 119. That is HUGE. I am not challenging you to do that, though I'd love to hear from you if you do. I would like to challenge you to sit with your teens and go through Psalm 119 verse by verse. Talk about it, explore its meaning, and pray for ways to apply it to your lives.

## → Connection Point

*Father, thank you for the treasure of your Word. Help me to impart passion to my teenagers for studying scripture. Illuminate your words to them that they will see and understand what You've prepared for them to know. Amen.*

## Thank You, Jesus
### Nicole O'Dell

Dear one,

The years have flown by. We stood together and smiled as we watched a beautiful baby bloom into an inquisitive child. Now we stand by in wonder as that child becomes a confident teenager who will naturally pull away to figure things out independently. Are you beginning to feel unseen? Unappreciated in your parenting efforts?

I understand. I'm a parent too.

Would you allow me to express how I feel about you?

I appreciate the nights you go to bed and cry out to me for your child's welfare and salvation more than you'll ever know on your side of heaven. I appreciate the hours you spend on the road driving from sporting event to church activity to friend's houses. I appreciate the thankless hours you sit on cold bleachers to celebrate a moment that will be remembered by no one but you – and me.

Dear parent, I honor you for the selflessness you've shown as you've set your own dreams aside. I've seen your sacrifice. I honor you for defending your child in the face of attack. I've seen the way you've ignored fear and relied on me. I honor you for the times you've disciplined even when it was difficult. I know how that feels.

I thank you for the relentless passion you display parenting despite rejection. I thank you for the overtime you put in every single day for no extra pay or recognition. I thank you for being my ambassador and preparing to leave a legacy in my name.

Thank you.

I love you,
**Jesus**

# Powerline365 Contributors

**Nicole O'Dell:** Project coordinator and contributor of almost 300 devotions, finalist for the ACFW's 2014 Editor-of-the-Year award, and the author of 26 books and founder of Choose NOW Ministries, a 501(c)(3) organization. A national speaker, Nicole is available to speak at your upcoming events.
Visit www.nicoleodell.com.

| Name | Website | Pages |
| --- | --- | --- |
| Cassie Beck | | 8, 83, 306 |
| Takiela Bynum | www.takielabynum.com | 48 |
| Valerie Comer | www.valeriecomer.com | 12, 94, 146, 214, 242, 358 |
| Claire Culwell | www.claireculwell.com | 158, 246 |
| Shannon Deitz | www.shannondeitz.com | 36 |
| Mary DeMuth | www.marydemuth.com | 134, 234, 298, 348 |
| Dr. Tara Fairfield | www.tarafairfield.com | 182 |
| Wendy Fitzgerald | www.ifthenmovement.com | 28, 79, 142, 198, 286 |
| Amber Frank | facebook.com/amber.frank.9 | 24, 114, 338 |
| Sara Goff | www.saragoff.com | 110, 238 |
| Tricia Goyer | www.triciagoyer.com | 138, 178, 218 |
| Tim Hageland | www.timhageland.com | 222 |
| J. Alden Hall | www.jaldenhall.com | 4, 360 |
| Jill Hart | www.jillhart.com | 68, 162, 230, 326 |

| Name | Website | Pages |
|---|---|---|
| Bethany Jett | www.bethanyjett.com | 44, 106, 154 |
| Sherri Wilson Johnson | www.sherriwilsonjohnson.com | 64, 126, 270 |
| Amy Joob | facebook.com/amy.robnikjoob | 72, 202, 314 |
| Laura Kurk | www.laurakurk.com | 130, 206 |
| Wil O'Dell | www.wilodell.com | 186 |
| Lyn Parker | www.lynparker.com | 166 |
| Cara Putman | www.caraputman.com | 56, 102, 270, 258 |
| Jason Lane | www.pastorjasonlane.com | 16, 32, 210 |
| Debi Lee | facebook.com/debra.m.lee | 91, 122, 174 |
| Dori Powledge Phillips | www.doripowledge.com | 40 |
| Steve Repak, CFP® | www.steverepak.com | 60, 290 |
| Janet Sketchley | www.janetsketchley.com | 87 |
| Laura L. Smith | www.laurasmithauthor.com | 20, 226 |
| Vicki Tiede | www.vickitiede.com | 118, 190, 322 |
| Brenda L. Yoder | www.brendayoder.com | 52, 98, 150, 194, 254, 274, 351 |

The Choose NOW Team would love it if you'd share Powerline365 with a friend. In fact, anyone can get 30 days of Powerline365 devotions emailed to them completely free. Just scan the QR code to the left or visit www.nicoleodell.com/product.spark30 and enter coupon code Spark30.

Inspiring experts write issue-focused columns for parents of teens. Learn how to set boundaries, how to guard against peer pressure, and how to keep your teens solid in the faith. We cover hot-button issues like teen pregnancy and eating disorders, parenting choices and lifestyle questions...and much, much more. Visit www.choose-now.com.

## Choose NOW Publishing

Family struggles, hot-button issues, sound biblical support...that's what you'll find in CNP publications. Books written from a Christian worldview will leave you challenged and inspired. Parenting & self-help books, devotionals, Bible studies, and audio resources...CNP provides tools for Christian parents and families. Visit www.choosenowpublishing.com.

## Choose NOW Speaker Team

Talented and anointed speakers are available to minister at your events on a wide range of topics, all focused on reaching people right where their real life is happening, making Jesus known to them in a new way. If you need help with your choice of a Christian keynote speaker, or you'd like more information about our team or about the work of Choose NOW Ministries, please visit www.choose-now.com.

www.ingramcontent.com/pod-product-compliance
Lightning Source LLC
LaVergne TN
LVHW051541070426
835507LV00021B/2353